The Lockington Gold Hoard:
an Early Bronze Age barrow cemetery at Lockington, Leicestershire

By
Gwilym Hughes

with contributions by

L. Bevan, D. R. Hook, R. Gale, J. Greig, S. Limbrey, J. Meek, N. D. Meeks, L. Moffett, A. G. Moss, A. Monckton, S. Needham, J. Watson, D. Williams, A. Woodward and R. Young

Oxbow Books
2000

Published by
Oxbow Books, Park End Place, Oxford OX1 1HN

© Gwilym Hughes and the individual authors, 2000

ISBN 1 84217 017 1

This book is available direct from
Oxbow Books, Park End Place, Oxford OX1 1HN
(Phone: 01865–241249; Fax: 01865–794449)

and

The David Brown Book Company
PO Box 511, Oakville, CT 06779, USA
(Phone: 860–945–9329; Fax: 860–945–9468)

Printed in Great Britain at
The Short Run Press
Exeter

Contents

Introduction 1

The Excavation 4

The Gold and Copper Metalwork *(Stuart Needham)* 23

The Prehistoric Pottery *(Ann Woodward)* 48

The Flint *(Rob Young and Lynne Bevan)* 62

The Cup Marked Stone *(Gwilym Hughes)* 76

The Charred Plant Remains *(Lisa Moffett and Angela Monckton)* 78

The Pollen Remains *(James Greig)* 82

The Buried Soil and Mound Materials *(Susan Limbrey)* 85

The Soil Phosphate Analysis *(A. G. Moss)* 93

Charcoal Identifications *(Rowena Gale)* 95

Discussion 96

Bibliography 104

Appendix 1 110
Appendix 2 114
Appendix 3 115

List of Contributors 116

In memory of

Bronwyn Robinson
1968–2000

One of the excavators at Lockington and a sorely missed friend

INTRODUCTION

This report details the results of excavations within an Early Bronze Age barrow cemetery near the village of Lockington in north-west Leicestershire (Fig. 1, SK466290). The work was undertaken between August and November 1994 in advance of the construction of the A564(T) Derby Southern Bypass.

The barrow cemetery lies on an area of sand and gravel surrounded by the alluvium of the Trent floodplain, at a height of approximately 30m OD. The confluence of the Rivers Soar and Trent lies approximately 3km to the north-east and the confluence of the River Trent and the River Derwent lies approximately 2km to the north-west. At the time of the excavation, the majority of the barrow cemetery was located within a triangle of land, bounded by the M1 motorway to the east, the A6 trunk road to the south-west and a branch line railway to the north-west (Fig. 2). Prior to the excavation, the whole of this area was under arable cultivation.

Various aerial photographs suggest the presence of at least six possible barrows, four associated with a single, circular ring ditch (Sites I–III and Site VI), one with a single, oval ditch (Site VII) and one with two concentric circular ditches (Site IV). The ring ditch at Site II appears to be associated with a number of internal 'pit-like' features. Prior to the investigation, a cluster of cropmarked features at Site V suggested the presence of a pit circle. Several other possible barrow sites in the area have been tentatively suggested although these are yet to be proven (Clark 1995; Meek 1995). Only one of the sites at Lockington has formerly been investigated; Site I, to the south of the present A6. This was partially excavated in 1954 by Merrick Posnansky (1955a). Traces of a cremation associated with a small bronze knife, two flint knives, a flint arrowhead and possible beaker pottery were recovered from under the central area of the truncated remains of a low earth mound. The mound was surrounded by a single annular ring ditch.

An evaluation of the area threatened by the construction of the Derby Southern Bypass was undertaken by the Trent and Peak Archaeological Trust in 1993 and included fieldwalking, geophysical survey and two trial trenches (T&PAT 1993, 21). The fieldwalking indicated a background scatter of material of prehistoric and medieval date and the geophysical survey accurately located the positions of the ring ditches at Sites II and VI on the ground (Stratascan 1993). A trial trench across the north-western side of the ring ditch at Site VI suggested the survival of a slight mound and a number of struck flint flakes were recovered.

The proposed road corridor threatened the whole of the barrow at Site VI along with parts of associated linear and curvilinear cropmarked features. The evaluation report recommended the complete excavation of the barrow prior to the start of the road construction. Following competitive tendering, Birmingham University Field Archaeology Unit was commissioned to undertake the work by Scott Wilson Kirkpatrick (Consulting Engineers) on behalf of the Highways Agency. This work conformed to a brief prepared by Nottingham University Consultants Limited. The construction of the road also necessitated the diversion of a mains water pipe. This operation threatened a second group of crop-marked features (Site V) 20m to the west of the barrow. The excavation of this site was undertaken by Leicestershire Archaeological Unit on behalf of Severn Trent Water Limited. Both excavations were undertaken simultaneously (Plate 3). In addition to the two area excavations, other areas threatened by activity associated with the road construction were sampled with regard to the possibility of further burials or archaeological features relating to the barrow cemetery (Fig. 2, Trenches B–P).

2   THE LOCKINGTON GOLD HOARD

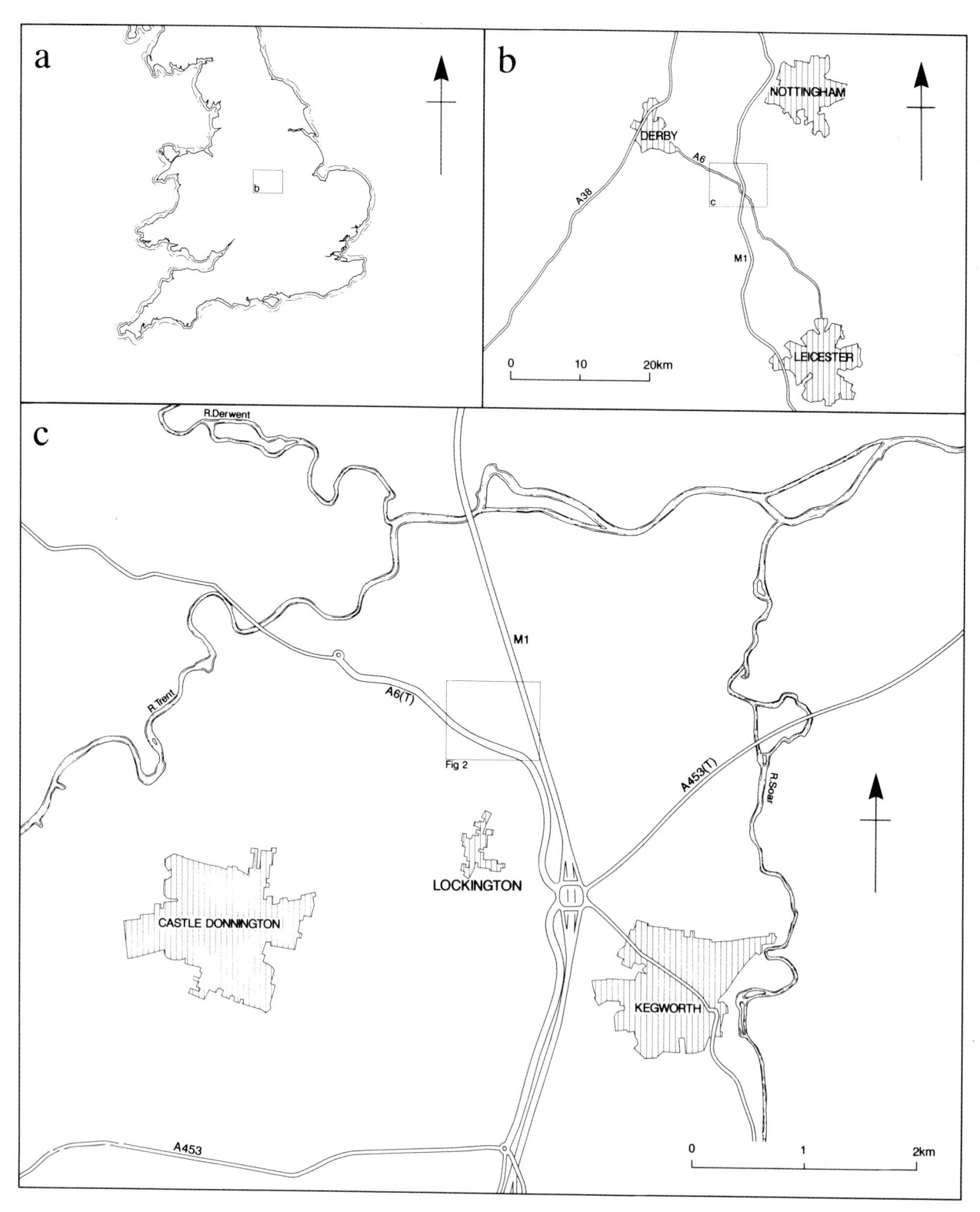

Figure 1: Location.

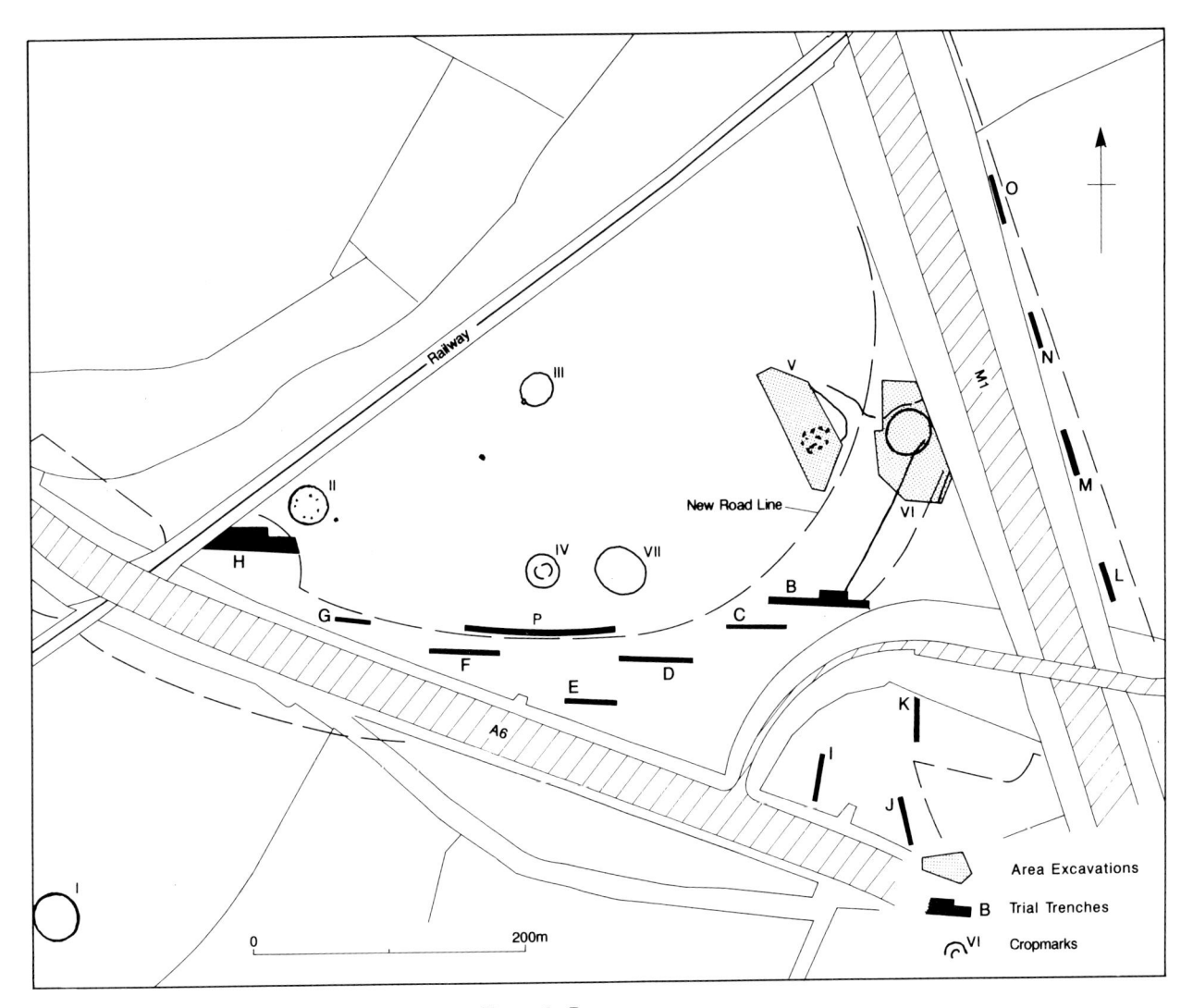

Figure 2: Barrow cemetery.

Arrangements have been made for the deposition of the archive and finds with Leicestershire County Council Museums, Arts and Records Service (accession No. A.166.1994). The two gold armlets have been declared Treasure Trove and are in the possession of the British Museum

THE EXCAVATION

Method of excavation

Prior to the excavation of Site VI only a slight trace of the surviving mound of the barrow, about 0.3m high, could be distinguished within the cultivated field. A resistance survey undertaken during the evaluation clearly located the ring ditch as an area of low resistance (Stratascan 1993). During this geophysical survey, two linear features, also identified on the aerial photographs, were detected to the south and north of the barrow. In addition, a series of parallel features with alternate high and low resistance readings were detected crossing the site from north-west to south-east. These were interpreted as ploughed-out ridge and furrow.

A contour survey of the barrow was undertaken prior to the commencement of the excavation. Two, one metre wide, transects were then laid out crossing just to the north-west of the estimated central point of the barrow. The modern ploughsoil (1000) from these transects was removed using hand tools in order to establish the depth of the top of the undisturbed archaeological deposits. This also allowed some indication of the density of artefacts present within the ploughsoil. The ploughsoil proved to be 0.25m deep and, where the two transects crossed, directly overlay the surviving barrow mound material. The remaining modern ploughsoil in this area was carefully removed by machine leaving two 1m wide baulks across the centre of the barrow adjacent to the original hand excavated transects (Fig. 3 and Plate 6). The barrow mound, in each of the resulting quadrants, was excavated as a series of three horizontal spits, each 0.1m thick (Plate 8). The mound material was planned after the removal of each spit, essentially each representing a horizontal slice through the barrow (Plate 12). The central portions of the baulks were subsequently recorded and removed in order to record and excavate the pre-barrow deposits in plan. The surrounding ring ditch was excavated as a series of eight segments separated by 1.5m wide baulks. These baulks were subsequently recorded and mechanically excavated at the end of the excavation.

Beyond the outer edge of the ring ditch, the modern ploughsoil overlay a sandy loam with many stones (1001), up to 0.3m deep, which contained occasional fragments of medieval and post-medieval pottery and tile. This was interpreted as a medieval and post-medieval ploughsoil and was also removed by machine to expose the surface of the underlying natural sands and gravels. The surface of this gravel was cleaned in order to define potential archaeological features. These were then half-sectioned. If they proved to be archaeological they were subsequently fully excavated. In total, an area of approximately 4000 square metres was opened around the surviving trace of the barrow (Fig. 3).

All finds from the excavation were individually numbered and their locations plotted on the appropriate plans. Following the excavation all the site plans and finds points were digitised using Autocad12, Tosca (Idrisi's digitising modules) and a digitising tablet to create drawing files. Finds records were entered into another database and the two related by find number. This allowed the production of proportional symbol maps showing the distribution of selected finds classes by phase, context or spit. Figure 4 is a plot showing the distribution of all finds of prehistoric date recovered during the excavation. A selection of other plots are used to illustrate the distribution of the principal artefact classes for each phase.

At Site V, the modern plough soil and the lower

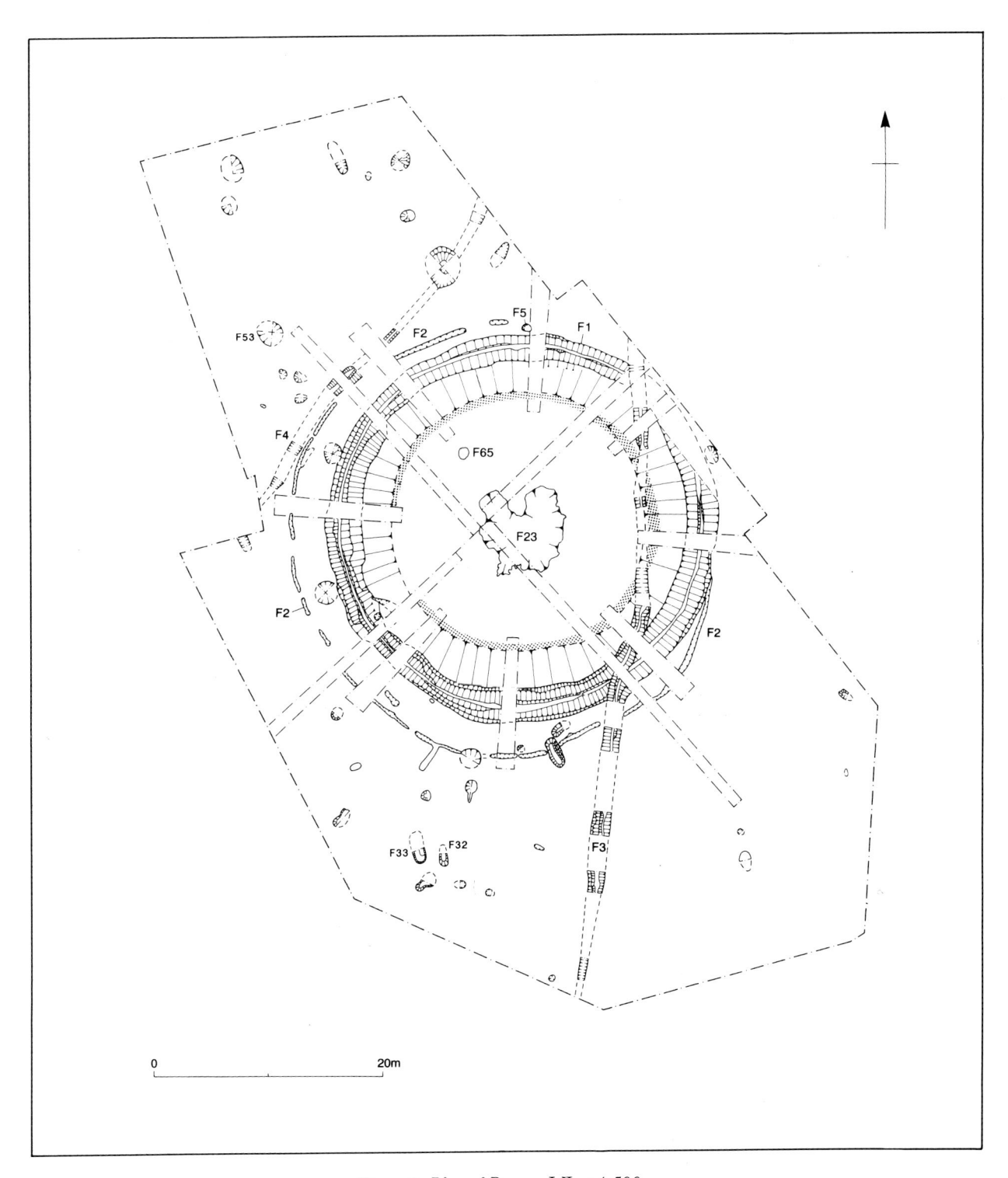

Figure 3: Plan of Barrow VI at 1:500.

Figure 4: Distribution of all finds from Barrow VI.

remnants of the disturbed medieval plough soil was also removed by machine and the underlying sand and gravel natural cleaned in order to define possible archaeological features. An area of 2,384 square meters was examined. Numerous possible pits and post holes were sample excavated (Fig. 16). It seems likely that a group of these pits in the southern part of the excavated area relates to the features identified on the aerial photographs.

A total of 14 other trenches were excavated within the area threatened by the proposed road construction (Fig. 2, Trenches B–P). Trenches B–F and P were designed to test for the presence of archaeological features on the periphery of the barrow cemetery which were not identified from the aerial photographs. Trenches G and H were intended to sample areas in the vicinity of ring ditch II which appeared to be masked by alluvium. Similarly, there was a suggestion of masking alluvial deposits in the areas to the east and south of the barrow cemetery. These areas were tested by Trenches I–O. In all cases the plough soil horizons were removed by machine. Where alluvial deposits were encountered, they were sampled down to the level of the underlying gravels.

THE RESULTS

The pre-barrow deposits (Fig. 5)

Within the area of the barrow platform, the sand and gravel natural (1009) was overlain by up to 0.2m of brown silty sand and gravel (1046). This was cut by a small pit (Fig. 6a, F65), 0.5m in diameter and 0.3m deep, containing a deposit of charcoal, burnt pebbles, flecks of cremated bone, fragments of flint (much of which was burnt) and a single sherd of possible Neolithic pottery (see below page 52). The impressions of two possible stake holes (F68 and F69) were recorded in the base of this pit. A radiocarbon date of 4375±80 BP (Oxa-5846) calibrated to 3350–2750 BC (see Table 1) was obtained from hazel charcoal from this pit.

Within the central part of the barrow platform, the sand and gravel (1046) and the small pit (F65) were overlain by a thinner deposit of relatively stone-free sandy loam (1088) up to 0.05m deep and covering an area 17m by 11m. The central area of this sandy loam, approximately 10m in diameter, was stained yellow/red (1044). This central deposit was cut by a large, shallow irregular scoop (F23), between 6m and 7m across and up to 0.2m deep (Fig. 7 and Plate 5). The edges and base of this scoop were very poorly defined except for those areas where they were associated with prominent iron panning. The scoop was associated with a number of smaller, but equally ill-defined shallow pits (F56–F58). These features were filled with a brown sandy loam with red/brown and pale brown mottles caused by iron staining (1043) and overlain by a thin spread of charcoal with an occasional fleck of cremated bone (1041). It was not possible to determine whether or not this cremated bone was human. A radiocarbon date of 3370±50 BP (Oxa-5847) calibrated to 1870–1520 BC (see Table 1) was obtained from hazel charcoal from this deposit.

The radiocarbon date and Neolithic pottery from the small pit (F65) suggests that it belongs to an early phase of activity predating the ritual activity associated with the barrow. Other evidence for Neolithic activity at the site is suggested by a fragment of a leaf-shaped arrowhead (Fig. 32, 4) from the sand and gravel (1046) overlying the natural gravel (1009) and by three flakes from a polished stone axe recovered from the mound of the barrow (see below page 66). It seems likely that the sandy loam deposits (1088 and 1044) overlying the natural gravels represent the remnants of pre-barrow soils. The red-yellow staining in the central area (1044) does not appear to be related to a burning episode such as the torching of a funerary pyre (see soils report below). A more likely explanation is that it represents iron staining caused by the decomposition of organic matter in the overlying mound. This implies that the actual cremation took place away from the site. The shallow scoop (F23) may have been intended to hold the redeposited remains of the cremation prior to the construction of the barrow. The deposit of charcoal and the associated cremated bone (1041) over the scoop may correspond with such cremation deposits.

A number of pieces of worked flint and fragments of prehistoric pottery were recovered from these pre-mound deposits. Their distribution is indicated in Figure 8. There is a noticeable concentration of flint to the northwest of the central scoop in the area of the possible Neolithic pit (F65), including 27 fragments from the pit fill itself. By contrast, the pottery fragments form an apparent northwest-southeast linear arrangement. These included several rim fragments with ribbed decoration, recovered from different contexts (1042, 1043, 1044 and 1088) and possibly from a single Enlarged Food Vessel (see below page 52 and Fig. 28, 1).

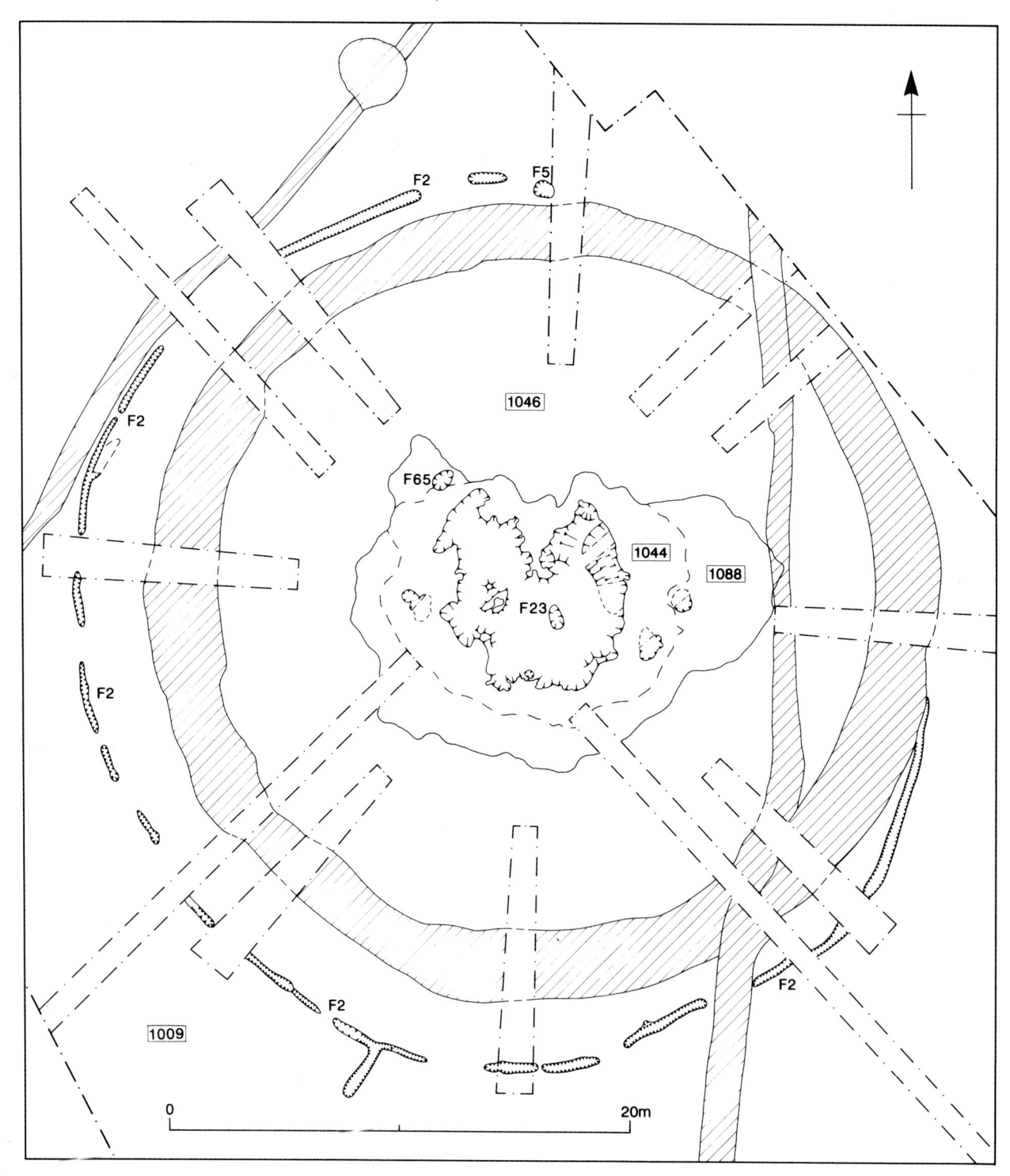

Figure 5: Pre-barrow features and deposits at 1:250.

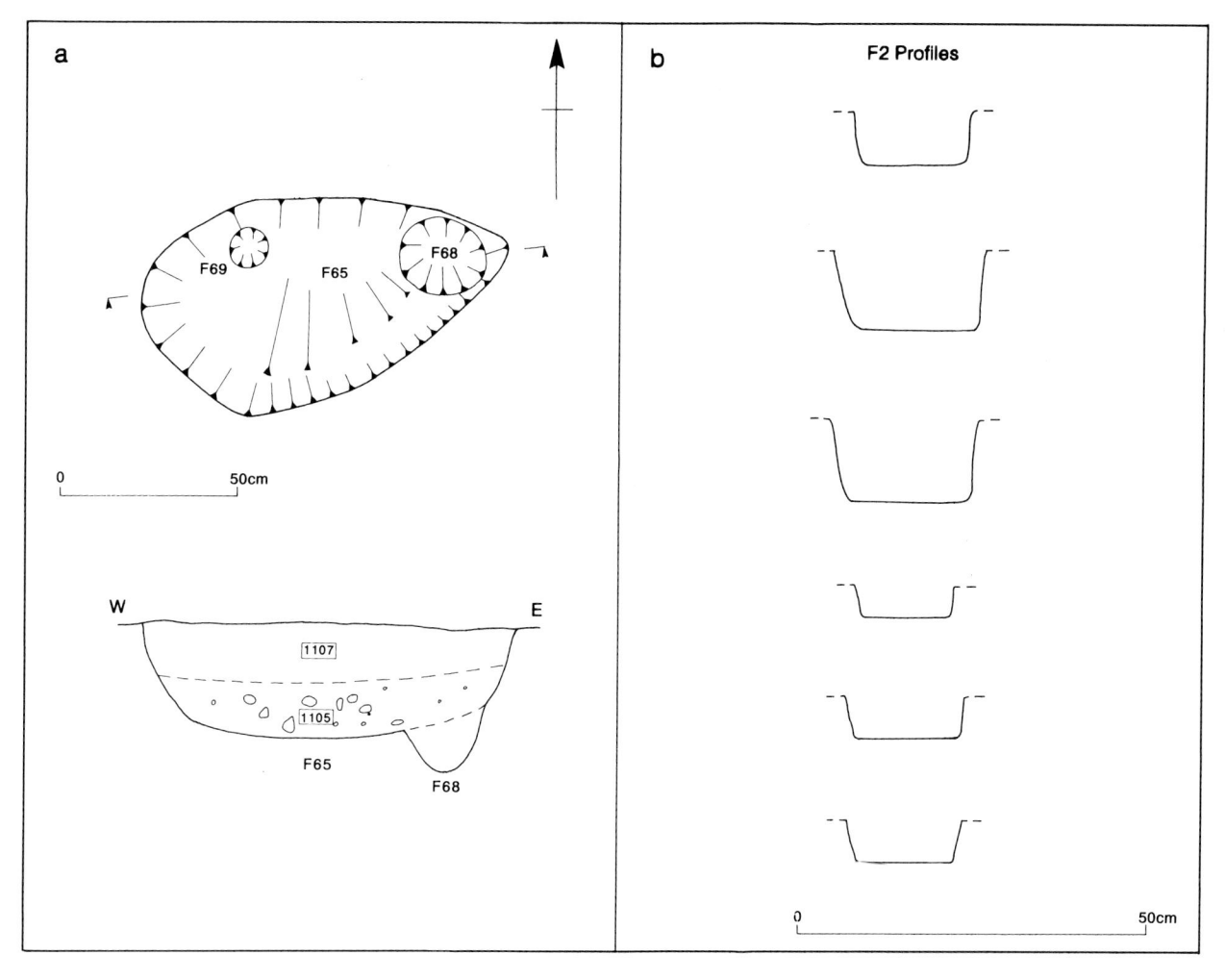

Figure 6: a) Plan and section of cremation pit (F65), b) profiles of palisade gully (F2).

The palisade gully and hoard

The pre-barrow features and deposits were surrounded by a narrow gully (F2), 0.3m wide and up to 0.2m deep (Plate 10). The gully appeared as a discontinuous feature on its northern and western sides with occasional evidence for post impressions (Fig. 5). It had a more regular square-shaped profile on the southern and southeastern side. The northeastern side of the gully had been removed by the cut of the later ring ditch. The only finds were occasional worked flints and the remains of several cattle teeth, the majority of which were recovered from the southeastern sector. It seems likely that the gully represents the foundation trench for some form of lightly-built palisade, pre-dating the construction of the ring ditch and the barrow. It appeared to have a polygonal plan, suggestive of a structure involving a series of prefabricated hurdles, and defined an area 36m in diameter. The narrow breaks on the western side may have been entrances. However, it seems likely that the principal entrance was on the north side where only faint traces of the feature could be discerned.

A small pit (F5) was recorded on the line of the northern side of the palisade close to where it converged with the later ring ditch (Plate 2). It contained a spectacular group of artefacts comprising two incomplete pottery vessels, two gold armlets and a copper dagger. The two pottery vessels were inverted, one inside the other, and partially covered one of the gold armlets

Table 1: Radiocarbon dates.

Lab No.	Result BP	1 sigma calibrated range	2 sigma calibrated range	Context
OxA-5846	4375±80	3270–3240 cal BC 3110–2910 cal BC	3350–2750 cal BC	Site VI, F65
OxA-5847	3370±50	1750–1610 cal BC	1870–1840 cal BC 1780–1520 cal BC	Site VI, F23
OxA-6173	3910±60	2560–2540 cal BC 2500–2320 cal BC	2580–2200 cal BC	Site VI, F5 Scabbard
OxA-6447	3630±55	2130–2080 cal BC 2050–1930 cal BC	2190–1880 cal BC	Site VI, F5 Scabbard
Beta-83721	3440±80	1875–1805 cal BC 1795–1645 cal BC	1935–1525 cal BC	Site V, F84
Beta-83722	3039±80	1425–1260 cal BC	1510–1120 cal BC	Site V, F174

(Armlet No. 2). The second gold armlet (Armlet No 1) and the copper dagger were immediately beside the pots (Fig. 9). These objects are described in detail below (pages 23–27 and 52–54). Traces of an organic scabbard attached to the copper dagger has produced two radiocarbon dates of 3910±60 BP (OxA-6173) calibrated to 2580–2200 BC and 3630±55 BP (OxA-6447) calibrated to 2190–1880 cal BC (see Table 1). The pit itself was little more than a shallow oval scoop, 0.7m long 0.5m wide and up to 0.15m deep cut into the natural gravel and overlain by the medieval ploughsoil (1005). The pit had no stratigraphic relationship with either the palisade gully or the ring ditch. However, its location on the line of the gully within the area of a possible entrance suggests an association. No trace of either a cremation or inhumation could be identified during the excavation of the feature or the sieving of its contents. Although it is unlikely that any unburnt bone would survive in the sandy soils, the feature would appear to have been too small to have contained anything but the inhumation of an infant and no trace of any body stain was identified. There was no increase in the level of phosphates when compared with the surrounding soil (see below page 94).

The barrow mound (Fig. 10)

The core of the mound comprised a deposit of reddish brown sandy loam (1033) with patches and streaks of black and yellowish red mottles. This deposit was approximately 10m in diameter and covered the central area of the barrow platform, including the stained area (1044) and the charcoal spread (1041). It was surrounded by a narrow, concentric band of dark reddish brown sandy loam (1034), approximately 1m wide, with more frequent black and yellowish red mottles (Plate 12). This in turn, was overlain and surrounded by a wider band of brown sandy loam with finer and less prominent mottles (1035). Finally, the edges of the mound were defined by a thin 'capping' of small rounded stones (1004/1036), in some places extending down to the inner edge of the ring ditch. In section (Fig. 11) these various deposits could be seen as a series of truncated, overlapping layers with a maximum depth of 0.25m. The outer 2–3m of the mound, which had survived plough truncation, gave some indication of the original profile of the barrow.

It is reported below that the mottling is the result of iron staining created during the decomposition of organic matter within the original soil. This suggests that the core of the barrow represents a heap of soil, including surface vegetation, derived from the former ground surface. However, there was no evidence for the stacking of turfs. The paler colour of the outer desposit of sandy loam (1035) and the less prominent mottling suggests that it represents a subsequent enlargement of the barrow. The gravel 'capping' presumably derives from the surrounding ring ditch.

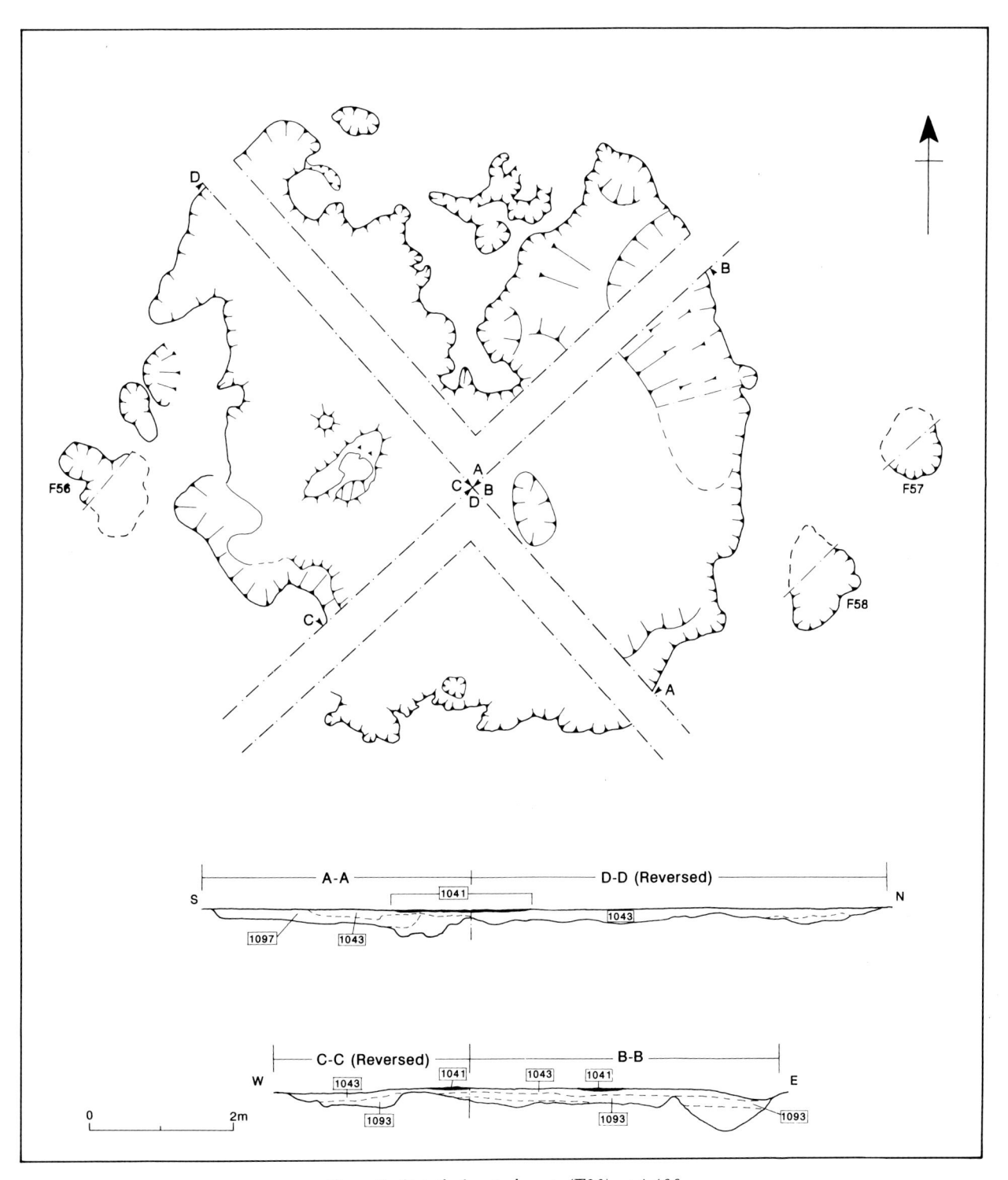

Figure 7: Detail of central scoop (F23) at 1:100.

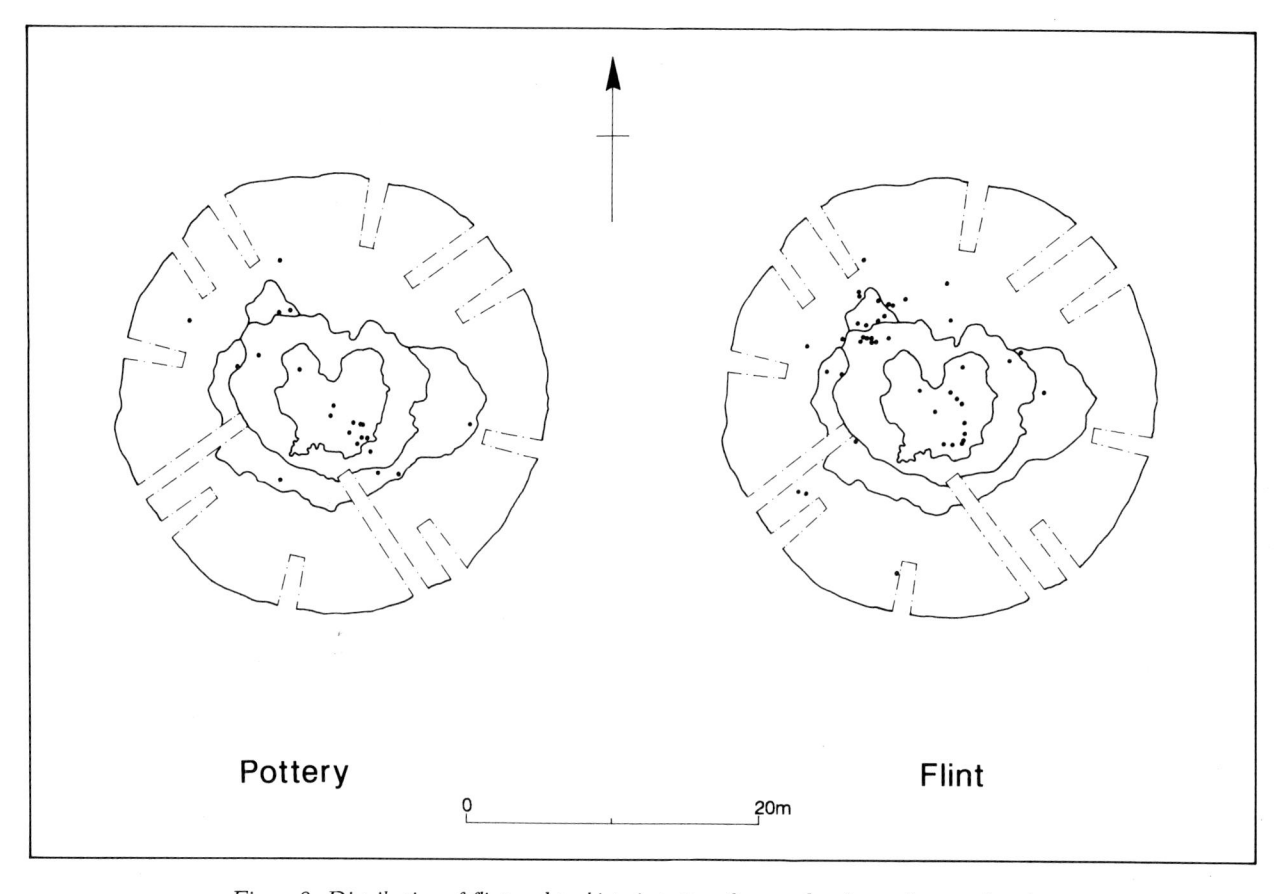

Figure 8: Distribution of flint and prehistoric pottery from under the pre-barrow deposits.

A general scatter of flint and prehistoric pottery was recovered from the various components of the mound. The majority of the prehistoric pottery fragments were of Bronze Age date but also included fragments from three different decorated beakers (see below page 55 and Fig. 28; 5, 8 and 9). The distribution plots (Fig. 12) appear to suggest a fairly even scatter of both pottery and flint within the make-up of the mound (although there are slight suggestions of more pottery in the southeast sector). Three struck flakes from a polished greenstone axe were also recovered from the make-up of the mound.

The ring ditch (Figs 13 and 14)

The outer edge of the primary cut of the ring ditch (F8) was 33.5m in diameter, and the ditch was between 2.5m and 3m wide, and up to 1.1m deep. It had an inverted bell-shaped profile with a fairly broad, flat-bottomed basal slot up to 0.4m wide (Fig. 13 and Plate 13). It was filled with a coarse deposit of sand and gravel (1015). A recut (F1) could be identified around the whole circumference of the ditch. It had a similar bell-shaped profile but was generally less substantial, up to 0.8m deep with a narrower basal slot up to 0.3m wide. The primary fill of the recut comprised a coarse sand and gravel (1014). This was overlain by a fill of pale brown sandy loam (1013) with occasional lenses of dark grey-brown silt and charcoal. The upper fill of the recut comprised a yellow-brown sandy loam (1010). Very few finds were recovered from the primary fills of the ring ditch. However, a number of pieces of struck flint and a few fragments of both prehistoric and post-prehistoric pottery were recovered from the upper fill (1010).

A stone block, probably sandstone, with a series of

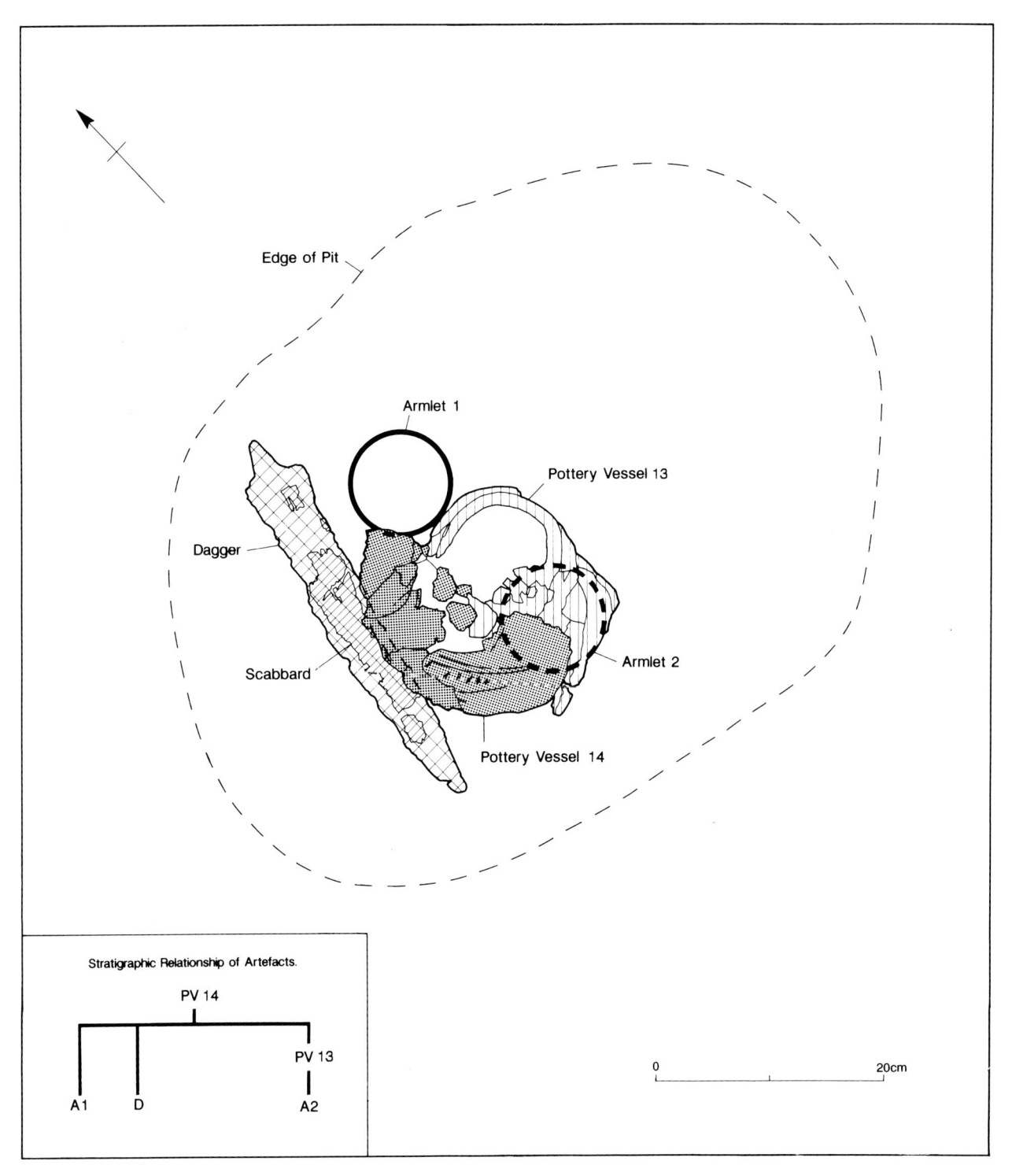

Figure 9: Detail of hoard in situ at 1:5.

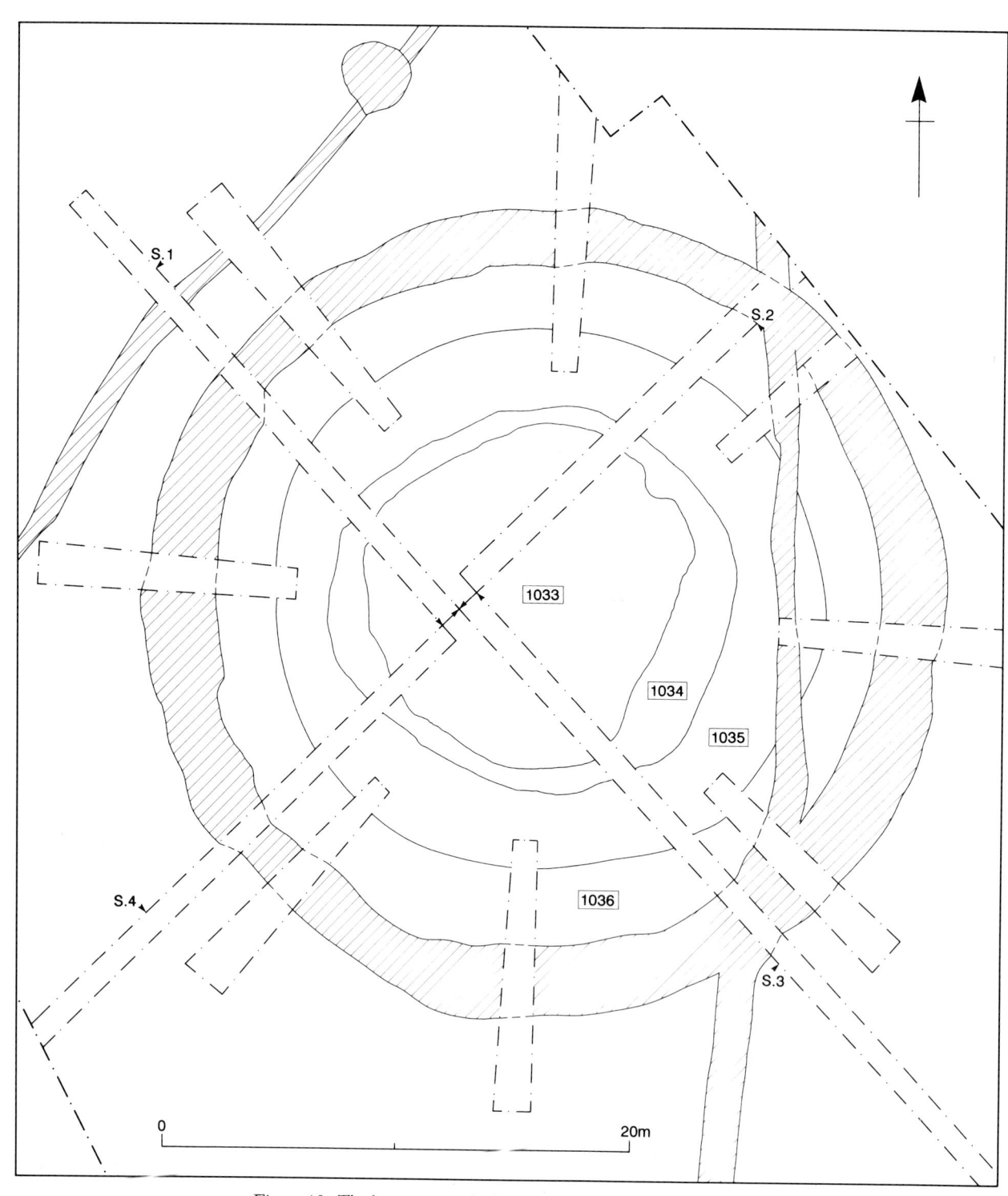

Figure 10: The barrow mound after removal of upper 0.1m at 1:250.

The Excavation

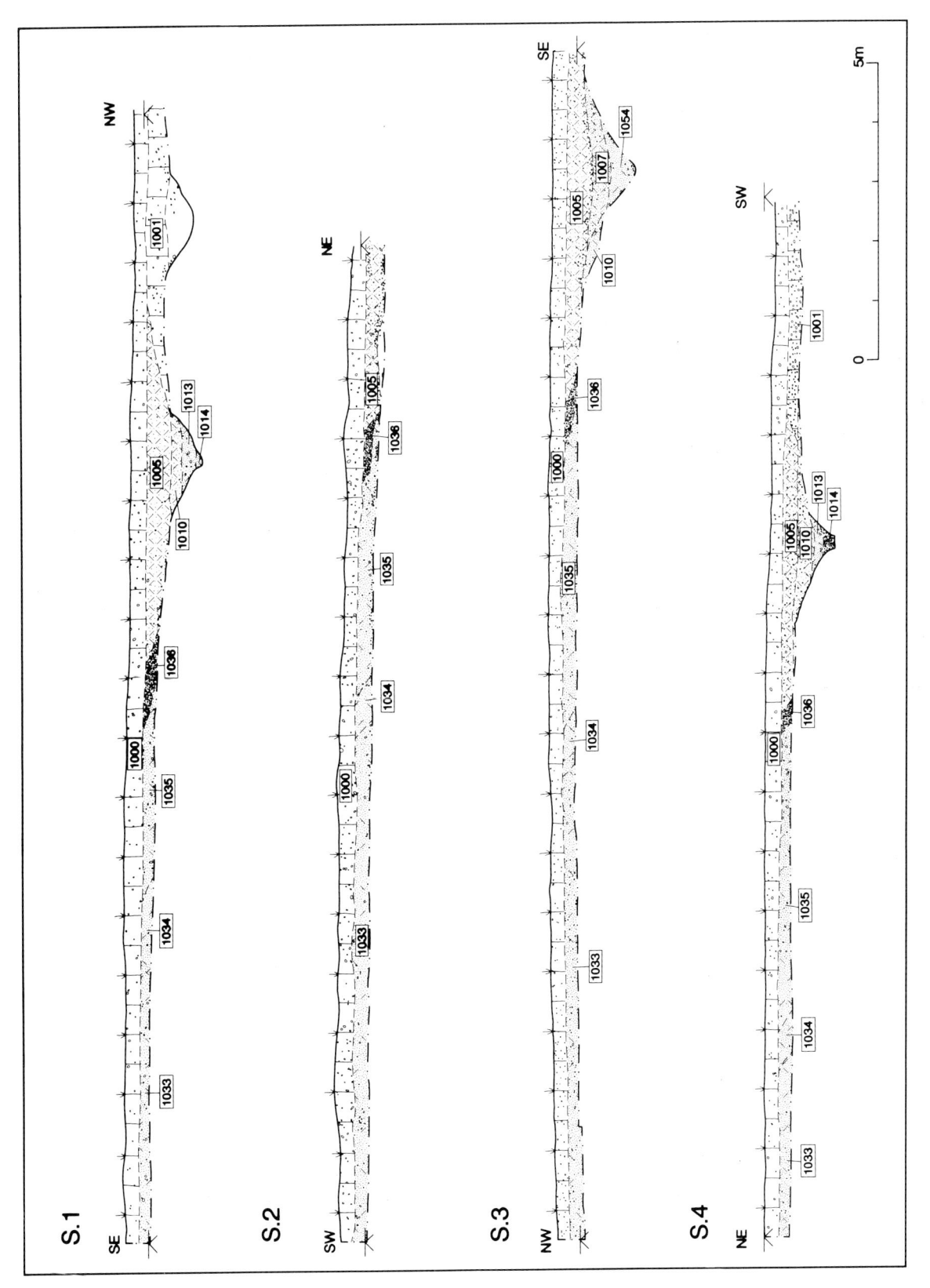

Figure 11: Sections through the barrow mound at 1:100.

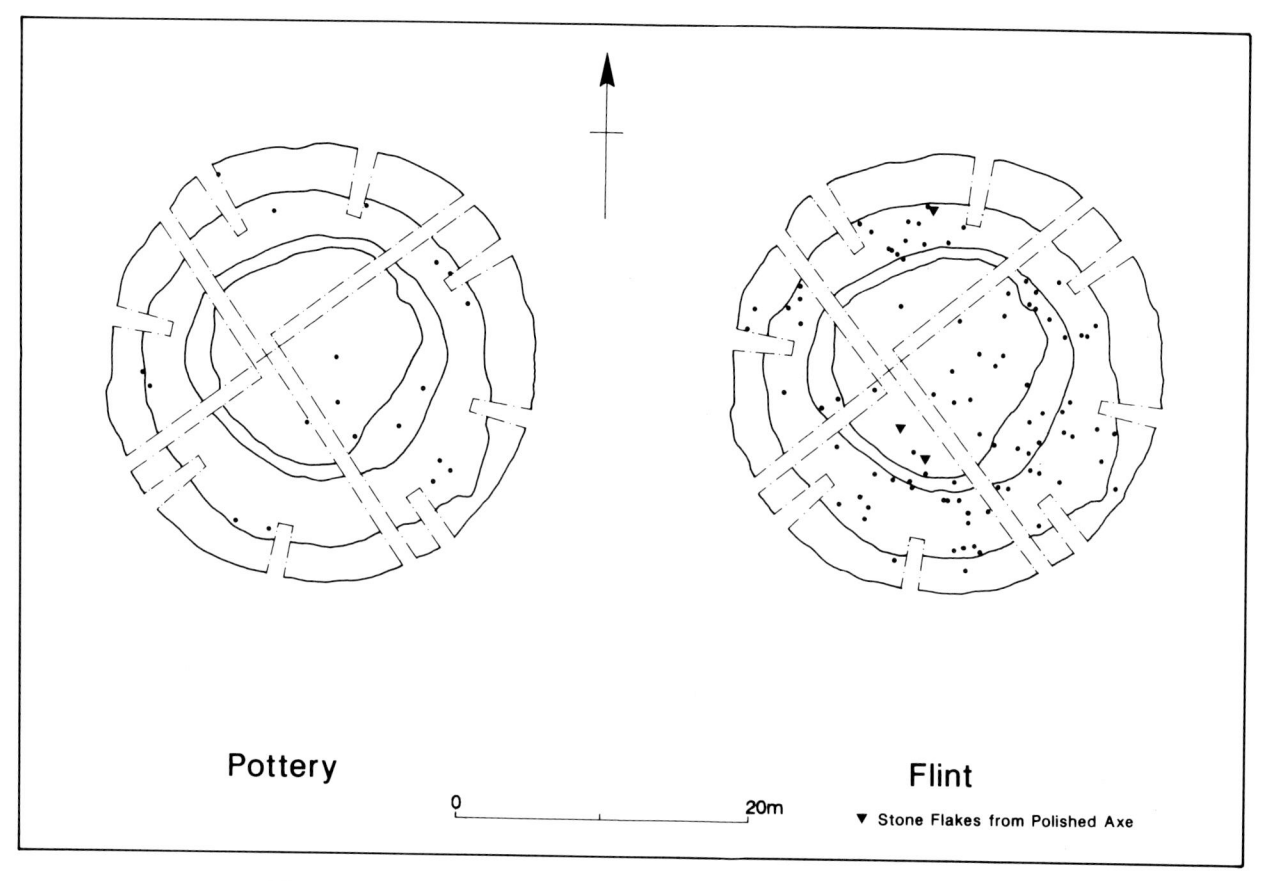

Figure 12: Distribution of flint and prehistoric pottery from the barrow mound.

shallow pits or 'cup-marks' pecked into one surface (see below page 76) was recovered from the fill of the recut (1013) on the north side of the barrow (Fig. 15). The principal concentrations of flint were recovered from the western half of the ring ditch fill. However, these concentrations may have been influenced by the patterns of deposition caused by later ridge and furrow agriculture (see below page 73). This in turn suggests that the main phase of backfilling did not occur until relatively recent times. This is supported by the presence of Late Bronze Age and Iron Age sherds in all the fills of the recut (F1).

The peripheral features

Numerous other features were recorded and excavated in the area around the barrow at Site VI (Fig. 3). The majority proved to be sub-circular or irregular shaped pits containing no finds or any other evidence of having an archaeological origin. It seems likely that the majority were from tree root activity perhaps relating to an episode of vegetation clearance. There were four exceptions which contained fragments of Iron Age pottery. Three were shallow, irregular pits (F32, F33 and F40) and each contained just a single sherd which may have been intrusive. The fourth was a large circular pit to the northwest of the barrow and was up to 2.2m in diameter and up to 0.5m deep (F53). The upper part of the sandy fill contained 28 sherds from 2 vessels (see below page 55).

Several sections were excavated through a curvilinear feature (F4) to the north of the barrow. This feature was originally identified from aerial photographs on which it appeared to skirt around the northern side of the ring ditch. It proved to have a U-shaped profile and was up to 1m wide and 0.5m deep. No finds were recovered from either the sand and gravel lower fill or the sandy clay upper fill.

A second linear feature (F3) cut through silt fills of the ring ditch and the eastern edge of the barrow. Only the lower part of its bell-shaped profile had survived in the area away from the barrow, perhaps as a result of plough truncation. The best preserved section, where it cut the ring ditch, was up to 1.8m wide and 0.85m deep (Fig. 14, S.7). There was, again, very little trace of the feature where it cut through the edge of the barrow. This perhaps suggests that it maintained a constant depth as it rose over the former mound and has subsequently been eroded away. The only finds were several flint flakes all of which were recovered from the area where it cut the barrow and ring ditch.

Site V features (Fig. 16) (J. Meek)

Numerous features of various sizes were recorded in the area of Site V. On the basis of the few stratigraphic relationships and morphological similarities these have been grouped into three phases.

Phase 1 comprised numerous post holes forming possible boundary markers or fence lines. The majority ranged in size from 0.23m in diameter to 0.8m × 0.54m and were between 0.11m and 0.46m deep. In addition to these post holes, two narrow linear features (F188 and F268) may also relate to this early phase of activity. The difficulty of assigning these small features to a particular phase is bourne out by a radiocarbon date of 3039±80 BP (Beta-83722) calibrated to 1510–1120 cal BC obtained from charcoal from one of the post holes (Table 1, F174). This date suggests that at least some of these features might be better placed in Phases 2 or 3.

Phase 2 comprised a group of oval or round pits with silty sand fills. The smallest was 0.8m × 0.6m and the largest was 2.13m × 1.2m. All contained occasional charcoal flecks. The most significant feature was a circular pit (F84) which contained cremated bone, pottery and a ceramic pully-shaped object with a dished surface and a grooved side. One fragment of the cremated bone was identified as the medial part of a distal right tibia of a pig (Baxter 1995). The pottery included five fragments from four different beakers and joining sherds from the lower portion of a large jar, probably of late Bronze Age date (see below page 56). A radiocarbon date of 3440±80 BP (Beta-83721) calibrated to 1935–1525 cal BC was obtained from charcoal recovered from the fill of the pit (see Table 1). Two Bronze Age sherds were also recovered from a second pit belonging to Phase 2 (F136).

Phase 3 comprised a narrow ditch bisecting the site from northwest to southeast (F10). The feature contained a single silty sand fill and was up to 0.67m wide and up to 0.31m deep. This ditch cut a number of the Phase 2 pits and it seems likely that it relates to the same system of later prehistoric land division as the linear ditches in Site VI (F3 and F4).

Medieval ploughsoil and silt over ring ditch

All the prehistoric features in both excavated areas were sealed by up to 0.25m of sandy loam and gravel (1001) associated with medieval and post-medieval ploughing. This contained a small, mixed assemblage of prehistoric, Romano-British, medieval and post-medieval pottery and pieces of worked flint. Traces of ridge and furrow were recorded within this ploughsoil, orientated northwest – southeast. This deposit merged with a yellow brown sandy loam (1005) overlying the upper fill and edges of the Site VI ring ditch and the base of the barrow mound. This formed a band up to 8m wide and up to 0.35m thick. It seems likely that it represents material removed by medieval ploughing from the top of the mound and redeposited over the top of the ditch. This particular deposit contained a large quantity of worked flint (Fig. 17). The distribution of this material shows a correlation with the patterns of ridge and furrow identified within the medieval ploughsoil (see below page 73).

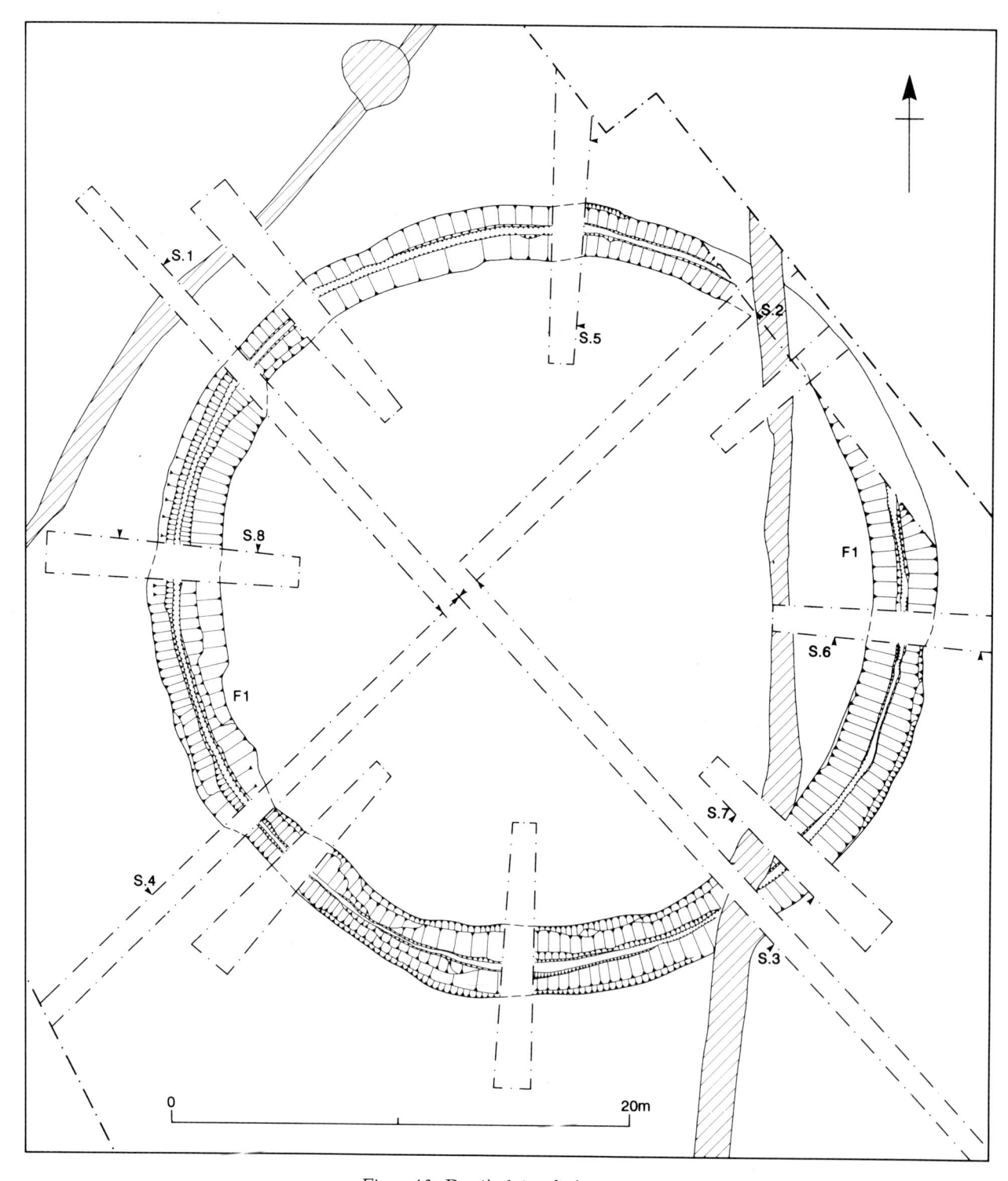

Figure 13: Detail of ring ditch at 1:250.

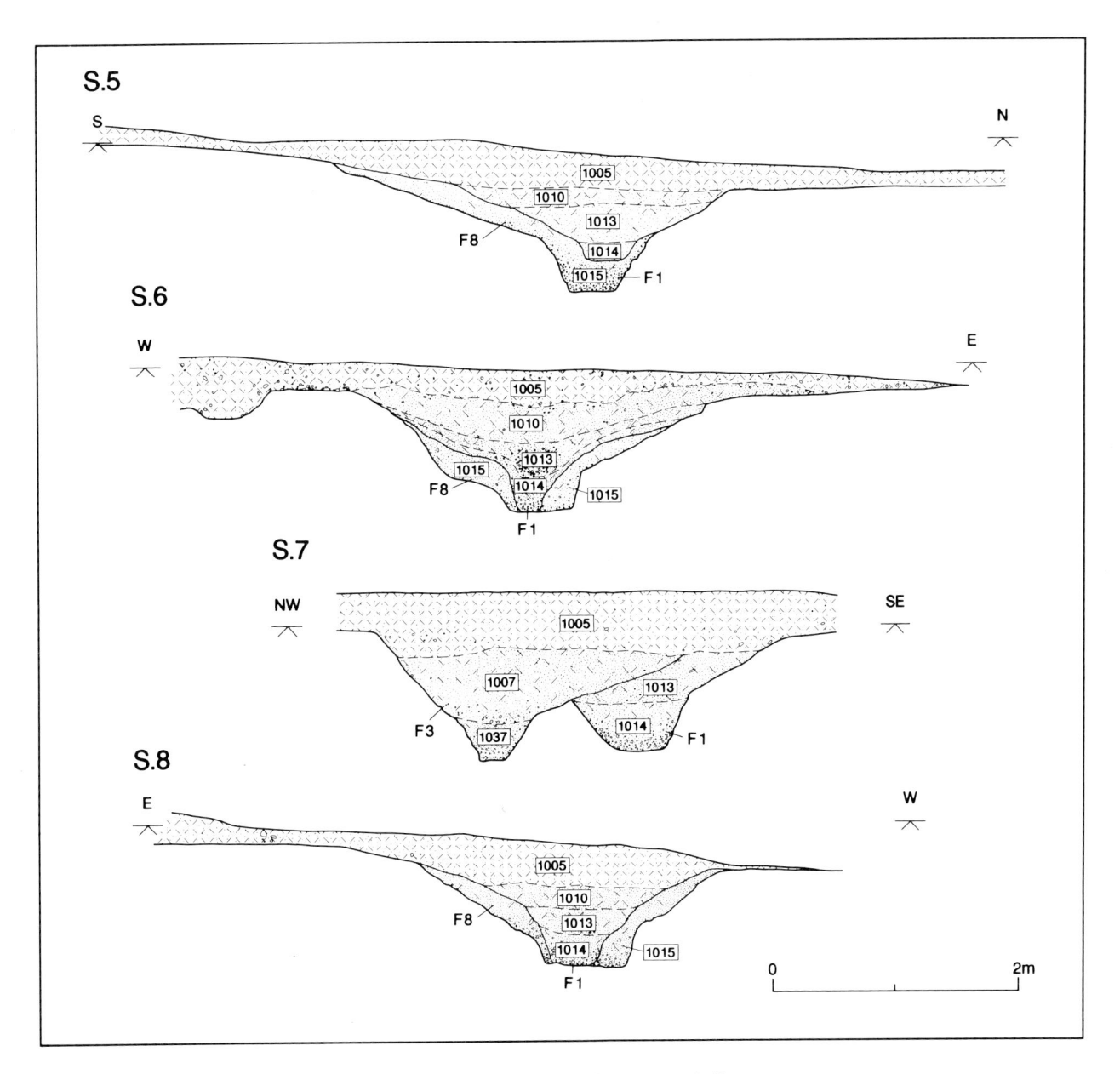

Figure 14: Detail of ditch section at 1:50.

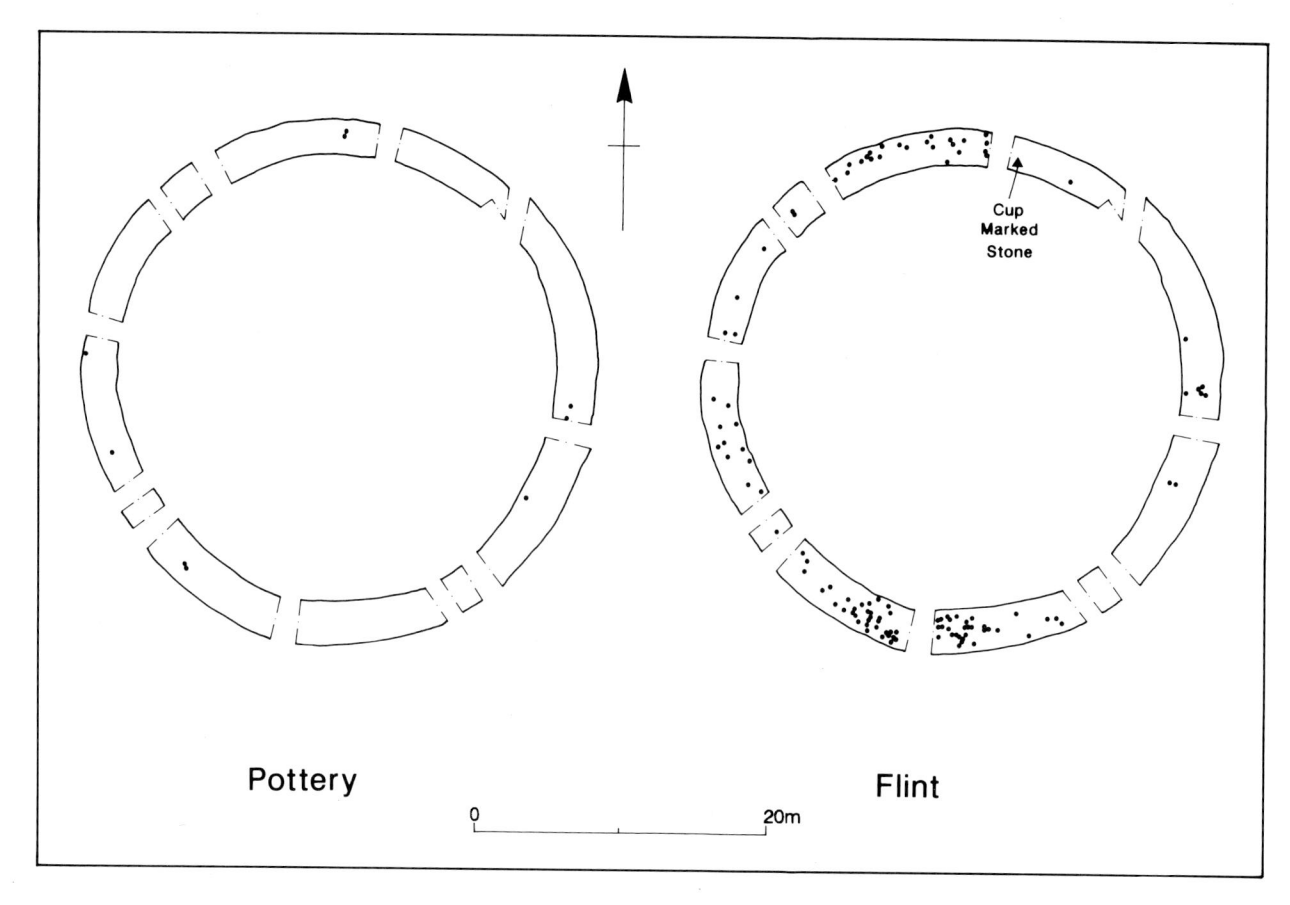

Figure 15: Distribution of flint and prehistoric pottery from the ring ditch fill.

Plate 1: General view of Barrow VI after excavation.

Plate 2: The board pit (F5) fully excavated.

Plate 3: Aerial view of the excavations in progress. photograph by S. Clouston.

Plate 4: General view of Barrow VI during excavation.

Plate 5: The central scoop (F23).

Plate 6: The west quadrant of Barrow VI after the removal of the ploughsoil..

Plate 7: Recording and samling the central scoop (F23).

Plate 8: Excavation of the barrow mound in progress.

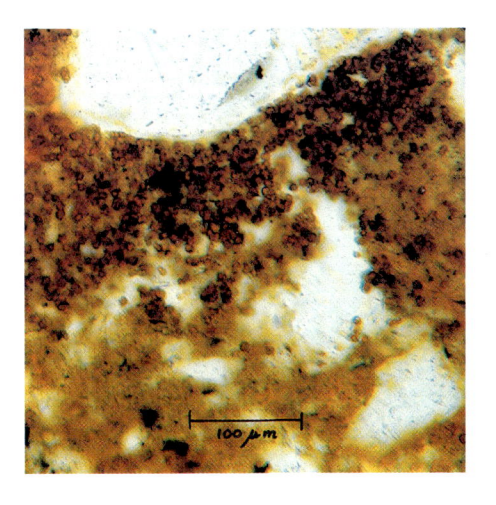

Plate 9: Microspherulites in the buried soil, Context 1044, seen in Plane polarised light. These are probably in an iron-humus complex of the calcite microspherulites formed in the gut of grazing or browsing animals (see page 91). Photograph by G. Norrie.

Plate 10: the palisade gully (F2).

Plate 11: Mark Allen, the excavator who first identified the pit containing the board.

Plate 12: The barrow mound during excavation. The darker band of sandy loam (1034) defining the edge of the core of the barrow is visible.

Plate 13: Ring ditch section (F1/ F8).

Plate 14: The two gold armlets. photograph by G. Norrie.

Plate 15: detail of the two gold armlets. Photograph by G. Norrie.

Plate 16: Armlet no.1 showing internal detail. photograph by the British Museum.

Plate 17: The dagger. photograph by G. Norrie.

Plate 18: The Cuxwold gold armlet (after Trollope 1857).

Plate 19: The Whitield gold armlet (after Herity 1969). Reproduced with the kind permission of the Society of Antiquaries of London.

Plate 20: The cup marked stone. photograph by G. Norrie.

The Excavation

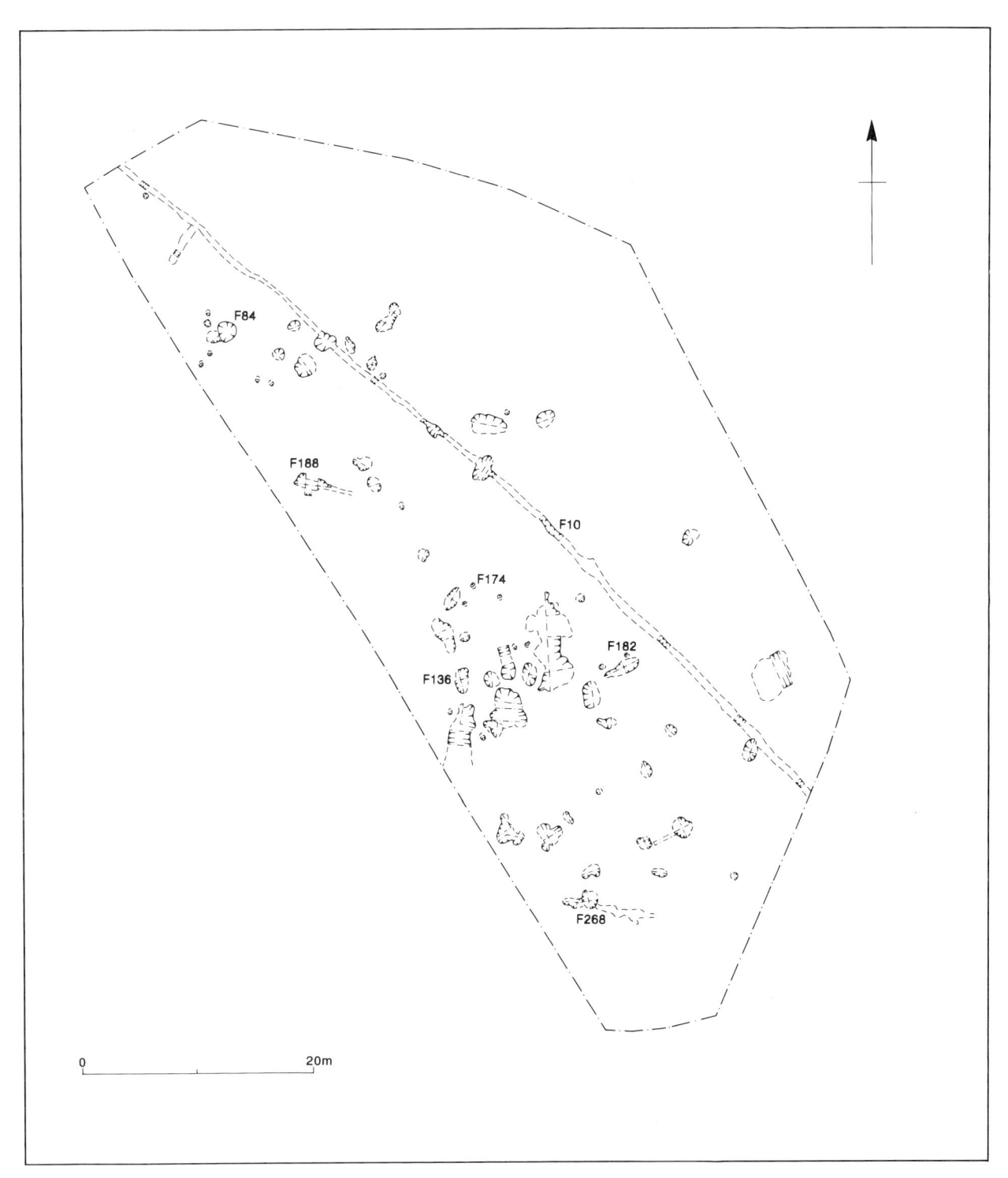

Figure 16: Plan of Site V pit group at 1:500.

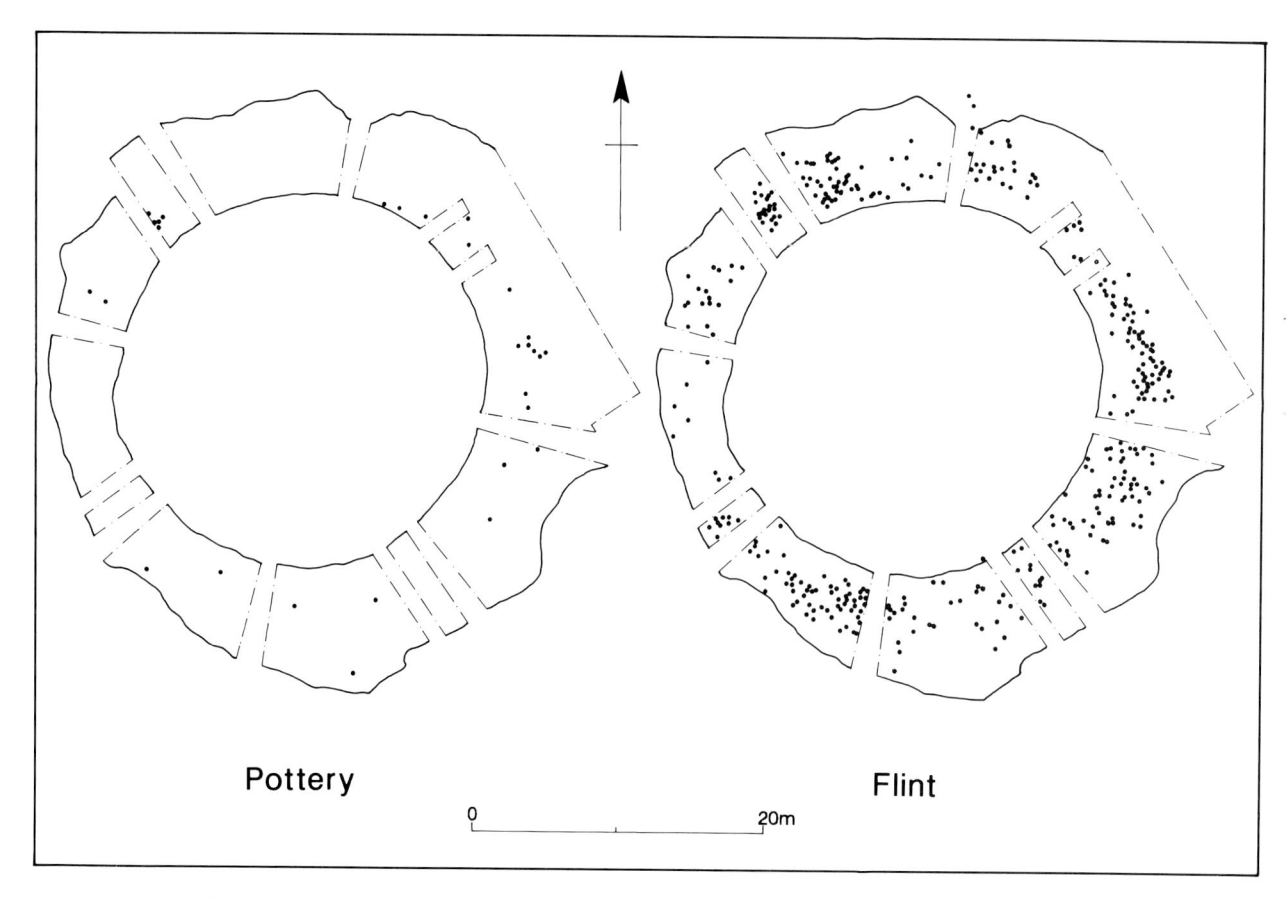

Figure 17: Distribution of flint and prehistoric pottery from the silt (1005) overlying the ring ditch.

THE GOLD AND COPPER METALWORK

By Stuart Needham

The three metal objects from the hoard were first seen by the writer in a cleaned state, having received initial conservation treatment at Leicestershire Museums Service. Notes on the method of recovery and cleaning were supplied by Mr Anthony Read. Most of the surviving sheath fragments had been consolidated and re-attached to the dagger blade having parted from it in the immediate post-excavation period.

ARMLET NO.1: LOZENGE-EMBOSSED (Fig. 18a and Plates 14–16)

Condition

The armlet has suffered no great distortion, localised areas of crushing being confined to the outer beadings. The under-turns feature a series of cusps where they have been pulled outward by a millimetre or two; these are the result of damage prior to deposition, and could for example have been formed in pulling out a backing material and/or wire supports (see Hook & Meeks' report).

On one rim there is a flat area of damage with coarse striations, a small tear and two tiny perforations. Generally there is a scatter of minor indentations pushed from the outside. One of the flat bands is locally marred by a 16 mm long 'chatter-line' of very small sharp strokes. There are some similar marks on the adjacent moulding and they seem to be later damage rather than a mistake caused during manufacture or decoration.

Most of the surface is in good, smooth condition and retains very fine striations presumed to be from the ancient finishing.

Form

A cylindrical band of sheet metal, annular with no join in evidence. In cross-section it is corrugated, with five bulbous ribs raised from a flat back. The ribs are evenly spaced with flat bands in between. The internal ribs each swell into lentoid bosses at eight points around the circumference. These bosses have a rounded profile whereas the linking narrower stretches of rib have a sub-triangular profile, still rounded along the apex (Fig. 19). Overall these ribs with their sinuous expansions and contractions give the impression of strings of barrel-shaped ('fusiform') beads. The two external ribs have a similar relief to the others but would originally have been of regular width, giving simple edge-beadings. The rim of metal has been curled right under these beadings to give strength and perhaps also to grip a backing material. Traces of a black substance were found under these lips, evidently a corrosion product of tin (see scientific report by Hook & Meeks).

The angles between ribs and the intervening flat areas are crisp and each is further defined by a neat row of pointillé (Fig. 19). The spacing varies between 11 and 14 dots per centimetre.

Dimensions

Maximum width 43.7 mm; minimum width 41.3 mm; external diameter 83.4–87.6 mm; internal diameter 77.5–79 mm; thickness at rim c.0.3 mm; weight 34.82 g.

24

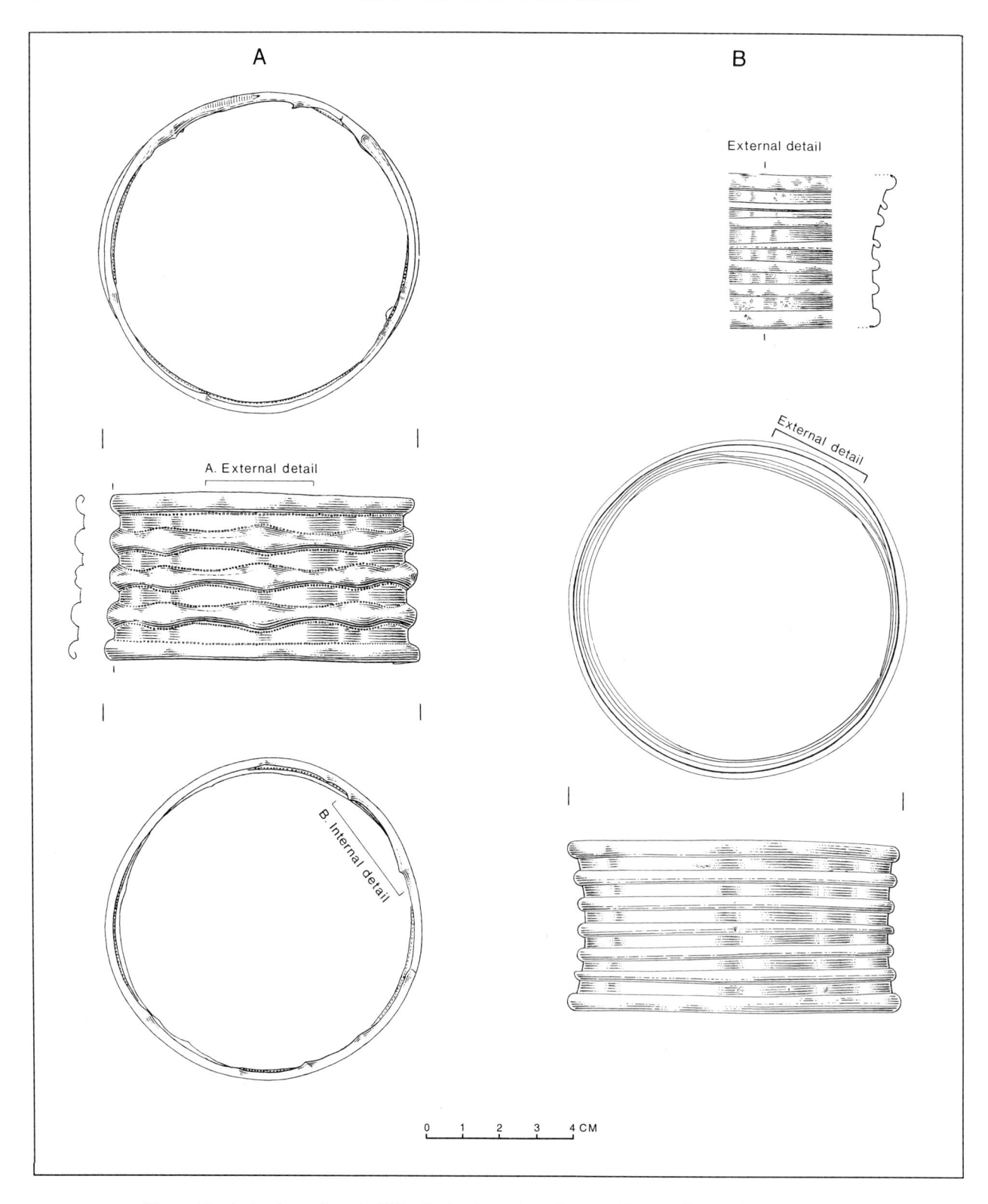

Figure 18: a) Armlet no.1; scale 67%. b) Armlet no.2; scale 67%. For detail of armlet 1 see Fig. 19.

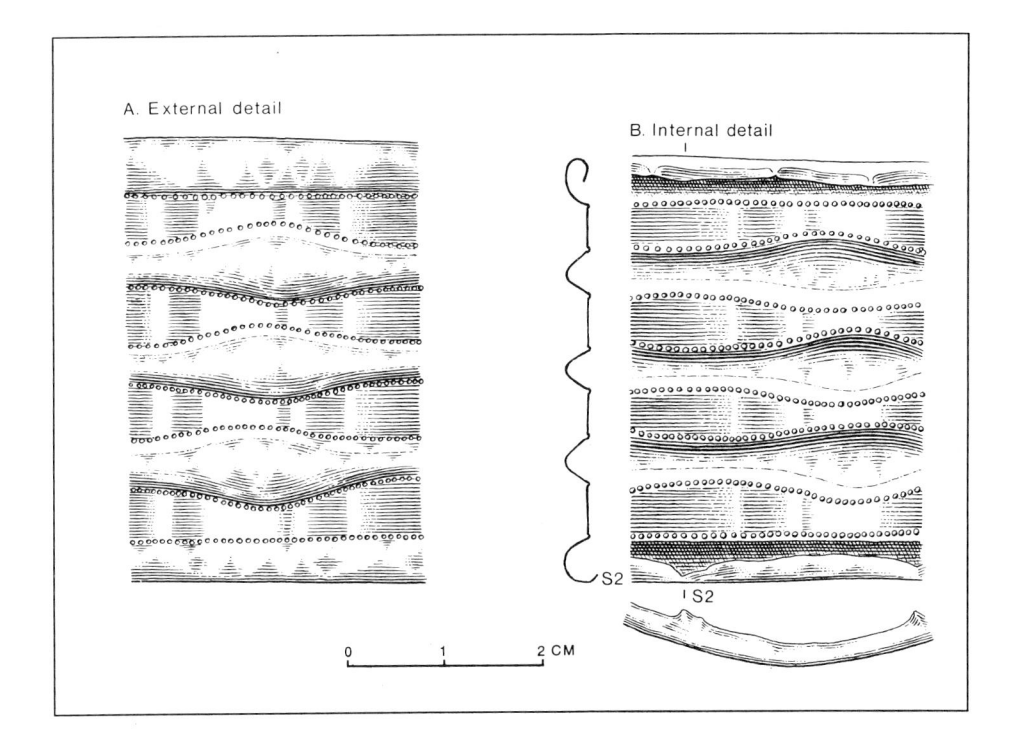

Figure 19: Armlet no. 1; detail.

ARMLET NO.2: PLAIN-RIBBED (Fig. 18b and Plates 14 and 15)

Condition

The armlet was little distorted by soil pressure in the ground, but instead the main disfigurement, the compression of one side by about 6.5 mm, resulted from resting directly underneath one of the pottery vessels. Two ribs have crumpled more than the others.

There are also several transverse creases across the flat bands, pushed from the inside, and a variety of other minor indentations from inside and outside. Both internal and external faces are carefully polished – very fine striations presumably from the ancient working are discernible. However, there are localised areas concentrated at the rim with coarser grinding marks which would seem to be subsequent damage. There are also two minute scars of brighter coloration on opposite sides of the armlet which are not readily explained.

Form

A cylindrical band of sheet metal, annular with no join in evidence. In cross-section it is corrugated, with seven bulbous ribs raised from a slightly concave back. The ribs are evenly spaced (where not damaged) and separated by flat bands with crisp angles at the junctions. The five internal ribs are essentially identical to one another, while the outer two are a little larger in both width and relief, thus emphasising the rims. The interior of all the ribs is hollow, having been raised by embossing. The rim along either edge is thin and is only slightly in-turned, but under magnification a tiny tight fold can be seen internally; in this way a neat, even rim has been achieved.

Dimensions

Maximum width 46.2 mm; minimum width (crumpled) 39.7 mm; diameter at edge beadings 89.4–91.8 mm, 89.8–91.7 mm; diameter at central rib 85.0–87.1 mm; internal diameter 79–83 mm; thickness rim 0.45–0.6 mm; weight 28.16 g.

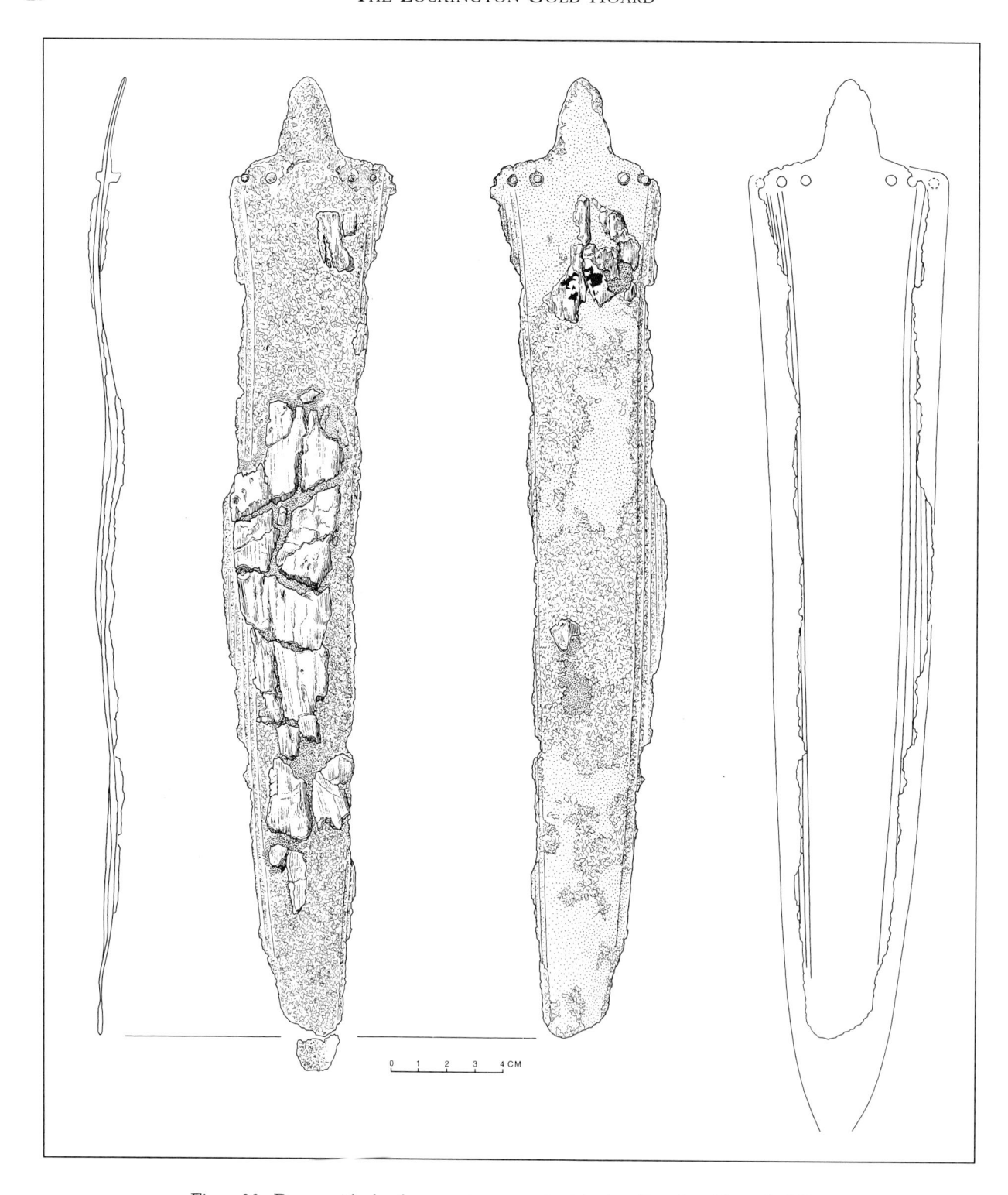

Figure 20: Dagger with sheath remnants; suggested original outline alongside; scale 50%.

THE DAGGER (Fig. 20 and Plate 17)

Condition

Corrosion has resulted in a very fragile object and the loss of most of the thin edges; the original outline thus has to be projected and cannot be verified in detail. The amount of loss is indicated by the survival of just a fragment of a third rivet hole on one shoulder, whilst one stretch of cutting edge projects much further beyond the inner two grooves than anywhere else on the blade.

The under-face of the blade retains a dark green smooth patina over some 50% of its surface, whereas very little patina survived on the upper face (that with more extensive sheath remains). The rest of the exposed blade has a light green powdery surface.

In long profile the blade exhibits gentle undulations which must be the result of ancient damage. Slight dimpling of intact patinated surfaces suggests hammering.

Form

Before distortion the blade would have been very slightly lenticular in cross-section, the faces being close to flat. It has not been possible to measure the thickness at the centre. On the evidence of the near intact part of its edge the blade was decorated with five closely set linear features. These have the general appearance of multiple grooves, but condition does not allow it to be ascertained clearly whether some were actually step mouldings rather than true grooves. It is possible that a combination of steps and grooves is involved.

The grooves follow a slightly sinuous line and the two sets are not perfectly mirror-imaged owing to the buckling of the blade. It seems probable that these ran parallel to the cutting edges and a gentle ogival shape may be presumed (as reconstructed in Fig. 20). The tip end has become detached and there is clearly some loss of metal here. However, it may not be extensive since the corrosion-chipped edges of the tip are all very thin. It thus seems likely that the tip shape would have been lingulate or bullet-shaped, rather than acute.

At the butt end a tang projects from almost horizontal shoulders, the top edge of which is in part essentially intact and surviving up to 2.0 mm thick. Only two rivet emplacements remain in one shoulder, but the edge of a third on the other, along with the loss to the cutting edges, indicates rather broader shoulders originally. The four surviving rivets are of the slender peg type. Traces of an omega-shaped hilt line are discernible in the corrosion products of one face, with tiny fragments of the hilt present above it (see Watson's report).

The sub-triangular tang has a lenticular cross-section with rather rounded, corrosion damaged edges. A slight hollowing just inside one side of the upper face may have been formed incidentally during manufacture. There is also a tiny but distinct indentation, perhaps punched, at one of the angles between shoulder and tang.

Dimensions

Length including detached tip 340 mm; maximum extant width 59 mm; maximum thickness c.3 mm; weight not currently ascertainable.

THE SCIENTIFIC EXAMINATION OF THE GOLD ARMLETS AND THE ANALYSIS OF A FRAGMENT FROM THE DAGGER

By D.R. Hook and N.D. Meeks

The gold armlets were examined under the optical microscope to identify the methods of manufacture used and to characterise the toolmarks which remain visible. The armlets were also analysed semi-quantitatively using X-ray fluorescence (XRF). In addition, a sample of a black substance from under the rim of one of the armlets was examined optically and analysed using XRF, X-ray diffraction (XRD) and Fourier transform infra-red spectroscopy (FTIR). A small, corroded fragment from the dagger was analysed qualitatively using XRF.

Visual and Microscopic Examination

The armlets are made from gold sheet, about 0.5–0.8 mm thick, with corrugated circumferential decoration. The corrugation of armlet no. 1 has lozenge-shaped swellings with additional tool marks defining the junction of the steep sides of the corrugation and the areas of low relief. The corrugation of armlet no. 2 is plain (see Fig. 18b). Both are in good condition with evidence of only a small degree of wear, although armlet no. 2 does have a compression damaged edge thought to be of post-depositional origin. The areas of the sheet between the corrugations are very smooth, showing accurate hammering and finishing. The surfaces are in a well-polished or burnished state, with many very fine striations in evidence. No obvious residual seam was observed on either armlet where the sheet gold may have been joined to form a band, but any overlapping joins could have been forged together leaving little trace. Alternatively, the armlets could have been hammered up from a blank which had originally been cast into a ring. There are no metallurgical features to suggest that the Lockington armlets were cast to their present thin forms. A visually similar ribbed bracelet of thin gold dating from the Late Bronze Age (*not* Middle Bronze Age – B. Armbruster, pers.comm.) found at Colos, southern Portugal is, however, reported as having been cast using the lost-wax process (Armbruster 1995).

Tool marks – Armlet no. 1 has repeating punch marks all along the edges of the corrugated decoration. There are some differences in their depth and spacing, clearly showing the use of a single-pointed tool. Occasional double stamps are visible where the tool probably "bounced". The punch marks show that the tool used had a tip which was basically round in cross-section but with a straight-edged facet, giving a characteristic "D"-shape. The tool was oriented differently from one row to the next, as indicated by the position of the facet. The angle at which the punch was used appears to have been approximately 45° at the junction of the corrugation and the flat sheet. Stress cracks are present around some of the punch marks.

The rims of the armlets – The rim of armlet no.1 has been formed by hammering over the edge of the sheet metal, thus giving extra strength. It is not, however, fully turned over and has outward pointing kinks in several places. This damage appears to have been caused by opening a previously tightly closed rim using a sharp tool or object. At several places inside the rim, a black substance was observed (see below). The damage to the rim may have been sustained when trying to examine or remove the black substance in antiquity. The damage is not thought to be associated with the original manufacture given the high finish of the rest of the armlet.

The sheet gold of armlet no. 2 has been turned over tightly at the rims, which are essentially undamaged.

X-Ray Fluorescence Analysis

The bracelets were analysed by XRF as part of the Treasure Trove process, using the analytical system described by Cowell (1998). As the bracelets were not part of the British Museum's collections at the time of the analysis, they had to be analysed totally non-destructively. Thus any potentially unrepresentative surface metal was not removed prior to analysis and therefore the following results should be regarded as semi-quantitative only:

Armlet	Lab No.	% gold	% silver	% copper
No.1	51633W	87	13	0.1
No.2	51632Y	85	14	0.3

The analyses have a precision (i.e reproducibility) of c.±2% relative for gold, c.±10% for silver and c.±30% for copper. Reliable figures for the accuracy of the analyses (i.e. a measure of how close the analyses are to the 'true' compositions of the body metal) cannot be quoted due to the unknown degree of any potential alteration to the composition of the surface metal during burial.

The analyses show that the armlets are similar in composition to other examples of Early Bronze Age metalwork (e.g. Hartmann 1970 and 1982). However, as the analyses are only semi-quantitative and limited to three major elements, detailed comparisons with other analyses of Bronze Age goldwork may be of little value.

Analysis of the dagger fragment – An already detached fragment from the dagger was analysed qualitatively using XRF to identify the alloy used. The fragment was found to be an arsenical copper rather than a tin bronze, which has major ramifications for both the dating of the dagger and the relationship between the dagger and the armlets (see discussion by Needham). The fragment was also found to contain traces of nickel, silver and antimony, possibly indicative of a *fahl*-type ore. The qualitative nature of the analysis precludes any detailed comparison with other arsenical copper metalwork. However, the presence of all these trace elements together is slightly unusual for an arsenical copper, certainly when compared to the analysis of British and Spanish material undertaken at the British Museum (e.g. Craddock 1985 and Hook *et al.* 1991).

Examination and Analysis of the Black Substance from Armlet no. 1

A sample of the black substance removed from under the rim of armlet no.1 comprised mostly a mixture of brown and black crystalline materials, with some tiny fragments of charcoal. The charcoal fragments were identified as *Fraxinus excelsior* (ash) using optical microscopy. The charcoal fragments may have entered the rim from the surrounding burial soil rather than necessarily being part of the armlet's original construction.

The crystalline brown and black materials were separated into two components. The brown component was slightly softer and less brittle than the black material, which easily broke under pressure into smaller crystallites. Both the brown and black components were sampled for XRD analysis and gave identical XRD patterns which corresponded to the synthetic mineral form of tin oxide (cassiterite, SnO_2; JCPDS pattern 21–1250).

Analysis of the brown/black material using XRF confirmed that tin was by far the major component, with traces of iron (probably absorbed from the soil), gold, silver, copper (probably largely absorbed from the armlets) and arsenic. Lead was not detected in the sample and therefore the tin was not present as the remains of a lead-tin soft solder.

The brown/black material was also analysed using FTIR to identify any organic media that may have been present. No peaks characteristic of organic substances were detected.

The black substance is therefore predominantly tin oxide, and it seems most likely that it represents the corrosion products of metallic tin. The fact that the sample consists of a mixture of brown and black cassiterite indicates that the substance may have been undergoing a transition towards the more brittle black form of the material. If tin metal was originally present under the rim, its presence would give the rim more solidity as the gold is relatively thin, or possibly the tin may have been present as a wire acting as a former around which the gold was hammered during manufacture. No other examples of the use of metallic tin in the manufacture of Early Bronze Age gold artefacts are known to the authors. Indeed, finds of metallic tin from the Early Bonze Age are rare (e.g. Needham & Hook 1988).

Conclusion

Both armlets are of hammered sheet gold with deep corrugated decoration which has been accurately formed. The gold surfaces are in a well polished or burnished state. One armlet (no. 1) has punched decoration which shows variations consistent with hand punching using a single tipped tool. This armlet also has damage to the rim which appears to be consistent with the opening of the rim with a sharp tool. The black substance present under the rim has been identified as cassiterite, without any associated organic binder and may have been present originally as a tin wire former round which the gold was turned. The major element compositions of the armlets are similar to each other and also generally similar to other examples of Early Bronze Age goldwork. The qualitative analysis of a tiny fragment of the dagger showed it to be an arsenical copper rather than a tin-bronze.

Early Bronze Age armlets in Britain

Form range and function

Various publications have drawn attention to particular types of armlet dating to the Early Bronze Age (Waterman 1948; Britton 1963; Henshall 1964; Coles 1968–9; Taylor 1980), but there has been no recent attempt at an overview of the full range known. The discovery of the Lockington armlets, which have so few close parallels, prompts a consideration of interrelationships.

Appendix 1 lists all armlets believed to be Early Bronze Age on the grounds of context or style. A few accepted in the past as Early Bronze Age are dismissed here: for details see Appendix 2. Form and decorative technique are rather diverse within the series as a whole and the initial impression is of a broad repertoire of trait combinations. Tabulation of their main attributes, however, (Table 2) suggests that the series can be split into three main groups, two of which show much conformity in choice of form, material and decorative elements. In addition there are three totally distinct finds in terms of form or material. This classification revises earlier ones, notably those by Coles (1968–9, 50ff) and Clarke (1975, 230ff).

Group 1 armlets are always made of copper or copper alloy and are consistently penannular flat-bands of thinnish ('sheet') metal. The band can be broad or narrow and is more often decorated than not, using longitudinal punched lines in combination with geometric infill patterns.

Utterly contrasting in form are thick bar armlets of 'D' to oval section which are again all copper/alloy (all analysed ones are bronze). They are, however, always undecorated and are classed here as *group 2*. Although the band is almost always seen to be broken, interestingly there was a systematic attempt to create a full annular form, by means of 'butt-jointing' the two terminals

Table 2: Early Bronze Age armlets in Britain and Ireland: summary of features.

	No	1	2	3	4	5	6	7	8	9	10	11	12	13	14	15	16	17	18
GROUP 1:																			
Knipton	1	B		X				X						X		X			?G
Bridlington	1	B		X				X								X			–
Normanton	1	B		X				X						X		X			G
Carnoustie	1	N		X				X											?G
Castern	1	N		X				X						X		X			G
Mill of Laithers 1	1	N		X				X						X		X			?G
GROUP 2:																			
Auchnacree	2	X	X			(X)													H
Port Murray	1	X	X			?X	?												H
Kinneff	2	X	X			X													G
Crawford	1	X	X		X														G
Ratho	1	X	X			fragments													?G
Netherglen	1	X	X			X													–
Stobo Castle	2	X	X			X													H/?G
Migdale	6	X	X			X													H
Uppat	2	X	X			X													?H
Mill of Laithers 2	1	X	X			X													–
Ingleby Barwick	1	X	X			?	?												G

Key:
1. Thin forms ('sheet')
2. Thick bar forms
3. Gold
4. Copper/alloy
5. Annular
6. Butt-jointed
7. Penannular
8. Simple ribs
9. Lentoid strung ribs
10. Floating lozenge bosses
11. Solid
12. Embossed
13. Long lines punched
14. Pointillé
15. Geometric punched
16. 'Ladder' milling
17. Rows of diagonal punch-strokes
18. Context: G-grave; H-hoard; R-ritual enclosure

B-broad; N-narrow

Table 2: continued.

	No	1	2	3	4	5	6	7	8	9	10	11	12	13	14	15	16	17	18
GROUP 3:																			
Ingleby Barwick	1		B	X		X			NB			X							G
Migdale	2		B	X		X			B			X					X	X	H
Mill of Laithers 3	1		B	X		X			NB			X			X		X		–
Shorncote	1	B		X			X		N			X					X		G
Williamstown	1	B		X		?	?	?	B			X			X				G
Melfort[iii]	2	B		X	X						X		X	X					G
Masterton[iv]	2	B		X	X riveted				B	X		X			X		X		G
Whitfield	1	B		X	X				B	X		X			X				?G
Lockington 1	1	B		X	X				B	X		X			X				H
Lockington 2	1	B		X	X				B			X							H
Cuxwold	1	B		X	X				B			X			X				–
OTHERS:																			
Luggacurran	2		X		X	overlapped													G
Lough Gur B	1	rod		X	?		?												R
Redlands Farm	1		X	shale	X		X												G

[i] Port Murray: one flattened terminal survives; three fragments heavily corroded; however, reconstructed they make near complete circuit (Piggott & Stewart 1957, GB31.6) – most likely butt-jointed.

[ii] Migdale: one group 2 armlet with overlapped terminals, bur probably originally butt-jointed.

[iii] Melfort: it is usually assumed that the second example, which crumbled on discovery, was of the same form as the extant one. Ribbing effect created by linear grooves which do not, however, punch through to flat back.

[iv] Masterton: rims tightly turned back; five major fragments plus number of smaller unconserved pieces – all erratically 'eaten' by corrosion; apex of one large fragment seems likely to represent a scarf joint behind the three-rivet terminal. (Fig. 4).

(Britton 1963, 271). An exception from Crawford, Lanarkshire, shows no sign of a joint and was presumably forged from an annular blank such as represented on certain stone moulds (Britton 1963, 266: Clarke *et al.* 1985, 94 fig. 4.17, 266; cf. Anderson 1886, 58–9).

The final group, *group 3*, is unified by the use of multiple ribs, but actually shows the complex mixing of elements seen in the other two groups, supplemented by some novel elements. This group, which includes the two Lockington examples, contains the more elaborate of the Early Bronze Age armlets, although not all of the highly decorated ones (see also group 1). Some in this eclectic group might be argued to belong elsewhere, for example the Migdale multi-ribbed bar armlets are

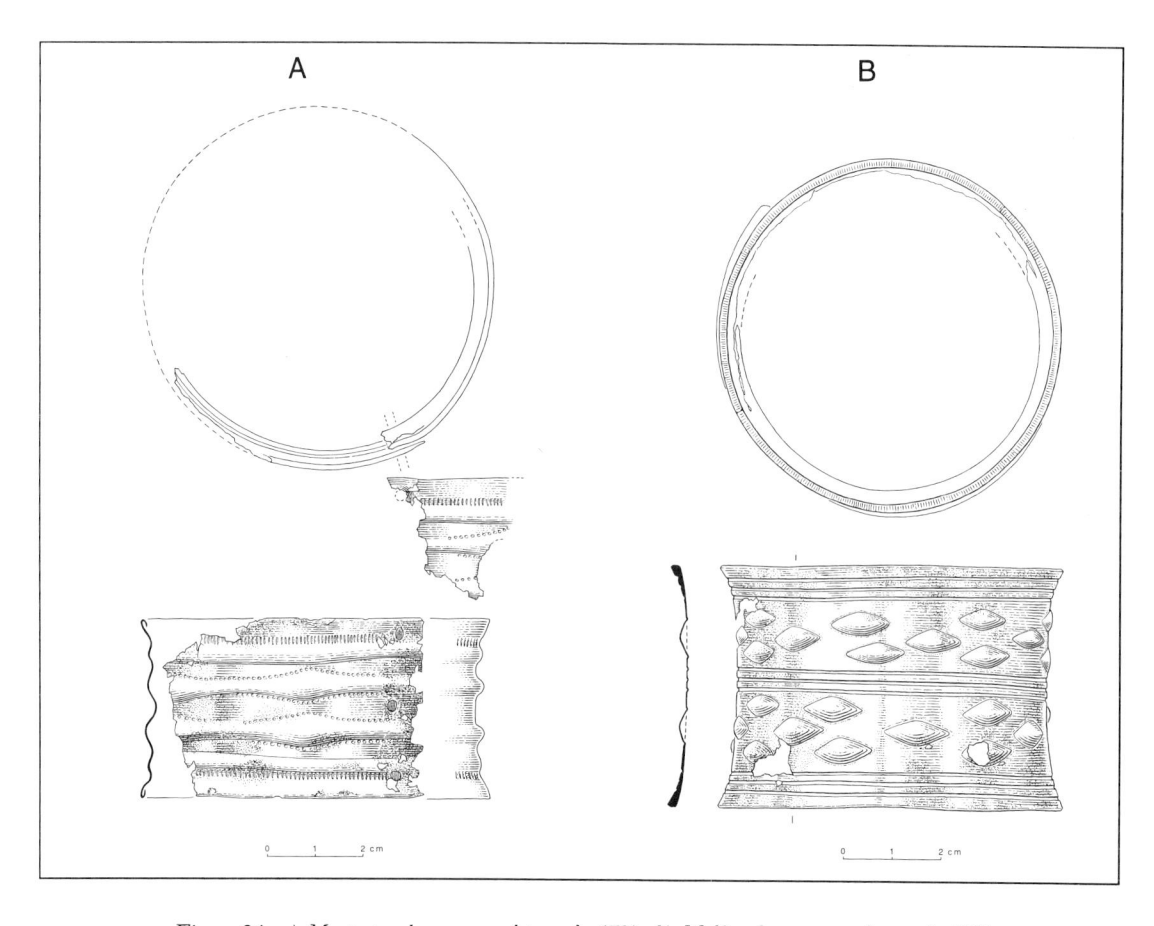

Figure 21: a) Masterton bronze armlet; scale 67%. b) Melfort bronze armlet; scale 67%.

obviously visually similar to multiples of simple bars of group 2. However, the application of ladder milling does link them to group 3. The group may be divided variously according to different criteria: the contrast between thin and thick forms, between annular and penannular, solid and embossed ribs, use of pointillé and ladder milling (Masterton and Mill of Laithers 2 have both), or the choice of gold or copper alloy. Some group 3 armlets have previously been referred to as the *Melfort type* (Taylor 1980, 51–2).

The four examples in gold, although not bearing an absolutely uniform set of features, nevertheless seem to form a rather coherent sub-group to which only the bronze examples from Masterton and Melfort have any real stylistic affinity (Fig. 21). The gold ones also seem to stand apart from their bronze counterparts in terms of internal diameters; the two Lockington armlets and at least one end of the apparently tapered Cuxwold example have much larger diameters (Fig. 22). This was probably also the case for the Whitfield armlet: its diameter is reported as 3 inches, but also to be 'so wide as to admit the arm of a man almost up to the elbow' (Herity 1969, 11 – quoting minutes of the Society of Antiquaries of London), implying an internal diameter of over 70 mm. In contrast the contemporary copper/bronze examples have internal diameters clustering between 56 and 66 mm (minimum undistorted measurement throughout). This would seem to offer some confirmation that the gold versions, being rather flexible, were backed by an organic band. The mean difference in their internal diameters compared with bronze armlets would suggest a backing material 5 mm or more thick, obviously on the assumption that they all tended to be worn on the same part of the arm. The bronze sheet armlets, although

The Gold and Copper Metalwork

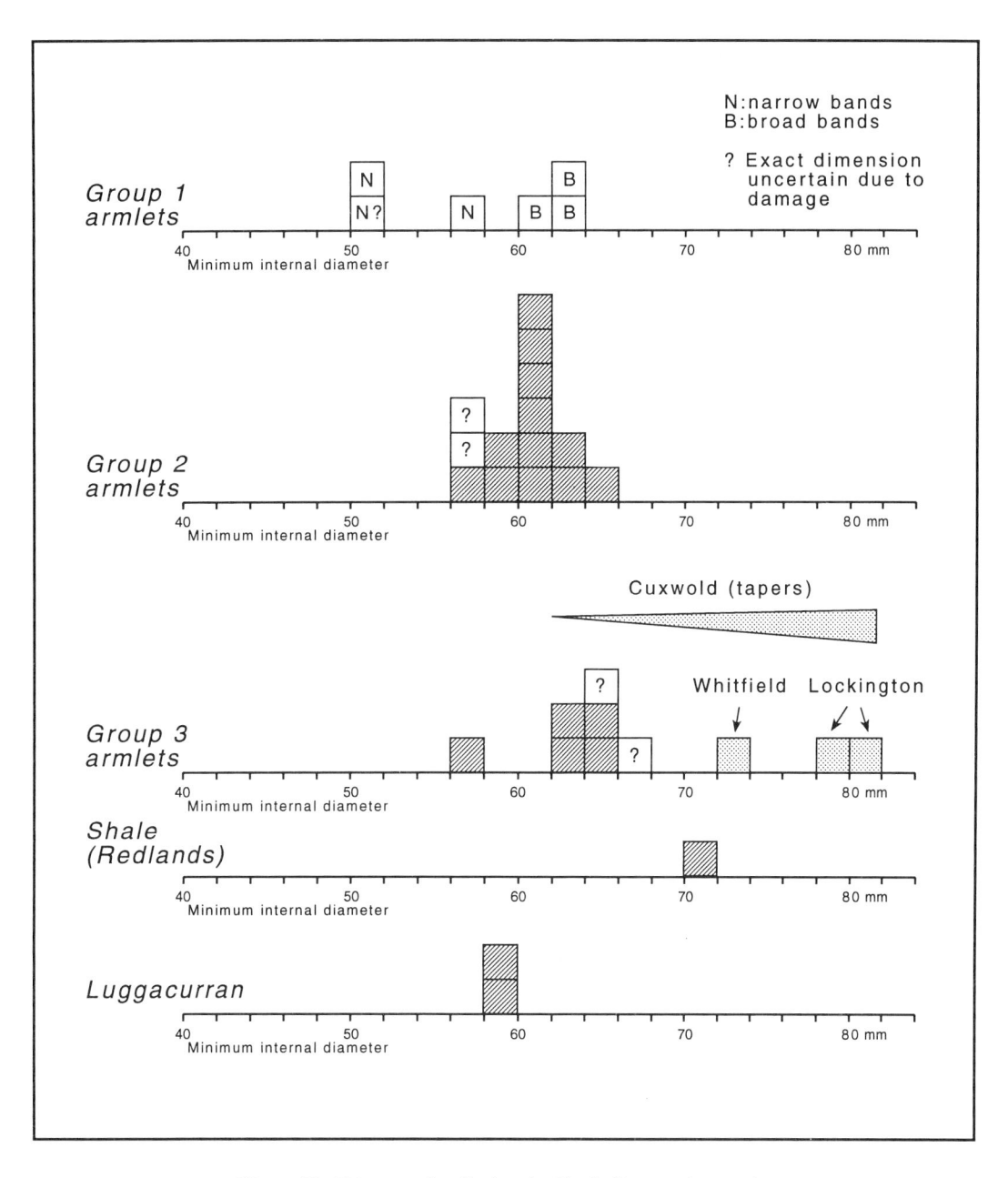

Figure 22: Diameter distribution for Early Bronze Age armlets.

generally of thin metal under 1 mm thick, would nevertheless have been rigid and resistant to distortion in normal circumstances. It may now be argued (see below) that the riveting present on the Masterton armlet served to clamp together two ends (Fig. 21a), rather than to affix an organic backing as was suggested by Coles (1968–9, 51).

Among the copper/alloy armlets there may be a subgroup of smaller size. The three known examples of narrow-band group 1 fall at the low end of the internal

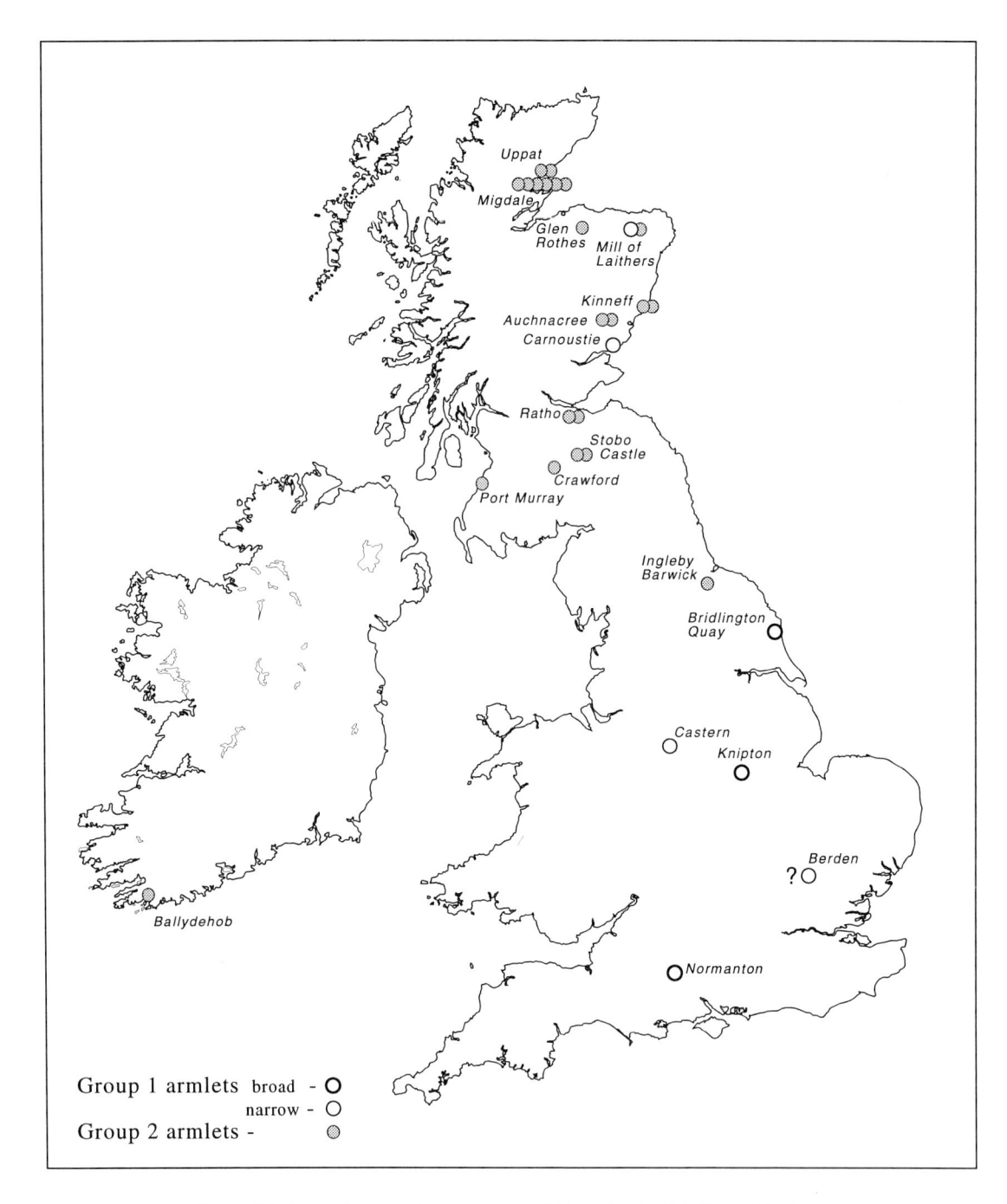

Figure 23: Map of recovery for groups 1 and 2 armlets in Britain and Ireland.

diameter spectrum, in two cases less than 52 mm. This type seems therefore to have furnished more slender wrists, presumably those of children or gracile adults, or were worn direct against the skin instead of over a garment.

Context and chronology

It is important to consider the background of the main groups and their interrelationships in chronological, contextual and geographic terms. The armlets from established contexts come from both graves and hoards; the distribution between these contexts may differ for each group, in particular there is a marked emphasis on graves for group 1 and a more balanced distribution for the simple bar armlets, group 2.

The chronology of these groups is difficult to establish with any precision. In general associations, stylistic and technological considerations suggest a date range focussed on late Period 2 and Period 3 (as defined in Needham 1996; *circa* 2200–1700 cal BC). The British Food Vessel associations (App. 1) should essentially belong to this date bracket. Although a few of the armlets are associated with Beakers, these offer little clarification of chronological position given current uncertainties over the significance of Beaker typo-chronologies (Kinnes *et al.* 1991; see also following papers). The radiocarbon date on human bones from the Shorncote grave points to a late part of the Beaker sequence (3480±60; BM-2892; 1980–1670 BC; 2–sigma calibration; Barclay & Glass 1995), while the Beaker and associated shale armlet from Redlands Farm has a similar date also on human bone (3450±45 BP; BM-2833; 1890–1670 BC; 2-sigma calibration). None of the other armlet-associated Beakers would traditionally be regarded as particularly early examples (Crawford, Berden, Knipton – Clarke's types N3, S2 and S3 respectively), although these types in general can now be accepted to have emerged during Period 2 (2300–2050 BC) on the strength of the combined radiocarbon evidence. Finally, there is a very recent radiocarbon determination on human bone from grave 6 at Ingleby Barwick, Teeside, of 3609±24 BP (2110–2090, 2040–1890 BC; 2-sigma calibration); two armlets – one of group 2, one of group 3 – were among the grave goods.

Four contexts in addition to Lockington contain other diagnostic metalwork in association with the armlets, either flat axes or daggers. All four are from sites in Scotland and all can be attributed to the Migdale metalwork assemblage on typological grounds, with a currency *circa* 2200–1950 cal BC (Needham 1996). The Migdale hoard now has a radiocarbon date in direct functional association (wooden bead core) of 3655±75 BC (OxA-4659; 2290–1870 BC; 2–sigma).

Finally there are the jet necklaces from Melfort and Masterton to be considered. Nine contexts in Britain containing jet or jet-like ornaments have yielded radiocarbon dates (Needham 1996, table 4); their one-sigma calibrations have ranges falling between 2180 and 1700 cal BC. Only one date is for a spacer-plate necklace comparable to that at Melfort, that for a grave at Risby, Suffolk, dated late within this bracket (3495±30 BP; GrN-11358; 1900–1740 BC; 2-sigma calibration). However, there is an early radiocarbon date of 3730 ± 35 BP (GrA-2157; 2290–2030; 2–sigma calibration) on human bone from an inhumation associated with a string of fusiform jet beads, from grave 13 at Keenoge, Co Meath, Ireland (Mount 1997, 23 fig. 17, 58).

Origin, distribution, technology and interrelationships

Although the broad chronology of these armlets seems secure, there is little refined evidence to assess how the various styles may have developed through the period in question. The whole idea of metal armbands seems likely to have been introduced to the British Isles from the continent given the widespread occurrence there of various forms, starting at an early date (Coles 1968–9; Clarke 1975, 230). For example, the Singen cemetery includes spiral forms radiocarbon dated to around the last quarter of the 3rd millennium cal BC (Krause 1988a). However, all or virtually all the extant British and Irish examples are insular in character suggesting that the introduction of the idea was rapidly overtaken by indigenous response.

D.L. Clarke argued for a close relationship between what he called the 'Knipton bracelet group' and Aunjetitz *manchettes* (cuff armlets) to the point that he envisaged 'Aunjetitz trained artisans working in Wessex' (1975, 231). (For some examples of Aunjetitz manchettes see Neugebauer 1995). The Knipton bracelet group was centred on group 1 armlets as defined here, but also included the now dismissed Cairntable example (Appendix 2), a neck ornament in similar style from Garton Slack, and the two rectangular gold plaques from Upton Lovell and Little Cressingham. These two gold

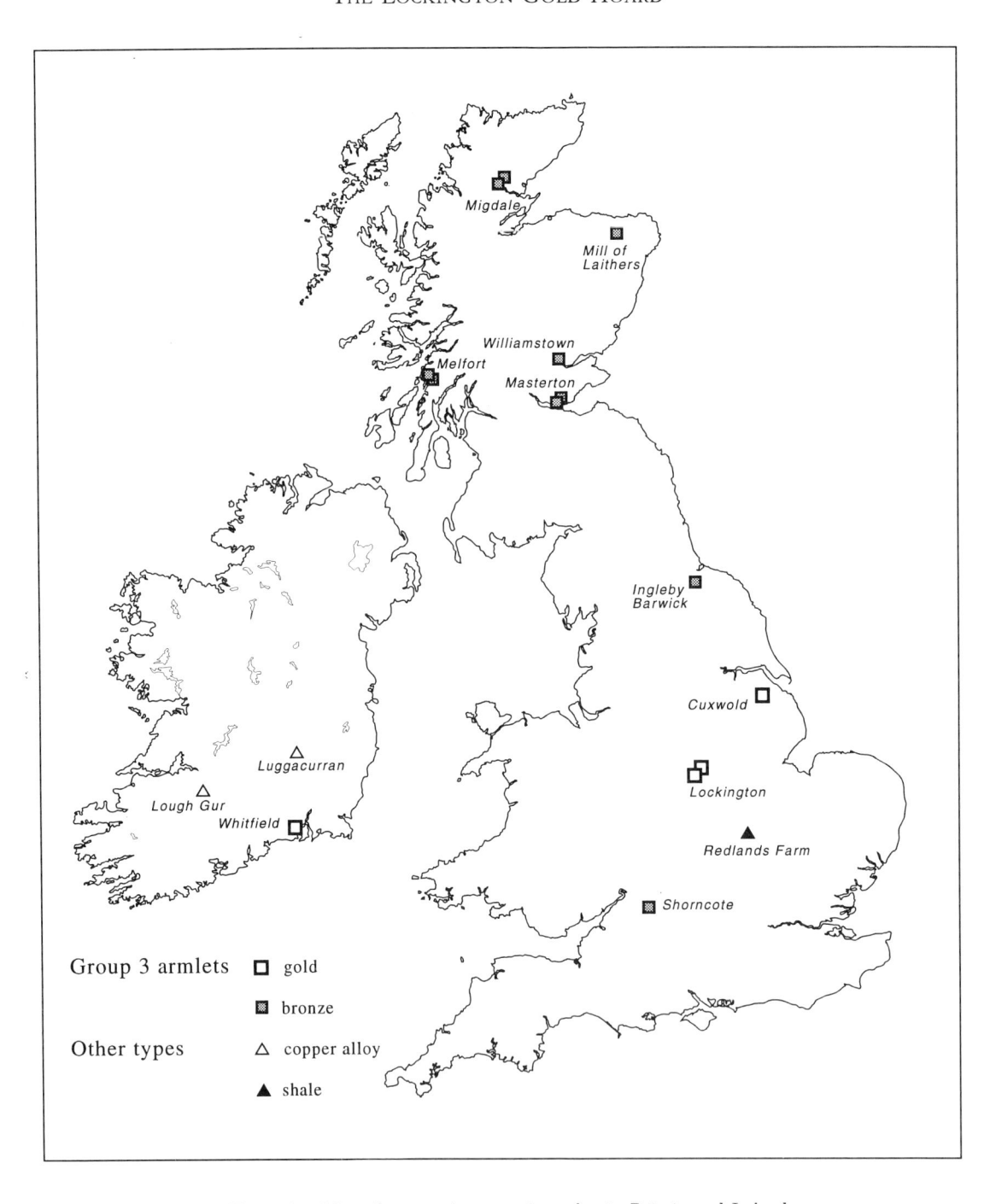

Figure 24: Map of recovery for group 3 armlets in Britain and Ireland.

pieces relate to the broad group 1 armlets only in carrying geometric ornament; the style is not very similar, especially in the case of Little Cressingham. Neither has Clarke's argument that the two gold ornaments are unfurled manchettes found much favour (e.g. Piggott 1973, 368). Their extant morphology, particularly at the edges, makes it hard to conceive that they could once have been so tightly curled (*vide* Clarke *et al.* 1985, pls. 4.29 & 4.57). Furthermore, the Little Cressingham piece, at only 92 mm long, could not in itself make an entire cover for an organic armlet, and it was in fact recovered from the breast of a skeleton (Norfolk Museums Service 1977, 32).

The comparisons in terms of geometric ornament linking British group 1 armlets to continental counterparts were probably overplayed by Clarke. With a longer Copper/Early Bronze Age chronology now established, it is possible to see a much longer ancestry and wide cognisance of complex geometric panel ornament, running back ultimately (in Britain/Ireland) to classical lunulae and middle stage Beakers, ie. Period 2. The appearance of such panels on armlets and other ornaments of, broadly, Period 3 demonstrates their shifting media context through time and space. This is further emphasised by the late transfer of complex panel designs onto the decorated axe series, appearing only late in Period 3 and continuing into early Period 4.

Although many of Clarke's conclusions about his Knipton group are no longer admissible, it is still most likely that group 1 armlets were the earliest developed in Britain. There is a high degree of mutual exclusion between the respective distributions of these and group 2. Group 1 shows a southern bias, being recorded from four, or perhaps five, locations in England and two in Scotland (Fig. 23). On the other hand group 2 has long been recognised to belong to an essentially Scottish metalworking tradition (Coles 1968–9, 50–1) – Britton's Migdale-Marnoch tradition (1963). Until a very recent find from Ingleby Barwick, Teesside, the type was confined to Scotland, where it is represented in ten finds.

Group 3 armlets are more evenly divided between north and south: eight examples from five findspots in Scotland, six examples from five findspots in England and south-east Ireland. Albeit based on few finds, there does appear to be an important distinction between a northern series in bronze and a southern series predominantly in gold. The one bronze example from the south, a multi-ribbed penannular piece from Shorncote, is not matched amongst northern group 3. Its inspiration might instead lie amongst the fine-ribbed penannular bracelets of the Únětician complex (e.g. von Brunn 1959; Uenze 1938; Krause 1988b; Vandkilde 1988, 118).

Arguing from a premise of developing complexity, given that skills had to be progressively acquired during the early stages of metalworking, it may be suggested that group 3 armlets were first developed from pre-established group 1 and 2 armlets. One strand in this process might be seen in the Migdale hoard with its multiple rib armlets at a date probably close to the turn of the millennium, early in Period 3. That hoard also shows that by this date metalworkers had developed the technique of embossing bronze sheet, as witnessed by a lentoid embossed strip, an object that has been interpreted *inter alia* as the metal cover for an organic spacer-plate (Stevenson 1956). Limited repoussé had been achieved earlier on the easier medium of gold on some Period 1–2 ornaments (discs and basket ornaments, followed by hilt bands – see Needham forthcoming b for full discussion of the developmental sequence). There seems little reason why the embossed forms of armlet could not have emerged by the time the Migdale hoard was assembled, in particular the association at Masterton also suggests a date either side of the Period 2/3 transition, *circa* 2100–1900 BC. Although the hypothesis presented sees the inception of group 3 armlets a little later than that of groups 1 and 2, the evidence gives no grounds for accepting a post-Wessex stage of development, which has been the traditional view (e.g. Taylor 1980, 51ff; Eogan 1994).

On the combination of typological, technological and associational evidence the Lockington armlets taken in isolation would seem best placed *circa* 2100–1700 BC.

Technology of embossed armlets

Some consideration needs to be given to the technique by which the embossing was achieved. The Masterton armlet was evidently formed by bending sheet bronze round into a cylinder, then riveting the ends together (Fig. 21a). The embossing could perhaps have been executed whilst still a little unfurled, but no appreciable degree of bending would be possible once the embossing had given the sheet a complex three-dimensional surface and thereby some rigidity. No join shows, however, on the Lockington and Melfort examples (although it should be noted that the full circumference of the latter survives only as a narrow band of metal alongside one rim, much of one side having been broken away). If forged from cylindrical or annular blanks, embossing these armlets with punches would have been technically rather difficult because the process of punching would have been confined to a very small space – the interior of the cylinder. There is no evidence from skewing of the boss profiles to suggest that long punches were applied obliquely so as to obviate this problem of confinement. (On the technology of Melfort see also Mancini in Powell 1953, 170).

However, an alternative method of production might be based on that suggested for the later highly embossed hats from western central Europe (Schauer 1986). After forming a cylinder of flat section, more or less of the dimensions required, the embossing would then be achieved by beating the band onto a carved wooden former placed inside. The former would have the shape of the desired mouldings in solid relief, but could only have represented a segment of the circumference, something like a quarter, in order that it could be freely detached after beating without disturbing the shaped metal. In this system the former would be moved round taking care to match up the relief pattern at the meeting points. In practice the full relief would probably have had to be built up gradually by going round the band repeatedly, and perhaps it would have been necessary to use more than one former at different degrees of relief. There are no indications on the Lockington armlets of former-junctions, but that is not too surprising; in a soft material such as gold small discontinuities could easily be ironed out with small hand tools afterwards. In the case of the Melfort armlet, the extant half shows no repeating pattern in the bosses; it is possible therefore that the putative former bore only a single boss, so that they would have been formed one at a time. This could explain the fact that the floating bosses are not very regularly distributed around the band and also vary slightly in orientation (Fig. 21b).

The complex working of sheet gold having a significant percentage of silver would have required annealing from time to time (Maryon in Powell 1953, 168; P. Craddock – pers.comm.). Nevertheless, the embossing of sheet bronze would in general have required greater technical skill than the equivalent treatment of sheet gold because of more rapid embrittlement. Given the innovative spirit of the earliest bronze-working in northern Britain, this should not necessarily be taken to imply the primacy of gold embossing over that of bronze. In the absence of closer dating evidence we might simply accept these as broadly parallel developments, tied also to another ornament type. The lentoid boss form has often been related stylistically to the use of fusiform beads in necklaces and bracelets (e.g. Simpson 1968, 205). Such beads are not a feature of Beaker associations – only one was recorded by Clarke, from Kirkcaldy (1975, fig. 1014). They occur instead in mature EBA associations and are presumably intimately linked to the creation of spacer-plate necklaces, themselves thought to be inspired by sheet gold lunulae. The earliest dating evidence as yet for fusiform beads is the directly associated radiocarbon date of 3730 ± 35 BP noted above for Keenoge grave 13, and this allows the form to have originated within Period 2.

THE LOCKINGTON DAGGER AND QUIMPERLÉ TYPE BLADES

The definition of Quimperlé 'swords'

At first sight the tanged form and arsenical copper composition of the Lockington dagger, bolstered by the association with Beaker pottery, could give the impression that it is very early, belonging to the phase of metalworking prior to the consistent practice of tin alloying. This is argued below however to be a misconception. While current interpretation does see a relatively swift and wholesale transition from copper to bronze in the British production of daggers, axes, and most smaller objects, there are a few exceptions for reasons that will become apparent.

With its flat blade, grooving close to the edges, near horizontal shoulders carrying six slender rivets and an intervening tang, the affinities of the Lockington blade in terms of British daggers are with the Armorico-British A type (Gerloff 1975). However, in detail it is not readily matched amongst British finds. It is unusually long, being matched only by the Armorico-British B blade from Bush Barrow, Wiltshire (Gerloff 1975, no. 124). This in itself need not be a problem, but when viewed in conjunction with its broad sinuous blade shape (as reconstructed in Fig. 20) and an unusually large tang, the piece looks rather deviant from the extant British series. Instead it finds very close matches in all its features with several amongst the parallel dagger series of Brittany.

The Armorican daggers contrast with those in Britain in including a number of long weapons, over 30 cm long, often referred to as *épées* (Briard 1984, 84–7). Amongst these is a group with slightly 'S' curved sides giving rise

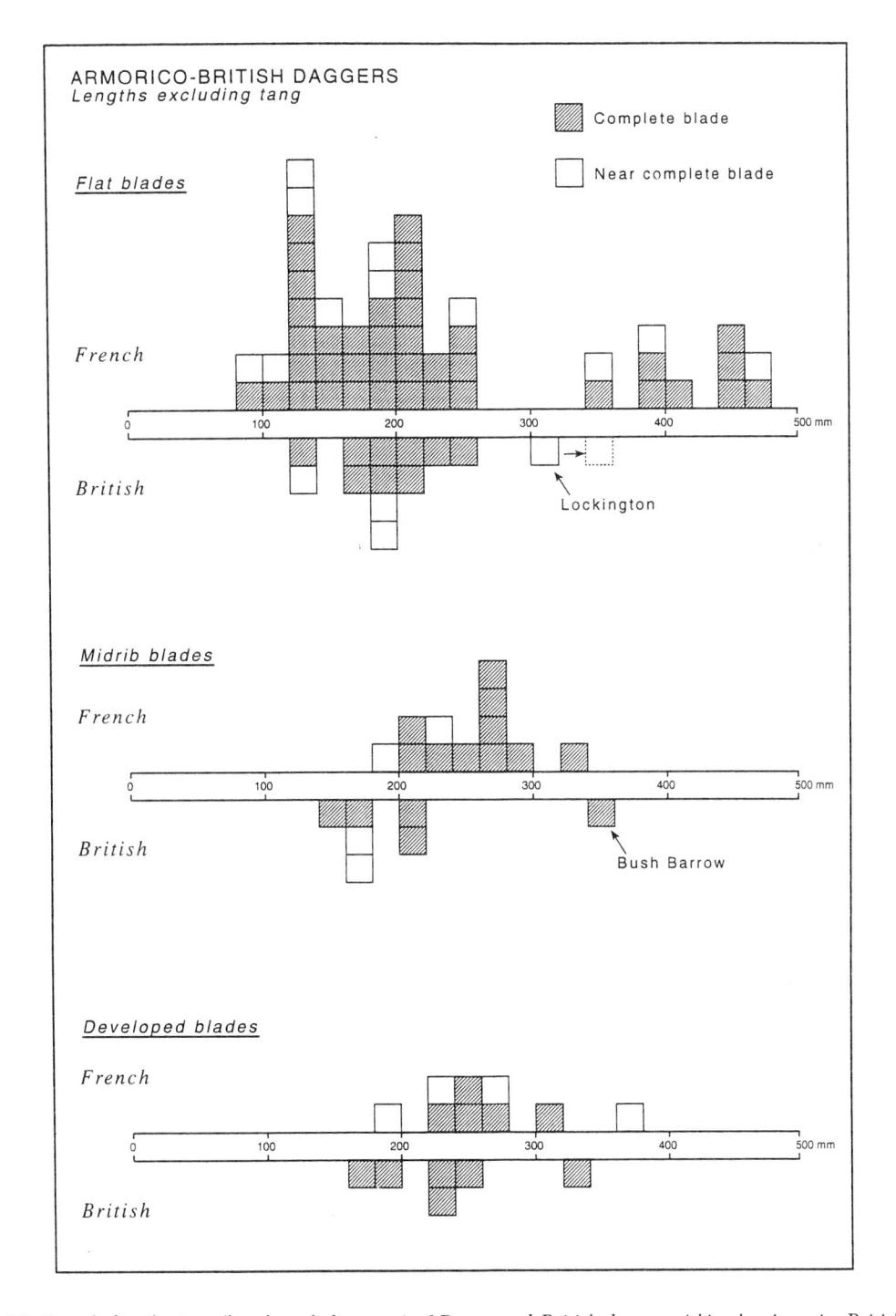

Figure 25: Length distributions (length excluding tang) of Breton and British daggers within the Armorico-British series.

to a virtually parallel central part of the blade, which then contracts bullet fashion to the tip. Briard (*ibid*) has described such daggers as having *lames larges avec double inflexion des bords*, which at times gives the impression of a leaf shape (*pistilliforme* – Briard & Mohen 1974, 55, 58).

In Gallay's classification they account for most of her *Langdolche der Art Rumédon* (1981, 93), a subset of form *Rumédon* from which she sees little distinction other than length. But it is clear that this long form of 'Rumédon' blades – whatever we wish to call them, long daggers or swords – should be treated as a conceptually distinct type. In shape they are not simply enlarged versions of the 'basic' Rumédon blades, being neither proportionally enlarged nor even extended preferentially on the long axis, which would result simply in longer *triangular* blades. Instead a new blade shape was formulated, the overall intention it would seem, being to maintain breadth for a large proportion of the blade. In addition to this distinction in shape, there is also clear bimodality in the length distribution indicating that the *Langdolche* are a discrete population (Fig. 25). The contrast with the modest length daggers is well illustrated by grave groups having both types (e.g. Tossen Kergourognon, Le Rumédon, Kerhué-Bras, Cosqueric – Gallay 1981, pls. 51B–C and 52B; Briard 1984, figs. 46 & 52).

The Lockington-like blades described cannot thus be regarded simply as falling at the longer end of a Rumédon spectrum. Briard's use of the term *Carnoët* type acknowledges this (1993, 184; 1995, 406), but he has not closely defined the type or its membership. To avoid confusion I propose to label them the *Quimperlé* type after the same famous grave group from the Forêt de Carnoët, Quimperlé (rather than Carnoët itself), which contains three splendid and well preserved examples (Briard & Mohen 1974; Briard 1984, 86–7 fig. 53). Although the Lockington blade may seem a little shorter than the Breton Quimperlé examples, reconstruction of its damaged tip would suggest a minimum blade length (excluding tang) of 340 mm, and possibly longer. This brings it into the length spectrum for Quimperlé blades (Fig. 25).

The identification of the Lockington piece as of a type otherwise unknown in Britain strongly suggests that it was imported. Brittany seems the most likely source given the concentration of Quimperlé daggers there (Fig. 26), but it should be recognised that this concentration may well be a function of the metal-consuming burial customs of the region. One other outlier, probably of this type but rather corrosion damaged, is a single find from Lafage, near Pamiers, Ariège, in the south-west of France (Guilaine & Briois 1984), whilst a lost *épée*, 40 cm long, found with 12 flint arrowheads at la Fosse-Yvon in the north of the Cotentin peninsula, could have been another of the type (Fig. 26 no. 17; Briard 1984, 193; Briard & Verney 1996, 573). Mention should also be made of dagger no. 2. from Gaubickelheim, Rheinhessen, some distance to the east (Fig. 26 no. 19; Hundt 1971) with similar blade form, length (c.350 mm), rivet arrangement, tang and decoration (in its first phase). Without the complication of the second-phase decoration, this piece would differ little from type Quimperlé, perhaps only in the tang shape and its contained seventh rivet (Briard & Mohen 1974, 57). A dagger from the Bassin de Penhouët, Saint Nazaire, Loire-Atlantique, has also been compared with the Quimperlé flat swords (Briard 1984, 280), but it has lost the butt and therefore any diagnostic features and it may not have been as long as the type defined here (Gallay 1981, no. 127).

It has been suggested that the long tanged dagger from Pinhal dos Melos, Beira Alta, Portugal, might have been modified from a long Breton blade (Brandherm 1995, 129). However, the argument hinges on the extant butt-line having been reduced in antiquity; the original butt-line is hypothesised to have contained a row of rivets. Even if this was the case, the well out-turned shoulders and the thinner taper to the blade tip would be at variance with the Quimperlé type proper. The present writer prefers to see the Pinhal dos Melos piece as one of a group of Iberian blades which relate closely to, but are distinct from the Quimperlé type (see further below).

Origins and comparanda of Quimperlé blades

The dating of the Lockington dagger (its manufacture rather than deposition) thus depends not so much on the dating of Wessex 1 in Britain, characterised *inter alia* by Armorico-British A daggers, but instead on the dating of the Armorican Tumulus series and the relative position of Quimperlé daggers.

There has been a tendency in the past to regard these unusually large blades as a relatively late development (e.g. Martin 1900, 163; Piggott 1938, 67–8; Briard 1984, 111). However, both Gallay's seriation (1981, 111ff) and the revised seriation put forward in Needham (forthcoming a) place Quimperlé daggers early in the Armorican sequence (Fig. 27). There is no evidence of a protracted Beaker phase in Brittany (e.g. Briard 1993),

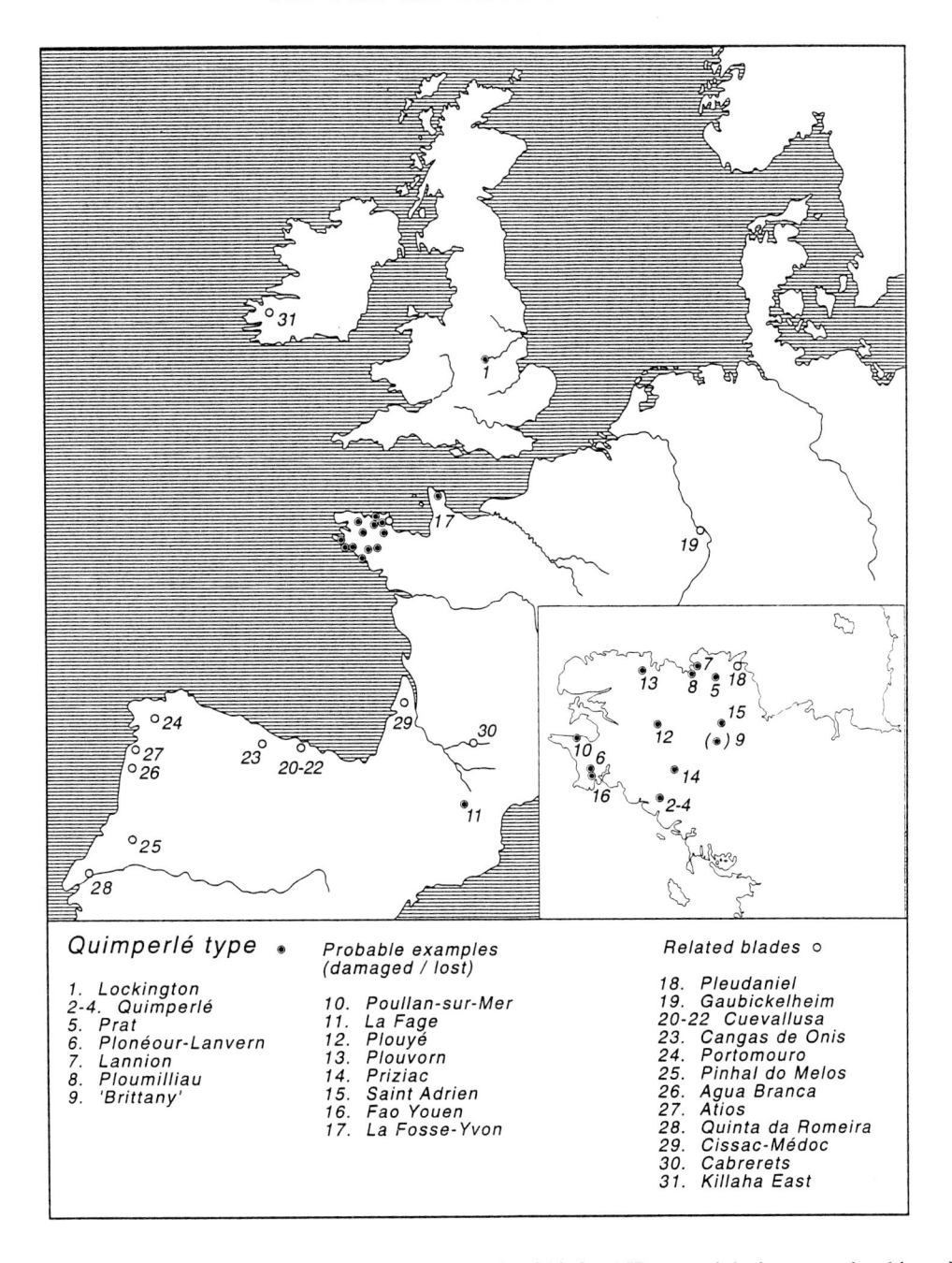

Figure 26: Map of recovery for Quimperlé type blades and related blades. NB some of the latter may be of later date.

unlike for example in Britain or Iberia, and it is argued that the Tumulus series began in the last quarter of the 3rd millennium BC (Needham forthcoming a). The Armorican daggers were part of a broad family of grooved triangular daggers emerging across western and central Europe at this time (Gerloff 1993, 74 footnote 48). The western groups may have owed something to pre-existing 'West European' tanged dagger forms, the developments in Brittany running potentially in parallel with those in Iberia (Briard 1984, 87, 203; Briard 1995, 406).

If this is broadly the dating and origin of type Rumédon, then there is nothing to argue against the parallel emergence of type Quimperlé given the association evidence (Needham forthcoming a). The basic West European Beaker dagger is of variable length, from modest to very short, but there are several much longer weapons of comparable type. These have come to be known as *épées épicampaniformes* (e.g. Briard 1991, 186). Only two examples in France have blade lengths around or over 300 mm: the celebrated pieces from Nantes, Loire-Atlantique and Le Vernet, Ariège (Briard 1965, 63ff; Gallay 1981, nos. 98 & 111; Guilaine & Briois 1984). Five others have blades between 170 and 230 mm long. Three finds from Britain fall within this medium to long range (Gerloff 1975, nos. 1, 2 & 5, perhaps also 3); whilst another, from Kenny Hill, Suffolk, has a blade 260 mm long (inf. C. Pendleton). It would appear thus that the development of long-bladed daggers (or 'swords') occurred whilst daggers in western Europe still conformed broadly to an international Beaker protoform.

In Spain and Portugal there are also medium to long plain tanged daggers, which Brandherm has classified as the Quinta da Romeira type (1995, 127ff; see also Almagro Gorbea 1976). Some at least show 'development' from the Beaker protoforms, featuring slightly leaf-shaped blades (*pistilliforme*) and sometimes groove decoration a little inset from the sinuous edges. The shoulders tend to be very pronounced with gently sloping tops. The longer of the two Atios weapons, for example, has a blade length of about 275mm, and that from Agua Branca, 340 mm. Those from Portomouro, Galicia, and Pinhal dos Melos, Beira Alta, have blade lengths of about 430 and 500 mm respectively. The blades give an overall similar appearance to those of type Quimperlé, but are more acutely tapered towards the tip. Once hafted, they may have differed significantly only in the hafting arrangement, notably in the lack of rivets. These can be viewed as the outcome of a parallel development to that in north-western France from *épée épicampaniforme* to Quimperlé (Almagro Gorbea 1976), although Brandherm emphasises that the evidence for sequence based on Iberian associations is still rather sparse (1995).

A small group of riveted flat blades in Ireland and Britain may also relate generically to the Quimperlé type; unfortunately most are not provenanced other than to 'Ireland'(Harbison 1969, nos. 24, 25, 32–34, 39, 40, 82; Gerloff 1975, no. 69). They are relatively long (between 200 and 320 mm) and have broad lingulate blades, just as some of their shorter parallels do; three or four even have slightly sinusoidal edges, reminiscent of that distinctive Quimperlé feature. The Killaha East example, moreover, has grooving and tang, which in combination are very suggestive of influence from type Quimperlé (cf. Sheridan & Northover 1993, 68), although it is not close enough in form to be regarded as an import. The Killaha hoard and the associations for the many closely related daggers of types Butterwick, Milston and Masterton (Gerloff 1975) all argue for a late Period 2 – early Period 3 date, *circa* 2200–1900 BC (Needham *et al.* 1985, iii; Needham 1996), indeed Killaha should be early within this bracket.

Overall, a simple progression would see longer Beaker tanged daggers emerging with time (e.g. Coffyn 1985, 13), perhaps as metal supplies became more widely available through the Atlantic zone, and then the subsequent development of distinctive regional dagger styles. In Brittany, Ireland and Galicia a tradition of long weapons (alongside standard-length daggers) was embraced and perpetuated, whereas in Britain there was an overwhelming preference for the shorter varieties.

The implications of the seriation of the Armorican grave groups is that the 'prestige' dagger types were essentially successive, with Quimperlé blades giving way to the Trévérec type (Needham forthcoming a). This transition is captured by the Armorican series 2 graves, which along with series 3 are argued below to be no earlier than Wessex 1, *circa* 1900–1700 BC. Reference to 'prestige' types introduces the elaboration of dagger hilts by the insertion of fine gold-wire studs, a phenomenon known on a number of Armorican dagger finds. The studding usually takes the form of outlining of the lower end of the hilt, where it grips the blade, most typically following the omega-shaped hilt-line. The daggers in question are sometimes fragmentary and not confidently classified, while in other cases gold-studded fragments of wood retrieved from a grave were not recorded as belonging to a particular dagger. Of those securely classified the majority falls within one or another of the 'prestige' types. One gold-studded dagger is attributed to the Rumédon type (Gallay 1981, no. 323) and it is possible that other examples may be among the fragmentary blades.

The addition of stout, well delineated midribs to daggers is an important change – conceptually as well as structurally. It is found widely in Europe on later Early Bronze Age daggers (e.g. Gerloff 1975, 87, 96). As far as the north-west is concerned an argument can be made for this adaptation first having been made in Britain, drawing the midrib from halberds which had always been strengthened in this way. Halberds had been current for four centuries or longer before Armorico-British B blades were developed and it may be no coincidence that this grafting took place just as halberds ceased to be used in Britain and perhaps generally in north-west Europe. [Note the uncertain Glomel association, Brittany, which would place the deposition of one halberd a little later – Briard 1984, 82–3]. During the concurrent use of daggers and halberds, with blades mounted in distinct manner they presumably had distinct symbolic roles and it may have been important to retain a fundamental morphological distinction to prevent ambiguity in their interpretation, especially when in an unhafted state. The strengthening of dagger blades may only have become 'permissible' once this differentiation no longer needed to be maintained. Furthermore, it is not inconceivable that daggers now carried both symbolic roles.

No use of the midrib is evident on north-west French daggers prior to type Tréverec, whereas in Britain a small group of daggers have plain blades with well defined midribs – Gerloff's group Ridgeway (1975, nos. 93–102). In other respects most Ridgeway daggers are not different from the pre-existing flat dagger series, and further evidence that they represent an early midrib form comes from the stratigraphy at Ridgeway barrow 7 (G8). The eponymous dagger was associated with an inhumation, already secondary in the mound (burial '1'), and was succeeded by a cremation deposit (burial '3') with a classic Wessex 1 grave group – here containing Armorico-British daggers without midribs (Gerloff 1975, nos. 114–116). Of course one cannot rule out some temporal overlap between daggers of group Ridgeway and the first real acceptance of the Armorico-British type in Britain.

It may be suggested then that daggers with midribs were developed in Britain early in Period 3, *circa* 20th century BC, as or after halberds declined in use. The standardised form of earlier bronze daggers was also being broken by other feature introductions, notably early versions of grooving on group Aylesford. In part these developments may reflect a greater receptiveness to cross-channel influences, a change which led to the adoption of the Armorican style daggers in Britain, perhaps along with selected other objects (discussed further in Needham forthcoming a). At this stage the Armorican assemblage comprised just Rumédon and Quimperlé blades and increase in contact may then have rapidly led to the midrib modification, resulting in Armorico-British B and Tréverec daggers.

The result in Brittany was thus the phasing out of Quimperlé 'swords' and their replacement by Tréverec daggers as the preeminent weapon. The Rumédon type continued alongside as a standard length dagger, but it is noteworthy that the Tréverec blades were rather shorter than Quimperlé ones, perhaps in part a recognition that a stout midrib and shorter length made a more functional weapon than the unwieldy and poorly strengthened Quimperlé blades. These new requirements of blades evidently continued unchanged through into the Bourbriac type (Fig. 25 – 'developed blades'), but blade strengthening was now achieved by thickening the whole of the blade centre between the groove-bands to give lenticular or sub-lozengic sections (Needham forthcoming a, fig. 2c). These blades are mostly between 220 and 320 mm long in Brittany and the associations do not give any real indication of a shorter series continuing alongside (only two possible sites). In contrast most blades in the roughly coeval Camerton-Snowshill series in Britain are under 200 mm long.

Displacement of the Lockington blade across space and time

The chronologies and correlations advanced here suggest that Quimperlé daggers had their *floruit* before Wessex 1 got underway and that the Lockington example, its production at least, is likely to have preceded *circa* 1900 BC. This would seem to be borne out by the radiocarbon determinations for the Lockington sheath (3910 ± 60 BP, OxA-6173; 3630 ± 55 BP, OxA-6447). However, these two dates are far from statistically compatible and the earlier one would give a surprisingly early date for Quimperlé blades, 2580–2200 cal BC at two sigma, implying a very rapid development from Beaker prototypes. Although there are several dates from Armorican tumuli of greater than 3800 BP, all suffer poor precision ($> \pm100$) and unhelpful contexts rarely directly associated with funerary goods (Briard 1984, 205; see also Needham forthcoming a). An exception, context-wise, at Kernonen en Plouvorn is a date of 3910 ± 100 BP for a *coffret* of oak associated with axes in the tomb, but it is considerably earlier than three others (3430 ± 120; 3200 ± 100; 3150 ± 120 BP) dating samples from the buried land surface and tomb fill (Briard 1970). In part, the earliness of this date might be due to the use of very mature wood for lining the grave.

The second Lockington radiocarbon date gives a calibrated range (2–sigma) of 2190–1880 BC. This correlates well with the sequence of dagger development outlined above, as seen against current views on absolute chronology. It should be emphasised that this has been drawn from a broad spectrum of evidence including accumulated radiocarbon dates from both Britain and the Continent (before the Lockington dates were available).

Whichever dating of the Lockington sheath is accepted, there is the possibility of significant time lapse between the manufacture and deposition of the dagger. A prestige object, found well away from the type's original sphere of use and reproduction, could well have experienced prolonged circulation. Had this involved multiple transactions, it could also have spanned several generations of people. However, one feature of the dagger may argue against prolonged circulation in this case.

It concerns the damage suffered by the Lockington blade which is broadly matched by a number of the Armorican parallels. The blade may well have been inside its sheath when the damage was inflicted, for re-insertion afterwards would presumably have been difficult even though the contortions are not pronounced. This could explain why possible hammer dimpling observed in the patinated surface is so slight. In the writer's experience the contortion of blades by mechanical pressures (rather than heat contortion from funeral pyres) is very exceptional on British EBA daggers, one rare example being that from Standlow, Derbyshire (Kinnes 1984, A14). This is difficult to evaluate comprehensively because side profiles are often overlooked in publications (e.g. Gerloff 1975). However, several Breton examples seem to have received similar treatment causing longitudinal bending and undulations (e.g. Briard 1984, 78 fig. 46.5, 82 fig. 48.7, 83 fig. 50; Balquet 1994, 71 fig. 25.1; Gallay 1981, nos. 288, 358 – and doubtless others lacking illustrated side profiles). Even the southern outlier from Lafage may have been treated thus, although here the mode of recovery leaves uncertain whether the damage was ancient (Guilaine & Briois 1984). There may thus be a strong association between this kind of deliberate damage and daggers emanating from Brittany. The implication is that a particular custom was involved, one peculiar to that region and its inhabitants. A further implication for the far-flung Lockington piece is that knowledge of that custom was transmitted with the actual objects. It would seem less likely that the object was transmitted in an already damaged state. We must then acknowledge the possibility that an individual from Armorica, or one with strong ties to Armorica, was responsible for the dagger arriving at Lockington, even perhaps for deposition of the hoard. This interpretation, however, does imply relatively quick and direct transmission from source area to final destination, that is, within a lifetime.

As an object manufactured abroad, the unalloyed copper composition of the Lockington dagger assumes a different significance. I have argued that Quimperlé type daggers were broadly coeval with British types Butterwick, Milston, Masterton etc., all of which are systematically made in tin-bronze. Such rapid consistency of alloying, however, does not appear to be matched at this date in neighbouring parts of Europe (if indeed anywhere on the Continent). That the depositon of the Lockington hoard post-dates this transition is suggested above all by the presence of metallic tin as a component of armlet 1. The Armorican dagger series could be made in either bronze or arsenic-rich copper (Bourhis & Briard 1985, 166; see Appendix A3 for Armorico-British daggers of arsenical copper). Examples of the latter composition can therefore appear anomalous against insular compositions, and indeed an unalloyed dagger at Bush Barrow (one of two full daggers) has previously been explained as intrusive from across the channel (Piggott 1973, 358; Needham et al. 1989, 392). It is possible that other Armorico-British blades found in Britain could also have been manufactured abroad (Needham forthcoming a).

GENERAL DISCUSSION OF THE METALWORK

The combination of objects in the Lockington hoard is extremely unususal; this is even true of the three pieces of metalwork. Daggers and armlets of the Early Bronze Age have only been recorded together in Britain on two definite occasions: in a grave at Masterton, Fife, and a hoard at Auchnacree, Angus (App. 1A). The Lockington hoard thus seems to have run against the grain of normally accepted rules of deposition (e.g. Needham 1988). This special case might be explicable in various ways, but it would seem significant that it was associated with an unusual context: a deposit made at the periphery

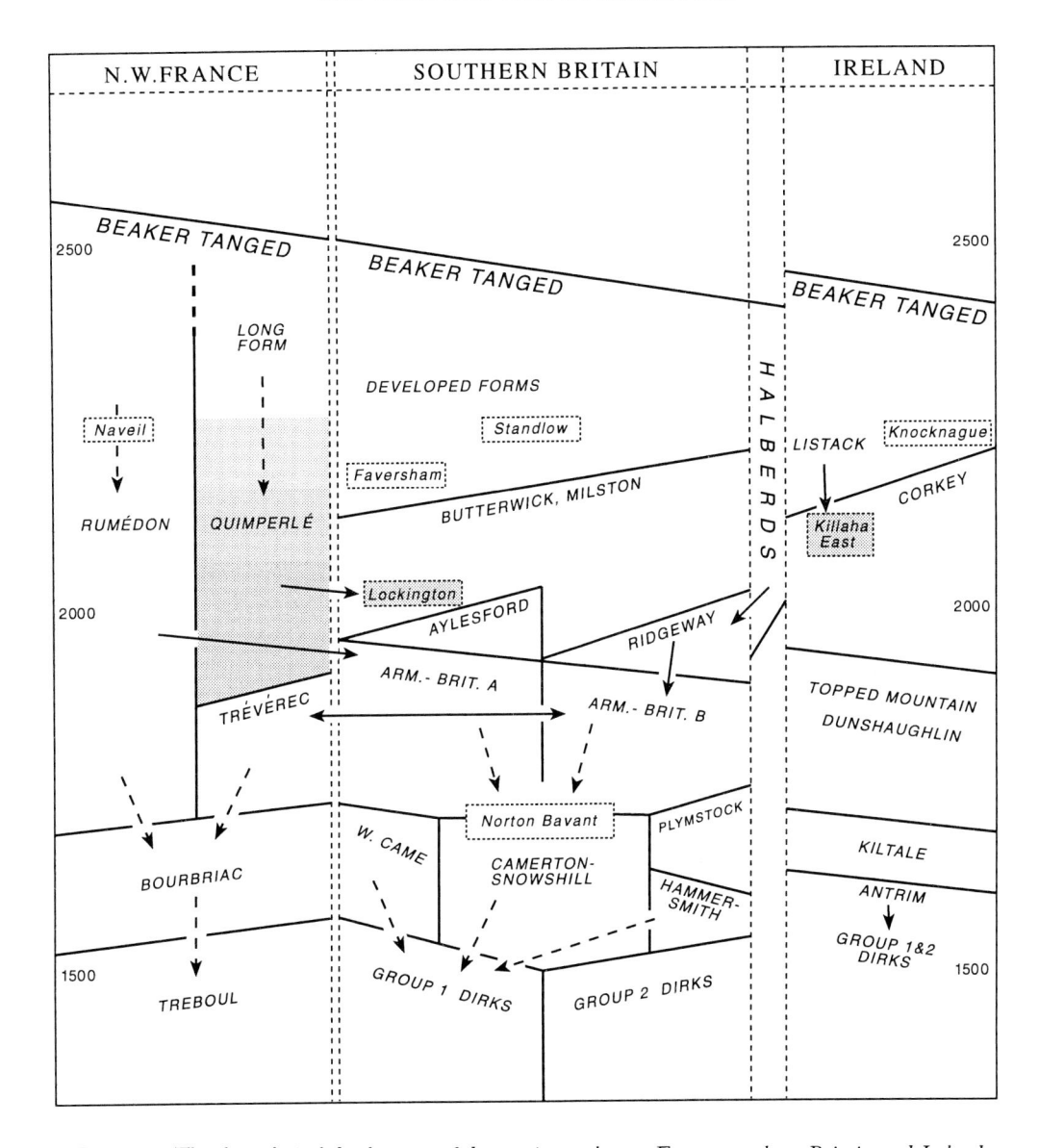

Figure 27: The chronological development of daggers in north-west France, southern Britain and Ireland.

of a mound and lacking any burial remains, yet comprising objects which, *taken individually*, are very familiar in graves. The position and contents of the hoard seem to refer conceptually to rites of burial and in this respect are of ritual intent.

One possible explanation for the 'liminal' siting with respect to the burial mound is that allowance was being made for the eventuality of retrieving the hoard; this could also explain why the hoard's composition seems so unusual, in that it was unusual for such a hoard to remain as a permanent deposit and thus potentially become part of the archaeological record. The tentative suggestion raised above, concerning a possible connection with an individual from afar, might be another factor in distorting the normal etiquette of deposition and we cannot exclude the possibility that this was in effect a surrogate grave group, the remains of the corpse actually being required elsewhere.

The Lockington hoard, with its Armorico-British dagger and fine goldwork, will readily evoke comparisons with Wessex grave groups. This however proves to be a false analogy on virtually every front. Firstly, the Lockington group was not placed in a grave, unlike the vast majority of Wessex 1 groups (although note the possibly anomalous context for the assemblage from the Clandon barrow – Needham 1988, 241). More fundamentally, however, there are clear distinctions in chronology, and in the technology and style of the goldwork.

On the chronological front, the richness and diversity of the Wessex associations has allowed their fuller characterisation, better opportunities for cross-correlation and therefore the prospect of a more reliable and refined chronology. Thus Wessex has become a natural reference point when trying to evaluate finds in other regions. This, compounded by a notion of a preeminently rich and powerful society in Wessex, has given rise to a tacit philosophy of *ex Wessex lux* – shades of *ex Oriente lux*. This has bedevilled the proper recognition of developments in other regions in Britain and Ireland which often had earlier roots than the emergence of the 'rich' Wessex grave rite; continual reference to the Wessex core has encouraged a belief that everything must stem from there. It is suggested that the analytical process employed has strongly conditioned our interpretation of developments and the transmission of ideas.

Around 1979 a chronological framework for the Early Bronze Age was consolidated, albeit heavily reliant on the metalwork sequence (Burgess 1979; Needham 1979). Although there is room for minor modification (eg. Needham 1996), this framework is finding increasing support in radiocarbon measurements (e.g. *Ibid*; Gerloff 1993). One feature is the relatively late placing of not only the Camerton-Snowshill series of graves (Wessex 2), but also the preceding Bush Barrow series (Wessex 1). The latter group is that of most interest in the context of goldwork for it has yielded virtually all of the classic Wessex gold objects which Taylor shows to be very uniform in style and technique (1980); she describes them collectively as *Wessex linear goldwork*. Although Wessex 1 is very poorly served by radiocarbon evidence, the coherence of the types present, in conjunction with the occasional inclusion of axes relatable to the hoard sequence, still argues for a mature stage of development. Many of the earliest developments of the full Early Bronze Age on this basis precede the 'Wessex culture'.

A case in point may be seen in the Lockington hoard. The armlets are best dated *circa* 2100–1700 BC, and the dagger to *circa* 2200–1900 BC. Given the likelihood that the passage of the dagger from source area to deposition was not unduly protracted, this favours a date for hoard deposition *circa* 2100–1900 BC. The associated fragments of pottery vessels are not inconsistent with this conclusion. The two armlets highlight a tradition of embossed sheet-metalworking previously represented by only a few finds. In addition to the two sets of bronze armlets and two gold armlets discussed above as the closest parallels (Masterton, Melfort, Cuxwold, Whitfield), we can add to the group the Rillaton cup (Kinnes 1994, A26), the Mold cape and another object associated with it (Powell 1953). Datable contexts make clear that this is a tradition of full Early Bronze Age date and it may be suggested that it evolved in northern and/or central Britain from *Primary Beaker goldwork*, by way of a group of finely corrugated hilt-bands, concentrated in Scotland (a sequence elaborated in Needham forthcoming b). This new embossed tradition, concerned with novel forms of adornment and vessels, seems to have eclipsed the primary repertoire of basket ornaments, discs, stud caps and lunulae, although there is also a shift in the distribution of these two groups from an Irish focus to a British one. The embossed tradition emerged before 2000 cal BC and had clear chronological primacy over any of the famous Wessex goldwork, although it is probable that the two then ran coevally. *Wessex linear goldwork* is utterly different in execution and indeed in the types of object made, and the two traditions present mutually exclusive geographical distributions (*ibid*).

ORGANIC MATTER ASSOCIATED WITH THE DAGGER

By Jacqui Watson

The dagger is covered in various organic materials which correspond to the hilt and a composite scabbard (Fig. 20). These have been preserved by the presence of copper salts which have prevented microorganism activity, but have not consolidated or replaced the organic structures. As a consequence some of the wood has shrunk during drying.

All the materials have been identified using a low-powered binocular microscope. Additionally samples were taken from the scabbard and mounted for examination in the Scanning Electron Microscope. These have been retained for future study (Watson, 1988).

The dagger has an omega-shaped hilt and the organic component is only represented by slight traces around the rivet holes. These could be either horn or antler, as there are translucent lacunae in one place, and in others it appears more fibrous. The organic evidence from other omega-shaped hilts suggests that this is more likely to be horn rather than antler, and in which case would probably have looked like the dagger from Drenthe (Clarke 1985, catalogue no. 170). The length of the rivets suggests that the hilt was around 11mm thick at the top of the blade. This is the typical width of these hilts. All four rivets holes appear to be packed with a fibrous material, possibly wood.

The scabbard is mainly made of wood, *Salix* sp. (willow) or *Populus* sp. (poplar) c.2mm thick with a tangential surface (SEM B732, fig. 2). These two woods cannot reliably be separated by microscopic examination. Both have the same general properties in that they are very light in weight and are resistant to splitting. Such thin pieces of wood would have been carefully cut or split and trimmed to shape probably with a knife. Some of the wood samples seem to be lined with animal pelt or textile attached with possible resin. There is a slight suggestion that the scabbard remains on the upper side of the dagger is decorated along one edge with parallel lines cut into the wood, imitating the decoration on the blade. In one place there is an almost perfect circular hole between the two sets of lines. It is almost certain that this is part of the decoration rather than a root hole. The top of the scabbard has a straight edge, rather than interlocking with the shaped hilt. As the wood has shrunk, the current position of the top of the scabbard is probably lower than at burial.

The exterior surface of the wood also appears to be coated with a black layer of resin which could either be a surface coating or an adhesive for a thin layer of leather that has not been preserved. A sample of the material in a KBr disc was analysed by Keith Matthews (Department of Scientific Research, British Museum) by FTIR and confirmed to be organic. The spectrum obtained was consistent with library spectra of a range of tree gums but no exact match was obtained. Unfortunately, because of the absence of suitable examples representative of degraded leather, this alternative source of the material cannot be ruled out. Hence the analysis is not sufficiently specific to provide a certain identification.

Underneath the wood there appears to be an animal pelt lining. At high magnifications it can be seen to be mainly very degraded skin with fine hairs (SEM B747). Unfortunately no scale patterns were visible so it cannot be identified.

Discussion

As stated above the hilt that bears the closest resemblance to the Lockington dagger is the one from Bargeroosterveld, Drenthe, Netherlands. This dagger has a single piece horn hilt attached with 4 bronze rivets and decorated with grooves and tin nails. (Clarke, cat. 170). Although not described as such in the catalogue, the dagger from grave 4 Winterbourne Stoke (Annable and Simpson, cat. 220) appears to have a horn hilt also.

Most of the omega shaped hilts that have been identified appear to be made from one piece of horn or wood occasionally ornately decorated with precious metal rivets – none are associated with this dagger. The copper dagger from Bush Barrow (Wilsford G5) in Wiltshire has a willow or poplar hilt decorated with gold pins (Annable and Simpson, cat. 169). The bronze dagger from Bush Barrow has a plain wooden hilt, and the photo indicates that one side of the blade was covered in hairs probably from a pelt and not wood as described in the text (Amiable and Simpson, cat. 170). From G.5 Winterbourne Stoke, Wiltshire, one of the daggers has a boxwood hilt with holes possibly for gold pins; and according to the catalogue a highly ornamented sheath, but no illustration (Annable and Simpson, cat. 263, 266).

Several daggers also have composite scabbards that could be similar to the Lockington example. The dagger grave group from Brun-Bras, Saint-Adrien Brittany, included fragments of a 'sword' with the remains of a composite sheath of wood and skin (Clarke, cat. 165.3). From Wilsford, Wiltshire, the dagger in grave 23 has a hilt made of wood and a possible composite sheath (Clarke, cat. 110.2). The dagger in grave 56 also has a wooden hilt. The scabbard has a transverse wooden strip and is thought to have been lined with textile (Annable and Simpson, cat. 159). In grave 27 the dagger has traces of a wooden sheath on the upper part of blade (Annable and Simpson cat. 346). There are the possible remains of a decorated scabbard associated with a knife from Barrow Hills, Oxfordshire (cremation Fl1, M8). This example is in a very poor condition, so it is difficult to tell whether it was made of resin or leather originally (Watson forthcoming).

THE PREHISTORIC POTTERY

By Ann Woodward

The barrow (Site VI)

A total of 276 sherds weighing 2005g were recovered. The overall mean sherd weight was 7.3g, varying between 16.6g for the pieces from the hoard pit down to 2.8g for the fragments from the mound material. Ten sherds could be ascribed to the Neolithic period, 154 were Bronze Age in date and 90 were of Iron Age type (see Table 3). The proportion of well-stratified material (96%) was extremely high.

Fabric

A series of 14 fabric types were defined macroscopically, and 13 samples representing eight of these fabrics were examined petrologically by David Williams (see separate report). Williams grouped the fabrics into four main categories, tempered with grog, quartz, sandstone deriving probably from local Triass deposits and, finally, igneous inclusions. They may have derived from local deposits but possibly could be matched with rocks in the Charnwood Forest area.

Fabric 1. Sparse angular inclusions of flint and quartz, ill sorted. Neolithic.
Fabric 2/3. Sparse quartz and mica, ill-sorted. Neolithic.
Fabric 4. Grog. Neolithic/Bronze Age/Beaker.
Fabric 5. Grog and sparse micaceous sand. Early Bronze Age.
Fabric 6. Grog with some sparse quartz. Bronze Age.
Fabric 7. Sparse small or large quartz inclusions, well-sorted. Bronze Age.
Fabric 8. Ill-sorted inclusions of small rock fragments, including sandstone and igneous types. Late Bronze Age/Iron Age.
Fabric 9. Sparse to medium density of medium igneous rock fragments. Late Bronze Age.
Fabric 10. Sparse quartz grains of varying size. Iron Age.
Fabric 11. Dense small quartz grains. Iron Age.
Fabric 12. Sand. Iron Age.
Fabric 13. Shell inclusions. Iron Age.
Fabric 14. Micaceous sand. Iron Age.

Amongst the Bronze Age sherds, grog was the most common tempering agent (66%) followed by grog with micaceous sand (22%). These figures are however dominated by the presence of three main vessels. The nineteen sherds of fabrics 8 and 9 are very distinctive and appear to be Late Bronze Age in character. The most frequently occurring Iron Age fabric is 10, sparse quartz inclusions, which accounts for 68% of the sherds of this period.

Few early prehistoric pottery fragments have been described in the East Midlands. However, grog-tempered Collared Urns are known from Conegre Farm, Notts. and Pasture Lodge Farm, Lincs. (Allen 1987, Fig. 10, nos. 53 and 54: Fig. 15, no. 24B). The urn at Willington contained coarse and angular grits (Manby in Wheeler 1979, nos. 108 to 112), whilst two Late Bronze Age or Early Iron Age vessels contained angular quartz inclusions (*op cit*. nos. 118–9). The Beaker sherd from Roystone Grange, which will be referred to below, contained grog and small calcite inclusions. The probably Late Bronze Age sherds at Lockington in the distinctive sandstone and igneous-tempered Fabrics 8 and 9 are of particular interest. Igneous inclusions, possibly from the Charnwood source, are known from Iron Age sites such

Table 3: Prehistoric pottery.

	Description	Total sherds	Total weight (g.)	Mean weight (g.)	Neo	BA	IA	Abrasion	Burnt	Notes
Site VI	Topsoil/ploughsoil	10	37	3.7	-	2	7	90%	-	1 scrap
	Silt over ring ditch	52	226	4.3	-	10	37	75%	6%	daub x 1 R-B x 4
	The barrow mound	36	102	2.8	-	33	3	60%	-	
	The ring ditch	32	310	9.6	-	14	12	41%	9%	daub x 4 R-B x 2
	Pre-barrow deposits	53	202	3.8	10	43	-	47%	4%	
	The hoard	62	1028	16.6	-	52	-	31%	-	
	Peripheral features	31	100	3.2	-	-	31	26%	-	
	Vessel A	29	187	6.4	-	29	-	7%	-	
	Vessel B	8	149	19	-	8	-			M/LBA
	Vessel C	2	43	21.5	-	2	-			
	Vessel D	9	56	6	-	-	9			
	Vessel E	8	22	2.8	-	-	8			
Site VI TOTAL		276	2005	7.3	10	154	90			
Site V Phase 1	Clearance	2	11	5.5	1	-	-	50%	-	Indet: 1
Phase 2	Pits	20	221	11	-	9	5	35%	-	Indet: 6
Phase 3	Ditch	20	101	5	-	1	19	95%	-	
Site V TOTAL		42	333	7.9	1	10	24			Indet: 7

as Gamston, Notts. (Knight 1992) and igneous fragments have been recognised in earlier Bronze Age urn pottery from Sproxton and Eaton in Leics. (Clay 1981, 14 and 1981, fig. 15, 1–3). Other Late Bronze Age pottery from the region displays a variety of sandstone (Tixover, Leics.: Elsdon forthcoming) or iron ore, limestone, quartz and grog tempering (Mam Tor, Derbys: Gerrish 1983).

Form and Decoration

The pottery will be described within a chronological framework based on the site phasing. Almost all the diagnostic items are illustrated in Figs. 28 and 29.

(a) pre-barrow deposits – One small feature contained a diagnostic piece of Neolithic pottery, no. 2 in fabric 2. There were also nine further fragments of fabric 1 Neolithic-type pottery. Otherwise there were 43 sherds of Bronze Age date. Of these 28 were in fabric 5 (micaceous sand and grog) with 13 of them definitely belonging to a single vessel, no. 1. There were also 12 pieces in fabric 4 (grog), one of which was from a Beaker (not illus.).

This context group produced the most sherds. They were of low to medium mean weight and displayed a low degree of abrasion (47%). Only 4% were re-fired even though many of the soils and deposits in this group were burnt. No Iron Age sherds were present, but a few Neolithic items indicated earlier activity. Neolithic/Beaker items displayed a very low average sherd weight of 1.3g and an even distribution across the area. The total sherd plot (Fig. 8) shows a concentration just S of centre and significant clusters at the N and SE. Vessel 1 (Early Bronze Age) sherds, mainly decorated rims, occurred mainly S of centre with one additional cluster to the N.

1. Seven rim sherds and at least six wall sherds, none joining from a large vessel with an internally bevelled rim and wide ribbed treatment to the area below the rim. Enlarged Food Vessel Urn. Fabric 5. Contexts 1042, 1043, 1088 and 1093. These were contexts sealed by the barrow mound and included the fill of the central scoop (F23).

The ridged profile of this plain vessel is matched on the Ridged Vase from Cossington site 2, Leics. (Vine

50 THE LOCKINGTON GOLD HOARD

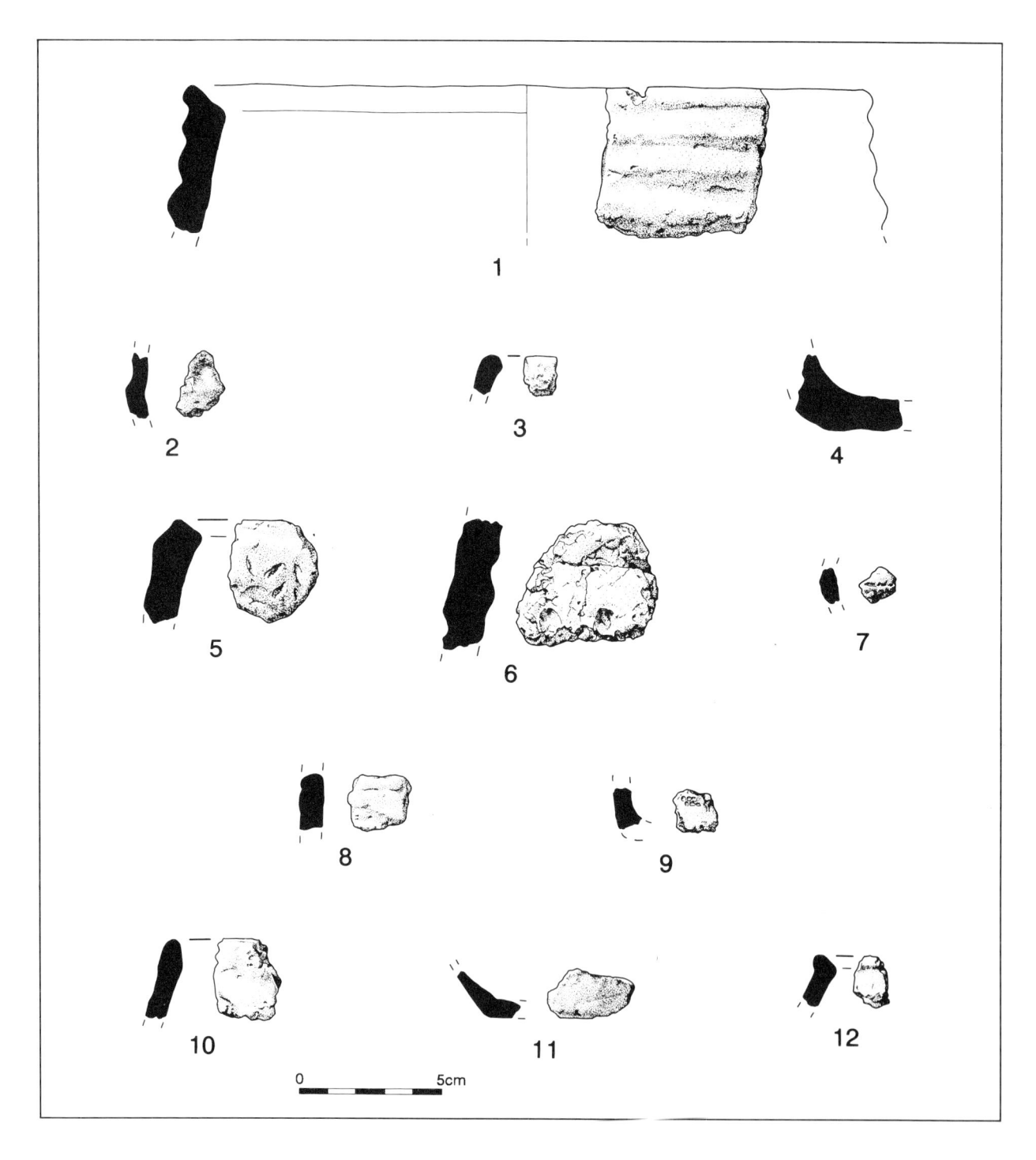

Figure 28: Pottery: Site VI. Scale: 1:2.

The Prehistoric Pottery

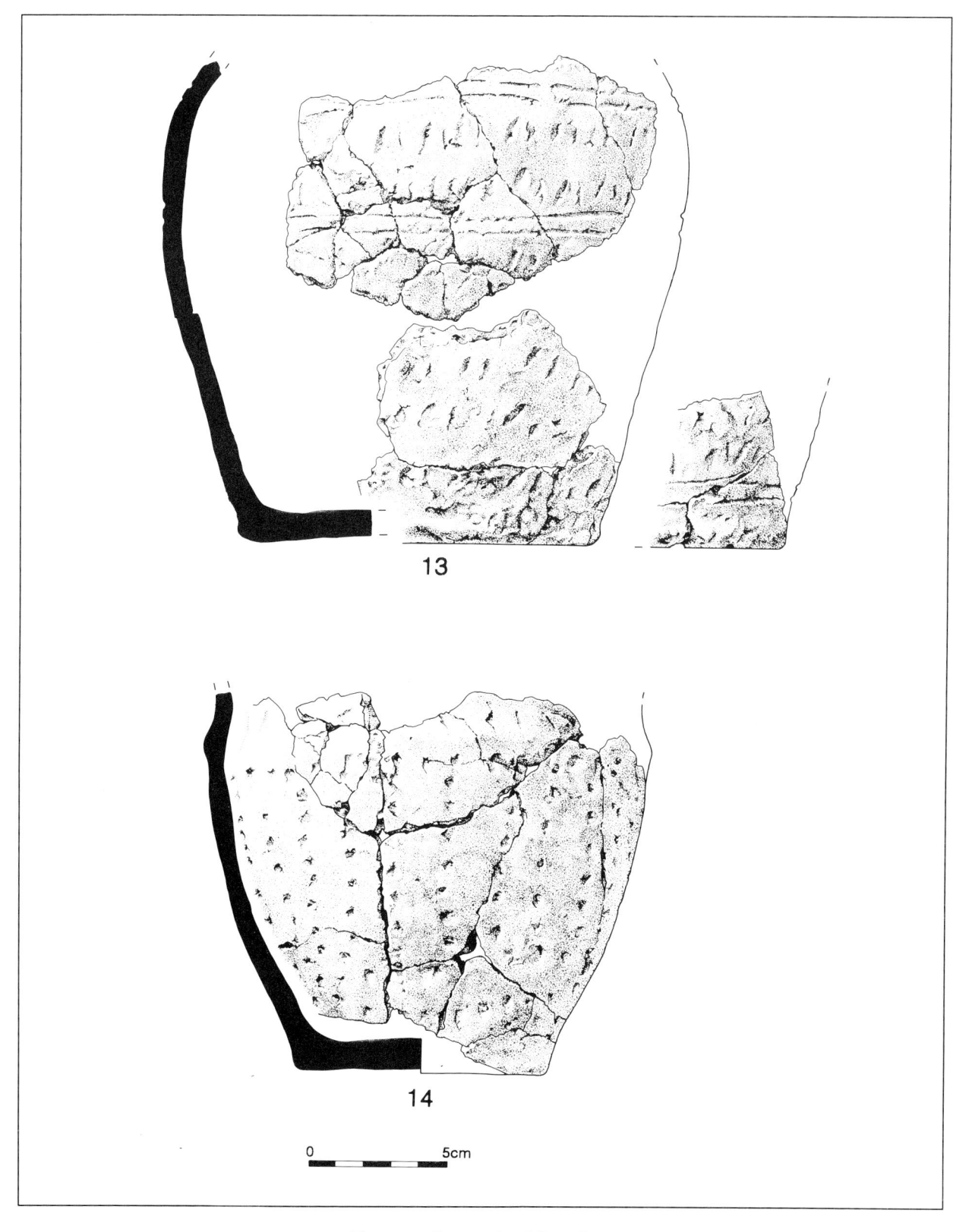

Figure 29: Pottery: Site VI. Scale: 1:2.

1982, no. 592), although that vessel is decorated and is of a size that falls within the Food Vessel range. Whilst Enlarged Food Vessel Urns are common in eastern England, they occur mainly from Yorkshire northwards. Ridged Urns are especially common in Yorkshire while Ridged Buckets are more common in southern England (Burgess 1980, Fig. 7). The Lockington profile is best matched by the urn from Friar Mayne in Dorset (Forde-Johnston 1965, fig.7).

The activities evidenced at Lockington are reflected well within the Amesbury barrow 71, where, in phase III, sixty non-joining sherds from an Enlarged Ridged Food Vessel were scattered on a platform which was a levelling layer above evidence for intense burning. The sherds were arranged in an arc, and the same layer produced a scatter of cremated bone and pieces of unburnt human skull (Christie 1967, 346).

2. Shoulder sherd from the carination of a plain thin-walled bowl. Earlier Neolithic. Fabric 2. Context 1107, F65, no 1021.

(b) Associated with the hoard – A total of 62 sherds were found within the pit and just above it. The main vessels were the two incomplete lower sections of pots, one, no. 14, in a single piece, and another, no. 13, in 14 large and 35 small fragments. There were also 11 other sherds, all in Fabric 4, representing at least three or four further vessels, one an urn, no. 4, and another a Beaker, no. 3. However, these sherds may not have been associated directly with the hoard. The mean sherd weight for the two vessels 13 and 14 was 19.4g, and for the other sherds, 4.9g.

The two vessels, both of which lack any fragments from the neck area or rim are difficult to reconstruct, and indeed their identification to type is not straightforward. The vessels have become the subject of much debate, and opinion has been divided. Contributions to the debate have kindly been offered by Arthur ApSimon, Humphrey Case, Alex Gibson, Ian Kinnes, Ian Longworth, Stuart Needham and David Tomalin. The general consensus is that both vessels are Beakers, although there remains a possibility that the smaller portion, no. 14, derives from a Collared Urn.

13. Forty-nine sherds representing 71% of the base and a substantial portion of belly from a large Beaker. Fabric 4. Context 1012, F5.

The substantial part of the base and lower wall, and non-joining fragments of the belly from a very large Beaker were found inverted over the smaller vessel (no. 14), gold armlets and dagger. The sherds had been dislodged by the plough. The rim and upper body were not represented amongst the sherds deposited; thus the vessel was already in portions when placed above the other items in the pit.

The fabric contains inclusions of medium-sized grog and occasional grits. A provisional restoration of the lower body profile is offered. This shows the flat base with slightly everted foot and rounded, thin-walled belly. The roughly executed decoration comprises pairs of horizontal incised lines defining zones which are filled with rows of paired fingernail impressions.

Beaker pottery spanned many centuries, between c.2500–1700 BC, and as the Lockington vessel belongs to the broadly defined category of domestic wares, it cannot be dated closely. The association of fingernail ornament and incised lines is extremely rare, although it does occur on a vessel from Zuidersee in the Netherlands (Gibson 1982, 542, no. 4). Large vessels such as this do not occur often in funerary contexts.

In the Midlands, typical assemblages of domestic wares are known from Stenson, Derbys. (Fowler 1953), Willington (Wheeler 1979) and from barrow 4 at Swarkestone (Greenfield 1960). A near complete rusticated vessel similar in profile to the Lockington example was found in ironstone working at Hauxton, Leics. (Clarke 1970, fig. 907), whilst a substantial sherd from another large vessel was recovered by Bateman from barrow 1 at Royston Grange, Derbys. (Hodges *et al.* 1989, 12–13). Unfortunately, whether this sherd derived from a pre-cairn, funerary or later ritual context is not known. In Aston-on-Trent barrow 1 the sherds of another part-Beaker, but this time the upper portion only, were found dispersed around the area of the primary burial (Reaney 1968, 72–3). The other barrow previously excavated at Lockington itself contained a central grave group of bronze knife, awl and plano-convex knives. Associated was a single sherd of decorated pottery, tentatively assigned to the urn tradition (Posnansky 1955, 20–21). A further late rusticated Beaker of similar profile comes from Buxton, Derbys where it was associated with a bronze earring (Clarke 1970, fig. 910).

A series of possible reconstructions for the full profile of vessel 13 are presented in Fig. 30, 1–3. All three are Late Style (now Style 3 according to Case 1993) forms. The first is a typical 'long-necked' profile, like those of the decorated Midlands Beakers of Clarke's S2 type from

The Prehistoric Pottery

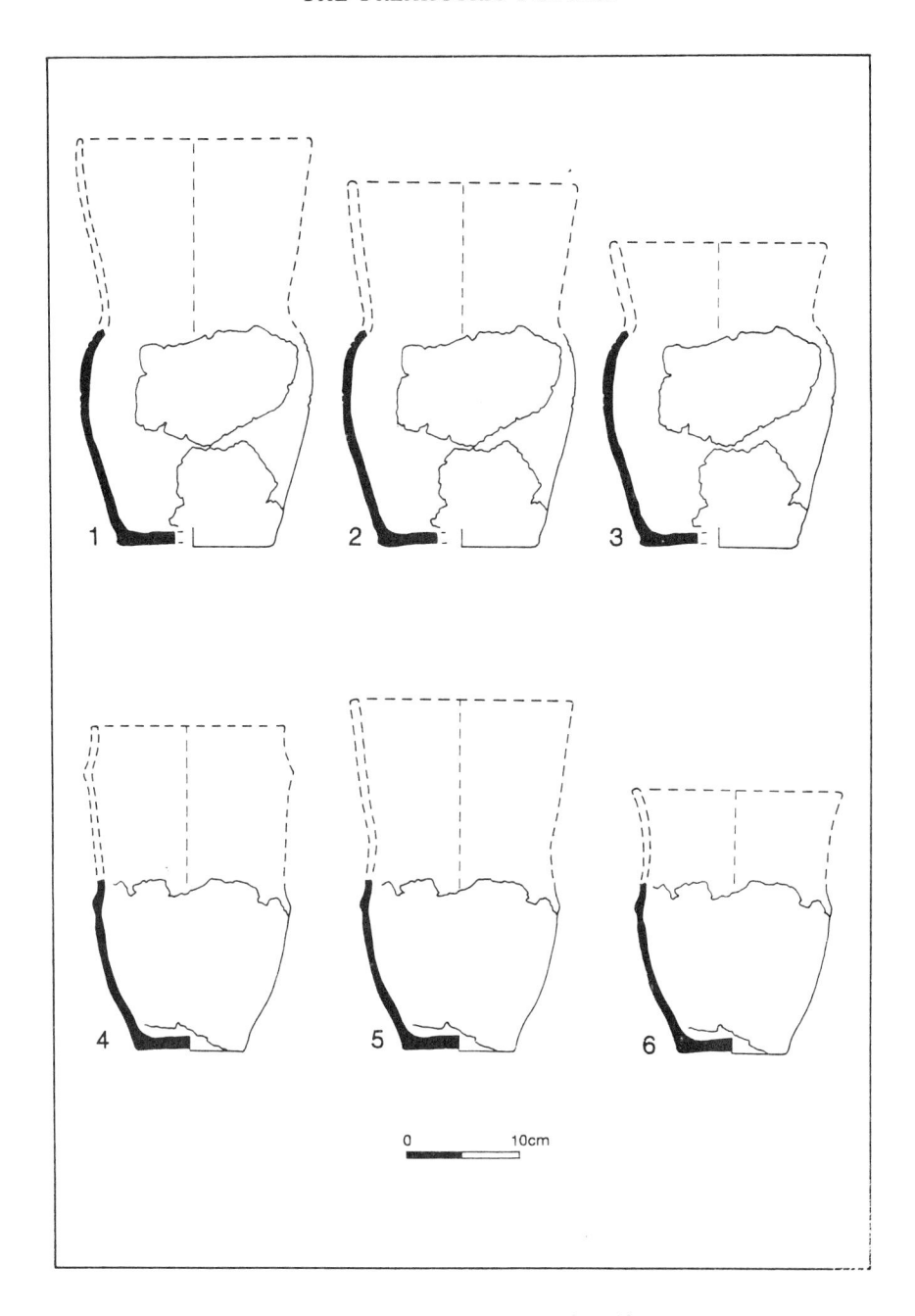

Figure 30: Pottery: reconstructed profiles.

Noseley, Leicestershire (Clarke 1970, fig. 852) or Fengate, Northamptonshire (*ibid.* fig. 856), whilst the second is based on the large vessel with paired finger-nail impressions from Buxton, Derbyshire, referred to above (*ibid.* fig. 910). Alternatively, the neck may have been much shorter, possibly with a slightly out-turned neck. Such a profile is presented in the third version, which is based on vessels of Clarke's N2 type, such as those from Stanton Harcourt, Oxfordshire (*ibid.* fig. 509) or Amotherby, Yorkshire (*ibid.* fig. 539).

14. Most of the lower portion, base to shoulder, of a smaller vessel, found inverted over one of the gold bracelets. Fabric 4. Context 1012, F5. The flat base has been damaged by ploughing and during discovery and excavation. As found, the rim and most of the collar (if any) and neck were missing. These portions had been removed in antiquity and, judging from the worn appearance of the breaks, this had happened some time before the deposition of the remainder in the pit.

The slightly sandy clay fabric is tempered with moderate quantities of medium and large fragments of grog. Above the convex lower body and weak shoulder only 15mm of the hollow neck survives. The remaining walls are decorated with a simple repeated device consisting of a small irregular three to four-sided impression, such as could be formed using the end of a bird bone.

With the total absence of rim sherds or fragments from the neck or collar area, it seems wise to offer a discussion which includes consideration of both Collared Urns and Beakers although the tentative reconstructed profiles presented in Fig. 30, 4–6 are of Beaker types. Collared Urns were used for burial between c.2100 and 1500 BC. As the rim and collar are missing, the potential urn cannot be classified in detail. The decorated lower body is an unusual feature, but does occur elsewhere in the Midlands, for instance on vessels from Stanton Moor, Derbys. and Milton, Northants. (Longworth 1984, nos. 1013 and 308). The Stanton Moor urn was associated with a cremation, a second urn, a clay bead, two fragmentary bronze implements and worked flints. In the Trent valley, Collared Urns are associated usually with primary or secondary cremations within ring ditches, as at Cossington and Sproxton, but deposits of sherds only are known from a secondary cremation at Bramcote (Longworth 1984, no. 1342) and from a pit at Swarkestone barrow 4 (Greenfield 1960).

Following the alternative identification as a Beaker, three possible reconstructions of the vessel profile are provided, as for vessel no. 13 (Fig. 30, 4–6). The first depicts a tall straight-necked container with a collared rim, similar to those found on Beaker domestic sites such as Hockwold in Norfolk (e.g. Bamford 1982, fig. 9; Gibson 1982, 429–430), or on decorated Beakers from the Pennines at Wetton (Castern), Staffordshire (Clarke 1970, fig. 861: group S3(E)) and from Top Low, Swinscoe, Staffordshire (*ibid.* fig. 939: group S3(E)) and at Castleshaw, Yorkshire (*ibid.* figs. 974–6), where a vessel with such a rim (of probably S3 type) was associated with two finger impressed vessels, the larger of which is not dissimilar in profile to the first suggested reconstruction of vessel no. 13 at Lockington (Fig. 30, 1). A simpler profile could have included a long straight neck as in the second drawing (No. 5), which is based on the vessel from Bury St. Edmunds (Clarke 1970, fig. 1046). However, it is also possible that the out-curving broken edge above the shoulder was the beginning of a weakly concave neck, more like the altogether shorter profile shown in the third sketch. This is based on pots of Clarke's S4 type from Linlathen, Angus (*ibid.* fig. 1018) and Dalton, Northumberland (*ibid.* fig. 1044). Bird bone impressions are not a common form of decoration within the fine ware Beaker tradition, but they are known amongst the domestic assemblages, for instance at Hockwold, Norfolk (Gibson 1982, 429).

3. Plain simple rim sherd from a Beaker. Fabric 4. Context 1012, F5.

4. Rounded plain base angle from an Early Bronze Age urn of unknown type. Fabric 4. Context 1012, F5.

(c) The barrow mound – There were 33 Bronze Age sherds, and three only of Iron Age date. The latter were very small and must have been intrusive; they were of fabric 10. Most of the Bronze Age items (55%) were in fabric 4. These included fragments of three different decorated Beakers, nos. 5, 8 and 9, and a fragment of urn. There were also seven sherds in fabric 6, one of them from a further Beaker vessel, no. 7, three sherds in Fabric 7 and, finally, two rim sherds and two wall fragments from the Enlarged Food Vessel Urn, no. 1 (above). These rim sherds, together with those from beneath the mound accounted in total for 28% of the vessel rim.

A medium number of sherds displayed very low mean weights, but only medium abrasion (60%). 92% of them were Bronze Age in date and they occurred as an even scatter with a slight concentration in the SE sector.

5. Rim, with internal bevel, from a large rusticated Beaker. The exterior surface below the rim is decorated with paired, diagonal finger-tip impressions forming a rough herringbone design. Fabric 4. Context 1033/SF 670.

This rim can be compared to vessels belonging to Beaker domestic assemblages. The rim form is best matched at Hockwold (Gibson 1982, 422, no. 5) whilst a decorated example occurs at Hockwold 'The Oaks' (Bamford 1982, 107, Fig. 24).

6. Three wall sherds (one illustrated) from a large vessel, probably an urn, decorated with two finger-tip impressions, possibly part of a row. Fabric 4. Context 1033/SF 92.

7. Small fragment from the shoulder of a Beaker, decorated with a long-tooth comb impression. Fabric 6. Context 1002/SF 553.

8. Worn wall sherd from a Beaker, bearing a single horizontal line, probably incised. Fabric 4. Context 1002/SF 553.

9. Wall sherd, near base, from a Beaker. The decoration is a double row of short-tooth comb impressions. Fabric 4. Context 1035/SF 617.

(d) The ring ditch – The filling incorporated 14 sherds of Bronze Age date and 12 Iron Age sherds. This represented a medium number of sherds, with the highest mean sherd weight. (9.6g) and the lowest abrasion (41%). The ditch also contained the highest number of burnt sherds (9%) although even this is a very low figure. The lower filling contained only Bronze Age sherds – all from a single vessel – six sherds with a mean weight of 17.8g. This compares with mean weights 12.9g for all the Bronze Age sherds and 3.4g for the Iron Age items. The plot shows Bronze Age sherds occurring mainly in the W and SE sectors, with the Late Bronze Age vessel sherds occurring mainly to the southeast and northeast, whilst the Iron Age sherds occurred mainly on the west side (Fig. 15).

Nine of the Bronze Age sherds, including the six from the lower filling, 1013, belonged to the base angle and lower wall of a large urn or jar, in igneous fabric 9, and probably of Late Bronze Age date (not illustrated). From the higher filling there were further plain Bronze Age sherds in fabrics 4 and 12, and six fabrics of daub. The Iron Age sherds were plain wall fragments in fabrics 8, 10, and 12, and two Roman sherds were also present.

(e) Peripheral features – A total of 31 Iron Age sherds comprised plain wall fragments in fabrics 8 (igneous fine ware), 10, 13 and 14. These indicate an Iron Age date for these features. The sherds have a low mean weight of 3.2g, but mostly comprise sherds from 2 vessels, in a single feature 1089. Degree of abrasion was very low at 26%. The main feature lay north of the ring ditch but other occasional Iron Age sherds were found to the south and southwest of it.

(f) Silt over ring ditch – The many sherds displayed a medium mean sherd weight and a 75% degree of abrasion. 71% of them were Iron Age in date and four Roman sherds were present also. The plot shows concentrations in the north and southeast sectors (Fig. 17). Sherds of a Middle/Late Bronze Age vessel (two in total) vessel were well scattered, and sherds of the Late Bronze Age vessel (derived from the mound material) and vessel no.1 (derived from the edge of the pre-barrow deposits) were present. The concentrations are due to the presence of clusters of Iron Age sherds. Iron Age sherds were larger (4.8g mean weight) than the Bronze Age ones (3.7g mean weight).

The presence of Roman sherds in these deposits, and in the ditch filling below, suggests that the upper ditch layers were not formed until the Roman period.

The ten Bronze Age sherds included items in fabrics 4, 5, 6 and 8, the only decorated piece being a ribbed wall fragment belonging to vessel no. 1 (see above). There were two possibly Late Bronze Age sherds in igneous fabric 8, and 35 Iron Age sherds in fabrics 6, 10, 11 and 12; 29 of them were in fabric 10.

10. Plain simple rim sherd, probably from a barrel-shaped jar. Fabric 11. Context 1005/SF 241.

11. Base angle from a thin-walled, round-bodied jar. Fabric 12. Context 1005/SF 315.

12. Plain rim sherd with internal rim bevel. Fabric 10. Context 1005/SF 374.

Nos. 10 and 11 are forms typical of the local Early to Middle Iron Age, whilst No. 12 could be of Early Iron Age, or possibly Late Bronze Age date.

(g) Ploughsoil and topsoil – There were very few sherds which were mainly Iron Age in date. They possessed almost the lowest mean sherd weight and 90% of them were abraded. A distribution plot showed a scatter with no concentrations, although Bronze Age sherds are more common to the south; Iron Age to the north. The plot suggests that sherds were in material dragged from the silt over the ring ditch by the plough.

The two Bronze Age sherds, in fabric 4, were very small. The Iron Age items included plain wall fragments in fabrics 10, 12 and 14.

THE SITE V PIT GROUP

A total of 42 sherds, weighing 333g, were recovered. The overall mean sherd weight was 7.9g, with the material from the Phase 2 pits giving a mean value of 11g and items from Phase 1 and the Phase 3 ditch being more fragmented (mean sherd weights of c.5g). There was one Neolithic sherd, 10 of Bronze Age date and 24 Late Bronze Age/Iron Age pieces (see Table 3). All material was stratified, but the phasing of features that could be attempted was not clear-cut, especially in the case of the Phase 1 possible clearance features.

Fabric

A series of nine fabric types were distinguished and five samples were examined petrologically by David Williams. As very few types correlated with those defined for the ring ditch site, a separate numbering system has been maintained. However, they can be grouped into three of the main categories defined by Williams, tempered with grog, quartz or igneous inclusions. Apart form the igneous material, which may derive from the Charnwood Forest area, the temper could have been obtained locally.

Fabric 1.	Sparse medium quartz inclusions and sand. Neolithic.
Fabric 2.	Grog. Beaker.
Fabric 3.	Grog and sparse large quartz inclusions. Beaker.
Fabric 4.	Sparse small quartz inclusions. Beaker.
Fabric 5.	Sparse sand. Beaker.
Fabric 6.	Grog and sparse small or medium quartz inclusions. Bronze Age.
Fabric 7.	Grog and sand. ?Bronze Age.
Fabric 8.	Sparse medium to large rock inclusions, probably igneous. Late Bronze Age to Iron Age.
Fabric 9.	Sand and sparse large igneous inclusions. Late Bronze Age to Iron Age.

Form and Decoration

Diagnostic pieces are illustrated in Fig. 31

Phase 1. There was one fabric 8 Late Bronze Age/Iron Age sherd from a probably natural feature and one Neolithic piece from a post-hole. The latter was similar in fabric to the shoulder sherd found in the feature beneath the mound at the ring ditch site.

Phase 2. There were two Bronze Age sherds in Fabrics 3 and 7 from pit 136; otherwise the only pottery recovered was an assemblage of 18 sherds from pit 84. These comprised five fragments from four different Beakers (fabrics 2, 3, 4 and 5, one of them a rim, no. 17 below) and one piece of fabric 6 Bronze Age pottery. The largest fragments, including joining sherds of base angle, belonged however, to the lower portion of a large jar, probably of Late Bronze Age date, no. 15. Four rim sherds, one of which is illustrated, no.16, may have belonged to the same, or a similar, vessel.

Also from pit 84 came the baked clay pulley-object, no. 18, which is an artefact of Early Bronze Age date. The relative disposition of this object, the Early Bronze Age sherds and the fragments of the Late Bronze Age jar were not recorded. However, it seems probable that the pit was dug first to contain an Early Bronze Age deposit, which may originally have been a burial associated with the pulley object, and that the Late Bronze Age vessel was inserted into the filling of the feature at a later date. The radiocarbon dates for pit 84 should relate to the earlier of these episodes. Similar reuse of a Neolithic/Bronze Age feature in the Late Bronze Age is known from the site of Wasperton in Warwickshire.

15. Two base angle fragments, representing 17% of the circumference, and three wall sherds from the lower portion of a large jar. The lower wall is rusticated with rough finger smearing. Late Bronze Age. Fabric 9. Contexts 132 and 4, pit 84.

The form and igneous fabric recall the vessel represented in the filling of the Lockington ring ditch.

16. Four plain simple rim sherds. Late Bronze Age. Fabric 8. Context 4, pit 84 (sample 6).

17. Plain thin-walled rim sherd. Beaker. Fabric 5. Context 4, pit 84 (sample 68).

18. A plain circular pulley-shaped object with dished surface and grooved side. Diameter 27mm. Fabric 2. Context 4, pit 84.

Such objects may have been used as studs or dress fasteners, or have been worn in the lobe of the ear. They are found with Early Bronze Age burials as at Stanton Moor 13, Derbyshire (24mm diam), Brenig, Llanrhiadr yn Cinmerch (a matching pair, 28mm diameters) or Gawsworth, Cheshire, all associated with Collared Urns (Longworth 1984, nos. 320, 2023–4 and 134 respectively). A slightly smaller example was found in the rich

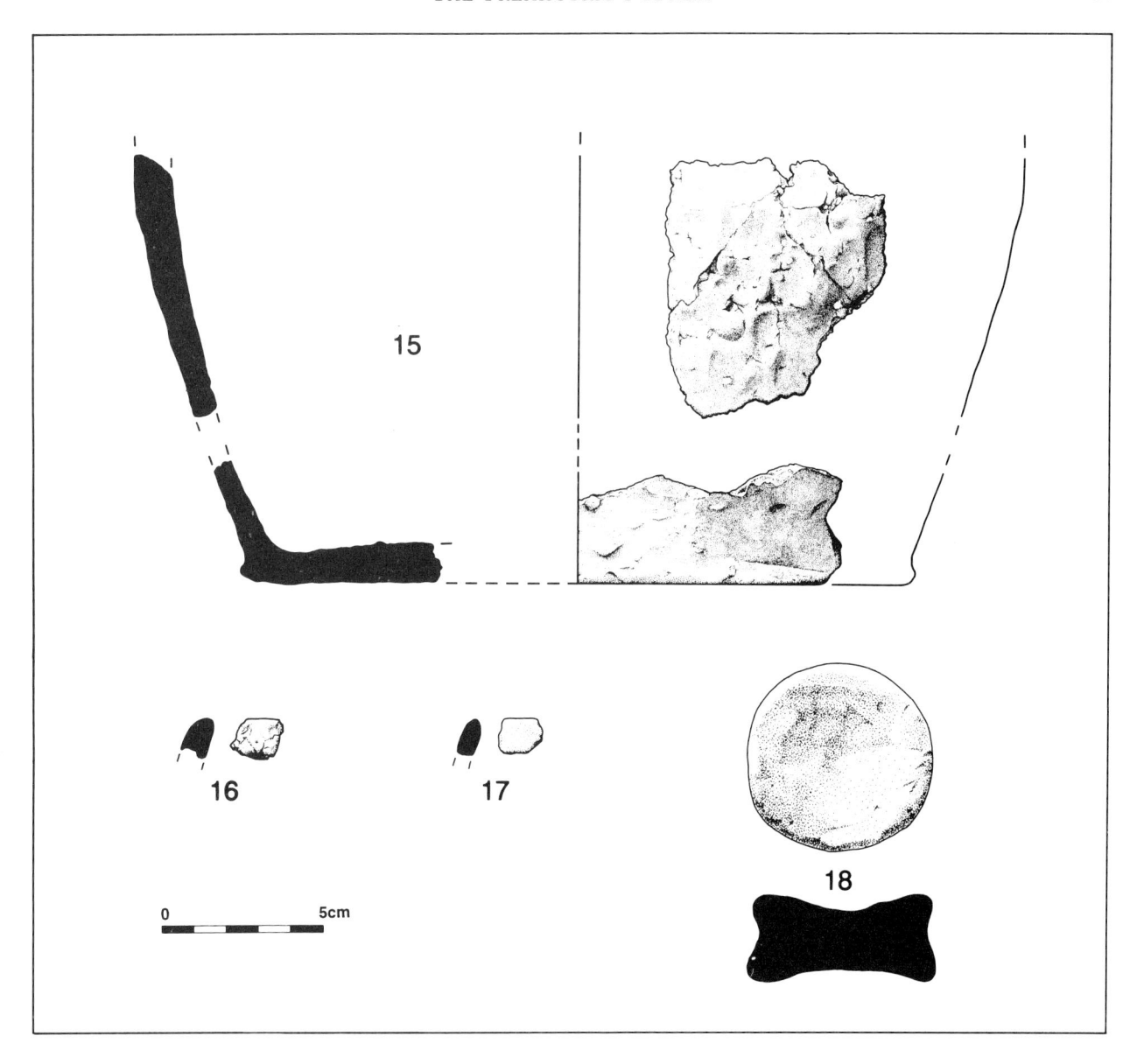

Figure 31: Pottery: Site V. Scale: 1:2, except no. 18: 1:1.

'Wessex' burial group from the Manton barrow (Preshute G1, Wiltshire, 20mm diameter, Annable and Simpson 1964, 101, no. 201). Thus this item may denote the former presence of a second deposit, possibly a burial, contemporary with the gold hoard from the ring ditch site.

Phase 3: ditch. A total of 20 sherds included one Bronze Age piece in Fabric 6 with the rest representing a very few sherds of Late Bronze Age type; these were in Fabrics 8 and 9. The igneous fabric of 16 sherds, and the general morphology suggested similarities with the vessel from Pit 84, and with the vessel from the ring ditch filling. This pottery assemblage indicates that the system of ditches may have gone out of use before the Iron Age.

Discussion

The association within the Lockington hoard of two part vessels, both of them probably Beakers, with a copper dagger and the decorated gold armlets is a unique occurrence. Discussion of the gold armlets (Needham below) would place them alongside a series of other armlets, in gold or copper alloy, which occur mainly in northern Britain and can be dated to c.2100–1700 cal BC. Such armlets occur both in graves and in hoards (see Needham Appendix 1). Some of the grave contexts include ceramic vessels. Two were of Food Vessel type, but the majority were Beakers. These included examples of Clarke's types S2, S3 (two examples) and N3 along with a further vessel probably belonging to the Southern series (see Needham Appendix 1 for details). Although the internal chronology of Beaker styles remains uncertain (Case 1993), two of the Beaker-associated armlets occurred in graves dated by radiocarbon to the later part of the Beaker series (an S3 Beaker at Shorncote, Gloucestershire; one probably of the Southern series at Redlands Farm, Stanwick, Northamptonshire – see Needham below). The dating of all these ceramic types is in accord with that suggested by Needham for the armlets, and the Lockington Beakers also fall stylistically within the later part of the Beaker tradition i.e. Case's style 3. The long copper dagger, with its Armorican parallels, probably dates from before c.1900 BC: it was probably an import and may not have been in circulation for very long prior to its deposition (Needham below). Another fairly long dagger is known from Bush Barrow in Wiltshire, and that piece was associated with a shorter dagger which is of arsenical copper, and therefore another probable import. Although this example was found in a rich Wessex 1 grave group, Needham argues that the main *floruit* of the dagger type evidenced at Lockington predated the sequence of rich Wessex graves. Thus the Lockington hoard was not connected, chronologically or culturally, with the Wessex graves. This is borne out by consideration of the ceramic associations found with these groups. Less than 20% of Wessex graves contain ceramic vessels (excluding the exotic incense cups and related material), and invariably these are Collared Urns rather than Beakers.

It is of particular interest to consider the possible motivation that lay behind the placing of two non-complete vessels, both of which may have been old at the time of deposition, around the Lockington artefact group. The pots seem to have been regarded as valuable and may have been family heirlooms or ancestral property. If this were the case, then it is pertinent to consider what may have happened to the missing portions. Perhaps the vessels became divided and shared amongst different segments of a family or lineage, or, maybe small parts of the special pots had been retained and ground up for use as grog in newly-manufactured vessels. Thus elements from the personal pots which possessed ancestral pedigrees might imbue identity and power to vessels made for use in a new generation. Recent research has suggested that, in the late Neolithic and Early Bronze Age periods ceramic containers were concerned more with personal identity than with community activities at the household, settlement or regional level (Woodward 1995). It is in these very periods that the use of grog as a tempering agent occurred most commonly (Cleal 1995, fig. 16.2). Furthermore, Boast (1995) has argued, on the grounds of fabric and surface treatment studies, that many Beakers which possess coarse fabrics in association with highly polished surfaces were not fine ware vessels for use in life but items which had been manufactured expressly for the grave.

The deposition of ceramic vessels as heirlooms within funerary deposits has been noted by some recent excavators. Perhaps the most impressive example is the complete decorated vase à anse found in a barrow at Gallibury, Isle of Wight in 1979. "The vase, which has an ancient modification to its damaged handle, appears to have been a worn heirloom when deposited in the grave" (Tomalin 1988, 208–9 and fig. 4,1). A second parallel with the Lockington group is afforded at Gallibury, for the heirloom vase had been placed within a nested group of vessels, covered successively by an upright urn and a larger inverted vessel (op cit. Fig. 5). Further examples of nested vessel groups are known from Dorset. At Frampton, a very small Collared Urn contained two smaller vessels one inside the other (Forde-Johnston 1958, 114–5, fig D), whilst at Long Crichel the partial remains of the rim, collar and shoulder of one Collared Urn were suspended over the shoulder of a second Collared Urn which was inverted with its base missing. Both these vessels, as at Lockington must have been in a broken state at the time of deposition (Green, Lynch and White 1982, 50–51). Examples of vessels occurring in pairs, or triplets, even in an unbroken state, are rather uncommon. Longworth records only 13 pairs of Collared Urns, but there are 16 examples of covering urns. In these cases usually a larger urn has been inverted over a small one, or a small vessel was placed inverted within a larger upright urn (Longworth 1984, 49–50). When Beakers occur in association with other vessels they are usually accessory vessels in the Beaker tradition. The only non-Beaker association appears to be that of an N3 Beaker with a Vase Food Vessel as Broughham, Westmorland (Clarke 1970, no. 1017). Nested groups do not occur in Beaker graves.

A process of breaking of fragments from ancestral pots for future use in grog preparation is well attested ethnographically (e.g. Sterner 1989). In order to test such a hypothesis in relation to Early Bronze Age Britain, it would be necessary to carry out a wide-ranging investigation into the occurrence of grogged fabrics within the known funerary and domestic assemblages, and a study of the degree of completeness of ceramic vessels found in graves. We have noted already the occurrence of Beaker and urn sherds within barrows at Roystone Grange, Aston and Lockington. However, information concerning the degree of representation of individual vessels has been recorded but seldom in the general archaeological literature. Preliminary studies of material from Wiltshire and the Upper Thames does indicate however that vessels found in burials often had portions missing at the time of deposition. Analysis of Wiltshire material has been assessed from the drawings in the Devizes Museum Catalogue (Annable and Simpson 1964; these vessels show accurately the absence and presence of the various vessel zones). It appears that two-thirds of the Beakers from burials were incomplete or represented only by key sherds. By contrast, most Collared Urns were deposited entire. In the Upper Thames region many Beakers appear to have been deposited entire. However, in two cases the rim was missing totally, and in three other cases parts of the base were absent. The latter phenomenon is of particular interest as it indicates that fragments may have been removed deliberately from the place where the resulting hole would be least visible. Further contextual studies are required, but at Stanton Harcourt, a Beaker with half its base missing displayed a break which was certainly ancient (Case 1956, No. 43). Meanwhile, at Barrow Hills, Radley there were three Collared Urns with major portions of the rim and collar or entire upper portion missing (Alistair Barclay pers. comm.). Like the Lockington example, two of these vessels were inverted and so the breaks must have been ancient.

The evidence to be sought in this enquiry is that for ancient breaks. It is necessary to establish that pieces or portions of a vessel had been removed before that vessel entered a particular grave or deposit. Such a line of research is hampered by the facts that drawings often do not show the exact degree of survival of vessel fragments and that many antiquarian and modern excavation reports do not record the condition of a vessel as it was found during excavation. In addition, modern damage such as ploughing has often removed a rim or base in the post-depositional phase. Therefore searching for degrees of brokenness amongst vessels in museum collections will not provide certain evidence of ancient breaks. What is required as clear evidence for the hypothesis is a series of written statements, by excavators, describing how vessels were found in a partial state, probably due to fragmentation in antiquity. Such statements are only likely to occur in relation to excavations published during the last few decades. An extensive, but by no means exhaustive, search of excavation reports relating to 20th-century barrow excavations has produced a convincing suite of possible examples covering a wide geographical range:

Park of Tongland, Dumfries and Galloway. An incomplete Collared Urn in Pit 2 was damaged while it lay on its side in the pit (Russell-White et al 1992, 318).

Ewanrigg, Maryport, Cumbria. An Accessory Cup (fig. 7,7a) with its rim edge lacking must have been damaged when placed in the grave. An inverted Collared Urn (fig. 10, 11) had had its collar removed prior to burial. (Bewley *et al.* 1992, 329–30 and 342).

Tallington, Lincs. Twenty-three sherds from grave 4 comprised only two-thirds of an S4 Beaker, associated with sheet-bronze earrings. (Simpson 1976, fig. 7,1).

Brenig, Llanrihiadr yn Cinmerch, Denbighshire. The semi-circular cairn of the later phases of the platform cairn 51 covered a small Collared Urn. The top of the rim had been damaged in antiquity (Lynch 1993, 111, fig. 10.8, Pot A). The very small Accessory Cup from the ring cairn 44, which contained cremations, a plano-convex knife and two pottery ear-studs, has two-thirds of its rim broken away prior to burial (ibid., 129–30, fig. 11.9, B4).

Trelystan, Powys. The upper part of the Food Vessel (fig 19, P21) in Barrow I, burial 4 'had been broken away before deposition' (Britnell 1982, 167–8).

Eagleston Flat, Derbys. The sherds of an incomplete accessory vessel were deposited inside Cordoned Urn 5. Only the bottom survived of Urn 6, the top 80mm of which had been 'smashed in prehistory and largely disappeared'. Urn 7 also had been smashed in prehistory. (Barnatt 1994, 309–10).

Pasture Lodge Farm, Lincs. Bronze Age Urn 19 contained a large fragment of grog which comprised a decorated rim fragment, probably from an Early Bronze Age vessel. Inside pot 24 was found a worn sherd which was part of a small collared vessel: this may have been included deliberately. Pot 10 contained grog inclusions which carried a 10% quartz content. This fabric was not recognised amongst the urns of the cemetery, so presumably derived from a very different, possibly earlier vessel. (Allen *et al.* 1987, 214).

Risby, Suffolk. The central burial was accompanied by part of a Beaker P2. Small pieces of a Food Vessel P8, found just north-east of the barrow centre, accounted for only just more than half of the vessel. (Vatcher and Vatcher 1976).

Roxton, Beds. Ring Ditch C. The primary burial B5 had been robbed in the Early Bronze Age and parts only of a Collared Urn were redeposited before a second funerary complex was constructed. Burial B6, in the ring ditch site, comprised the inverted lower half only of a bucket-shaped vessel. (Taylor and Woodward 1985, 103 and 119).

Woodchester, Glous. A Beaker, Pl.XI,D, was 'damaged or decayed prior to deposition' (Clifford 1937, 160).

Winterbourne St. Martin, Dorset. Martinsdown Barrow I contained a damaged handled Beaker, reminiscent in treatment to the Gallibury heirloom discussed above. 'The handle, in which the chief interest centres on account of its rarity, was not lost during the removal of the food-vessel, but was evidently deficient at the time of interment'. The stumps of the handle did not present clean fractures and the missing portions were not discovered after considerable search. (Gray and Prideaux 1905, 18).

Rimbury, Dorset. Two Beakers excavated from a grave displayed ancient fractures. (Woodward 1980, 99).

Rams Hill, Oxon. The Collared Urn from the ditch, undoubtedly a deliberate deposit, lacked its base. (Bradley and Ellison 1975, 92).

These examples suggest that there may have been a widespread tradition during the Early Bronze Bronze Age which involved the removal of fragments of portions from vessels prior to their deliberated deposition in funerary or other contexts. Some at least of these fragments were themselves revered, and were ground up for incorporation as grog within newly-made vessels of a similar or different kind.

Detailed study of the Lockington sherds has led to proposals that, in prehistory, the selection of temper in pottery was not determined solely on functional grounds. Alternatively, the temper played a strong cultural and symbolic role whereby fragments from existing artefacts with known histories and biographies were deliberately incorporated into new vessels. Thus the essence of important pots belonging to significant individuals or families could be preserved and passed down through the generations in a finite and often visible form. The fabric of a pot may have indeed assumed a far greater social and symbolic importance than either its form, or its decoration. Sometimes the pot may have incorporated the actual remains of a specific human ancestor. The record of calcined bone temper at Balneaves, Angus (Russell-White *et al.* 1992, 299) may provide stimulus for a more wide-ranging study of pottery fabrics in the Early Bronze Age.

THE PETROLOGY OF THE PREHISTORIC POTTERY

By D.F. Williams

Eighteen, on the whole, quite small samples of mainly Bronze Age and Iron Age pottery from the excavations at Lockington were submitted for fabric analysis by thin sectioning and study under the petrological microscope. The site is located close to the River Soar, and lies partly on Keuper Marl and partly on Post-Glacial Alluvium and River Terraces (Geological Survey 1″ Map of England sheet No. 141).

Petrological groupings

Grog tempered
1 Beaker – Site VI: Context 1044/SF 1005
2 Beaker – Site VI: Context 1012 /F5 (Fig. 29, 13)
3 Probably Beaker – Site VI: Context 1012 /F5 (Fig. 29, 14)
4 Early Bronze Age Enlarged Food Vessel – Site VI: Context 1093/SF 994 (Fig. 28, 1)

5   Bronze Age – Site VI: Context 1033/SF 92
6   Bronze Age – Site V: Context 4

All six of these sherds contain angular pieces of grog scattered throughout the paste (i.e. previously fired pottery that has been pounded up and then deliberately added to the clay by the potter prior to the forming of the vessel). The majority of these samples display a fairly fine-textured clay matrix containing mainly silt-sized quartz, together with a few larger grains, shreds of mica and some iron oxides. No. 4 is a little coarser than the rest, with a slightly larger size-range of quartz grains. Due to the common range of the non-plastic inclusions present in all of these sherds, it is difficult to suggest with any degree of confidence a particular source or sources for these samples, local or otherwise.

Quartz

7   ?Neolithic – Site VI: Context 1088/SF 1020.
Moderately frequent well-sorted subangular grains of quartz generally below 0.40mm in size, shreds of mica, some argillaceous material and iron oxides. Source unknown.

8   Iron Age – Site VI: Context 1089/SF 977.
Frequent ill-sorted quartz grains ranging up to over 0.80mm in size, together with flecks of mica, a few discrete grains of felspar, some quartzite and a little iron oxide. Sources unknown.

9   Bronze Age – Site VI: Context /SF 440.
10 Middle/Late Bronze Age – Site V: Context 4.
11 ?Bronze Age – Site V: Context 10.
12 Iron Age – Site VI: Context 1010/SF 437.
13 Iron Age – Site V: Context 10.
14 Iron Age – Site VI: Context 1005/SF 486.

All of these six sherds contain a scatter of large white angular grains of quartz, some of them polycrystalline, which can easily be seen in the hand-specimen. Also present are quartz grains of a smaller size-range, particularly frequent in No. 14, flecks of mica, quartzite and iron oxides. The angularity of the large quartz grains suggests that these could represent crushed tempering material deliberately added to the clay by the potter. Pebbles of white quartz and quartzite can commonly be found closeby to the site in the Pleistocene and recent deposits (Fox-Strangways 1905), and these may possibly be the source for such tempering.

Sandstone

15 Iron Age – Site VI: Context 1010/SF 750.
Frequent fairly well-sorted subangular grains of quartz normally below 0.50mm across, flecks of mica, several pieces of sandstone, a little quartzite and some iron oxides. Sandstone is a common constituent of the local Triass deposits, and may therefore indicate a possible local source.

Igneous

16 Middle/Late Bronze Age – Site V: Context 4.
The most prominent inclusions present in the clay matrix are made up of several pieces of an altered acid igneous rock, possibly a granite or a granodiorite. Also present are some discrete grains of felspar, large plates of biotite mica and grains of quartz.

17 Middle/Late Bronze Age – Site VI: Context 1013/SF 842.
Inclusions of an altered igneous rock are scattered in the clay matrix, together with grains of quartz, discrete grains of felspar, flecks of mica and a little argillaceous material.

18 Iron Age – Site VI: Context 1061/F34.
A fine-textured clay matrix containing sparse large inclusions of a siliceous rock, together with some grains of quartz, shreds of mica and a little iron oxide.

The local drift deposits in the Lockington area are known to contain fragments of granite and other rocks (Fox-Strangways 1905), and so it is possible that the range of inclusions present in these three sherds merely reflect a local source. However, an alternative origin worth considering would be the wide-range of igneous and associated rocks of the Charnwood Forest area, the northern outliers of which are to be found some 6 miles to the south of the site (*ibid*).

THE FLINT

By R. Young and L. Bevan

The Barrow (Site VI)

A total of 953 pieces of lithic material was recorded from the excavation of the barrow mound, and related contexts. Thirty three finds from peripheral features are dealt with in a separate section below. Total lithic finds from the barrow can be broken down by context group as follows:

Unstrat/topsoil	188
Silt over ring ditch	386
Barrow mound	102
Ring-ditch fill	170
Pre-barrow deposits	107
Total	953

Artefact categories are as follows:

TYPE	Pre-barrow	Mound	Ditch	Siltover ringditch	Unstrat / Topsoil/ fieldwalking etc
Primary Flakes	5	3	7	17	4
Secondary Flakes	26	37	72	187	88
Tertiary Flakes	38	19	20	59	29
Scrapers	3	1	–	5	8
Knives	1	–	–	–	1
Arrowheads:					
PTD/CHISEL	–	–	–	–	1
LEAF	1	–	1	–	–
Blades	–	1	–	2	2
Bladelets	–	–	–	–	1
Blade segments	–	3	–	–	–
Utilised/retouched flakes/blades	5	4	2	8	9
Cores/Core Frags	2	10	19	22	9
Chips/chunks	23	17	44	86	36
Natural Pieces	3	3	5	–	–
Greenstone flakes	3	–	–	–	–
TOTAL	110	98	170	386	188

Raw material

With the exception of three greenstone fragments (possibly from a polished axe) from the barrow mound, pebble flint was the main raw material exploited and all of this is readily available in the drift clay and gravel deposits local to the site. In terms of colour the flint can be broken down by context group as follows:

FLINT COLOUR	Pre-barrow	Mound	Ditch	Silt over ringditch	Unstrat/ Topsoil/ fieldwalking etc.
Grey flint	57	96	136	354	171
White flint	8	–	3	10	3
Black/brown flint	14	1	27	11	11
Fawn/grey flint	–	–	–	–	2
Burnt flint	28	2	4	11	1

Some 680 pieces (just over 71% of the total recovered) retain cortex to a greater or lesser degree and this can be broken down by context group as follows:

	No.	%finds from context	%total finds
Pre-barrow	42	39	4.4
Mound	68	67	7.2
Ring ditch	142	84	15.1
Silt over ring ditch	289	75	30.8
Unstrat/topsoil	139	74	14.8

In general the material is fresh but many pieces from the topsoil and the re-deposited silt deposits show traces of plough damage.

Technology

The low representation of primary flakes and cores and

core fragments throughout all of the recorded contexts would imply that primary knapping was not heavily represented in the assemblage. However, both hard and soft hammer direct percussion techniques are dominant throughout, and pressure flaking was certainly used to thin and finish off the arrowheads. An examination of extant bulbs of percussion and platform types on flakes can be used to gain an insight into technological processes and these can be classified as follows:

	Pronounced Bulb	Diffuse Bulb	Plain Butt	Facetted Butt	Cortical Butt
Pre-barrow	21	18	26	2	11
Mound	17	41	42	3	13
Ring ditch	26	63	51	3	34
Silt over ring ditch	117	99	94	14	105
Unstrat/topsoil	33	78	62	6	43
Total	214	299	275	28	206

From the above it can be suggested that soft hammer striking (producing diffuse bulbs of percussion) is slightly better represented than hard hammer techniques (producing pronounced bulbs). The lack of butt facetting is of interest here. As Whittaker has outlined, facetting is a method for removing platform irregularities (1995, 101) and it can also be used to change exterior platform angles, helping to lengthen flake removals. The lack of the technique here is probably a reflection of the nature of the raw material being exploited. A detailed discussion of the material by phase will now be presented.

PRE-BARROW DEPOSITS

Excluding 23 miscellaneous chips and chunks and two natural pieces from the overall total of 107 finds from these deposits, it is immediately obvious that there is a high proportion of broken pieces present in the pre-barrow contexts (49 out of the remaining total of 82 finds). This point will be returned to in the general discussion below.

Cores and Core Fragments

One small grey flint core with multi directional flaking (not illustrated) (Max dimensions: 31mm × 16mm × 6mm. Weight: 5gms) (Context 1043/SF 964), and one shattered fragment from a keeled core, also in grey flint, (Weight 10gms) (Context 1088/SF 1058) was recorded.

Scrapers

Three examples, all on secondary, grey, flint flakes, retaining hard pebble cortex were recorded. Only two are illustrated. Fig. 32, 1 (Context 1088/ SF 1102) is a fragment of a possible disc scraper (Weight 5 gms) broken transversely at its distal end. Fig. 32, 2 (Context 1046/SF 1057) is a short end scraper with a cortical butt and pronounced bulb of percussion. It is retouched around the distal end and the right edge (Weight: 6gms). The third piece weighs 5gms and is also an end scraper on a broken flake (Context 1046/SF 1012).

Knives

One was identified, on a grey, plano-convex sectioned inner flake from a blade core. The flake is broken transversely at the distal end and exhibits steep retouch on the right edge and lighter invasive retouch on the left (Fig. 32, 3) (Weight: 6gms) (Context 1088/SF 1104)

Arrowheads

One fragmentary leaf shaped arrowhead (Fig. 32, 4) was recovered. It exhibits fine invasive pressure flaking and has been broken transversely at the base (Context 1046/ SF 1004).

Miscellaneous retouched /utilised pieces

Five pieces showing traces of utilisation were recorded (Contexts 1043/SF 965, 1088/SF 988, 1043/SF 1002, 1046/SF 1010, 1088/SF 1103). All are blades or flakes and SF 965 and SF 1103 are broken. Complete examples range from 52mm to 24mm in length with a mean length of 41mm and in breadth from 23mm–17mm with a mean breadth of 29mm. None are illustrated.

Chunks and Chips

Fourteen chips and 9 chunks were recovered Of these, one chunk (Context 1043/SF 1022) is certainly a natural piece from the clay/gravel and only one (Context 1043/ SF 990) shows clear traces of flake removals. Of the chips, 10 come from Context 1105 and are the result of sieving material from F65 and 4 come from sieving Context 1041.

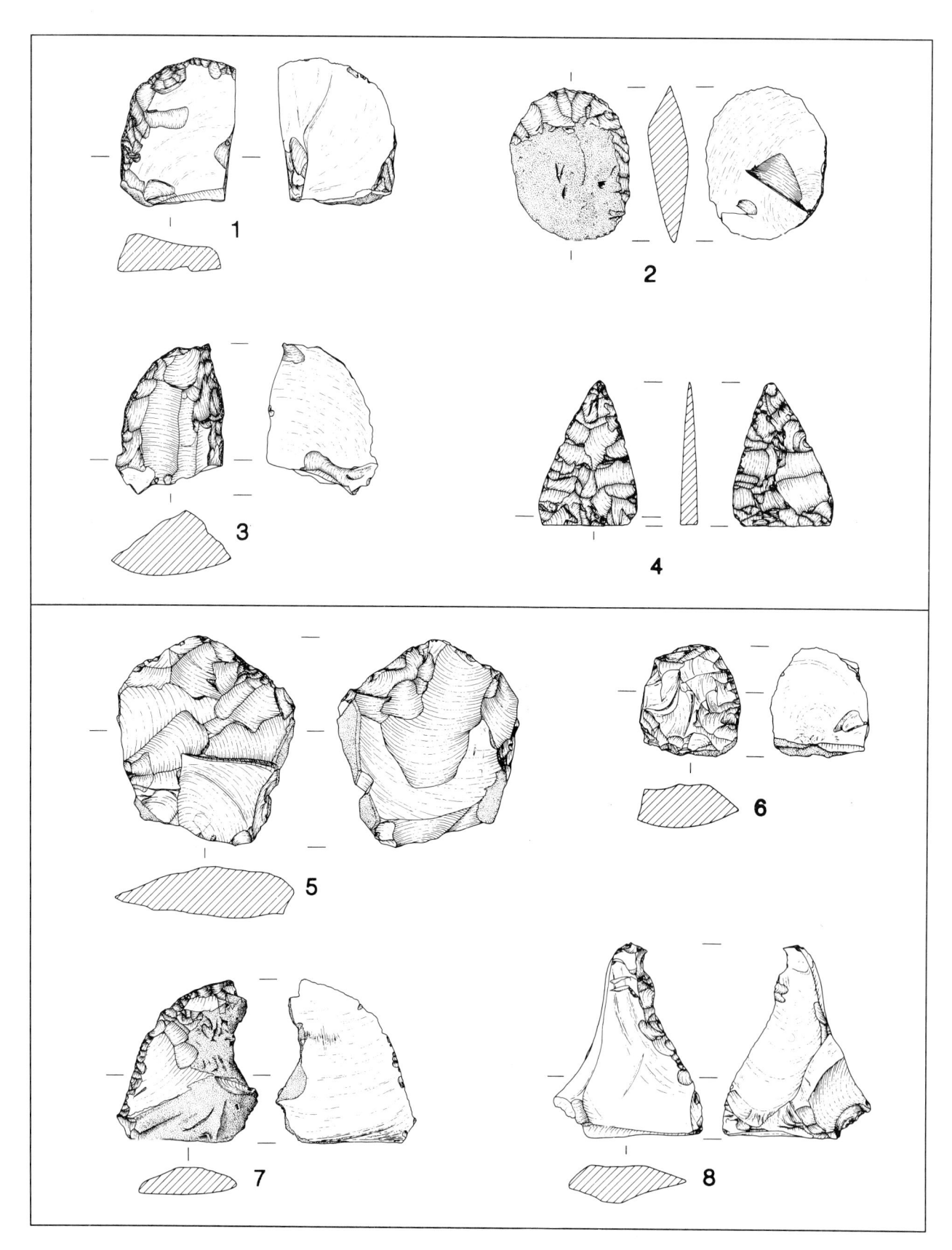

Figure 32: Flint: Site VI, a) Pre-barrow deposits b) The barrow mound. Scale 1:1.

Unretouched/Waste Flakes

Sixty nine examples were recorded as follows:

	Complete	Broken
Primary Flakes	2	3
Secondary Flakes	14	12
Tertiary/Inner Flakes	19	19
TOTAL	35	34

Complete secondary flakes range in length from 11mm to 37 mm with a mean length of 21.4mm and in breadth from 4mm to 31mm with a mean breadth of 21.6mm. Only two of these flakes attain blade like proportions. The majority of the broken flakes seem to have been intentionally fractured. Breaks do not seem to be the result of trampling of *in situ* material. One natural 'potlid' flake was also recorded from F65, Context 1105/SF 1028.

THE BARROW MOUND

The deposition of lithic material throughout the mound contexts is of interest with the highest number of finds coming from the turf core (1033/1034) and silt (1035) deposits:

Context No.	No. Finds
1033/1034	39
1035	32
1036	6
1022	8
1004	1
1003	1
1002	15

The possible significance of this pattern will be discussed below.

Cores/Core Fragments

Three complete cores (Contexts 1002/SF 713, 1034/SF 927, 1034/SF 931) and 7 fragments (Contexts 1002/SF 554, 1033/SF 610, 1035/SF 851, 1022/SF 862, 1035/SF 919, 1034/SF 925, 1034/SF 928) were recovered. Only one example, a discoidal core weighing 15gms (SF 931, Fig. 32, 5) is illustrated. The remaining complete cores are both single platform types. SF 713 weighs 13gms and SF 927 weighs 26gms. Both retain hard pebble cortex on their unworked faces (Max dimension: No. 713: 24mm × 21mm × 12mm; No. 927: 28mm × 28mm × 16mm). Only two fragments show evidence for plough damage.

Scrapers

One short example on the distal end of a dark grey secondary flake was recorded (Context 1034/SF 929: Fig. 32, 6). The piece has a cortical butt and a pronounced bulb of percussion and weighs 4 gms.

Miscellaneous Retouched/Utilised Pieces

Four examples (Contexts 1033/SF 669, 1002/SF 719, 1035/SF822, 1022/SF 863) were noted. Two are illustrated. SF 669 (Fig. 32, 7) is a light grey secondary flake which exhibits retouch on the left edge, dorsal face, and which retains hard fawn pebble cortex. It has a plain butt diffuse bulb and hinge termination. Some small irregular chips have also been removed on the bulbar face, left edge. Weight: 4gms. SF 863 (Fig. 32, 8) is also on a light grey secondary flake, broken transversely at the bulbar end. It exhibits retouch on the right edge, dorsal face, and retains hard fawn cortex. It has a feather termination and weighs 6 gms. SF 719 is a thick inner flake which measures 22mm × 28mm × 12mm and weighs 12gms. It has a plain butt, pronounced bulb and a feather termination and exhibits some plough damage and definite evidence for utilisation on both edges. SF 822 is a light grey inner flake, broken irregularly at both ends. Both edges show retouch. Weight 1 gm.

Blades/Blade Segments

Three blade segments (Contexts 1002/SF 718, 1035/SF 914, 1033/SF 694) and one complete blade (Context 1034/SF 895) and one broken example (Context 1035/SF 745) were recorded. None are illustrated. All of the segments are on inner flakes and only one (SF 718) exhibits controlled transverse fracturing at both ends. The complete and broken examples are also on inner flakes SF 895 measures 18mm × 3mm × 2mm and weighs less than 1gm. It has a plain platform, diffuse bulb and feather termination.

Chips and Chunks

Thirteen irregular chunks and four chips were recorded. Ten chunks and two chips come from the turf core and silt deposits. Five chunks (SF 940, 935, 911, 672, 691) show clear evidence of plough damage, while SF 897 and SF 796 from Context 1002 have been burnt.

Greenstone Flakes

Three flakes, probably from a polished axe, were recorded, two from Context 1033 (SF 898 and SF 900) and one from Context 1035 (SF 934). SF 900 and SF 934 are broken but the dorsal faces of all three flakes are polished. SF 934 exhibits some flake scaring on its dorsal face and these may have been from previous reworking of the axe. It is suggested that all three pieces are from the same source. None are illustrated.

Unretouched/Waste Flakes

Fifty nine examples were recorded and these can be classified as follows

	Complete	Broken
Primary Flakes	2	1
Secondary Flakes	26	11
Tertiary/Inner Flakes	13	6
TOTAL	41	18

Complete examples range in length from 10mm to 34mm with a mean length of 18.85mm and in breadth from 6mm to 24mm with a mean breadth of 15.31mm. Only four flakes attain blade like proportions. Two natural flakes (SF 910 and SF 939) were recorded SF 910 is a pot-lid flake.

THE RING DITCH

Cores/Core Fragments

Seven complete cores and twelve fragments were recorded. Of the complete examples, only one (Context 1010/SF 888) is illustrated (Fig. 33, 9). This is an angular piece in dark grey flint, which retains hard pitted cortex on its unworked faces and which shows evidence of multi-directional flaking (Weight 19gms), The remaining six complete cores (SF428, SF 475, SF 686, SF 758, SF 765 and SF 838) are all from Context 1010. Two (SF 428 and SF 686) are single platform examples while the remainder show multi directional flaking. Cores range from 7gms to 27gms in weight with a mean weight of 17.6gms

Arrowheads

One example (Fig. 33, 10) (Context 1010/SF 668) was recorded. This is a pressure flaked piece, nominally in the category of 'leaf' shaped arrowhead but with an incipient tang at the base. It is difficult to be sure whether the piece was of one manufacture or whether the tang was a modification to a simple leaf shaped point.

Miscellaneous Retouched/Utilised Pieces

Only two were recorded (Context 1010/SF 789 and Context 1010/SF 683). None are illustrated. SF 789 is a secondary flake 13mm × 16mm × 3mm, which exhibits retouch across the distal end and SF 683 is a primary flake broken at the distal end and retouched across the break.

Chunks and Chips

Forty one chunks and 3 chips were recorded. Of these 31 chunks and 2 chips come from the upper layers of the ditch fill (Context 1010) and 11 of the chunks exhibit plough damage. Seven chunks (one showing plough damage) come from Context 1013 and three come from 1014 (of which one shows possible plough damage). The final chip comes from sieving of F8, (Context 1015). Indeed the almost total lack of flint from the primary silting of the ring ditch (1015) is an unusual feature and the higher incidence of plough strikes on pieces from 1010 is probably indicative of the mixing of material at the interface with the redeposited silt material over the ditch which is thought to have come from the ploughing of the mound.

Unretouched/Waste Flakes

Ninety-nine were recorded as follows:

	Complete	Broken
Primary Flakes	6	1
Secondary Flakes	42	30
Tertiary/Inner Flake	11	9
TOTAL	59	40

Complete examples range in length from 8mm to 40mm with a mean length of 21mm and in breadth from 6mm to 43mm with a mean breadth of 19mm. Only two pieces have blade like proportions and the majority are short squat flakes. Eighty one examples (of which 5 show definite plough damage) come from Context 1010 and the remaining 18 (including 5 further plough struck pieces) are from Context 1013 (3 were recovered during sieving material from Section G).

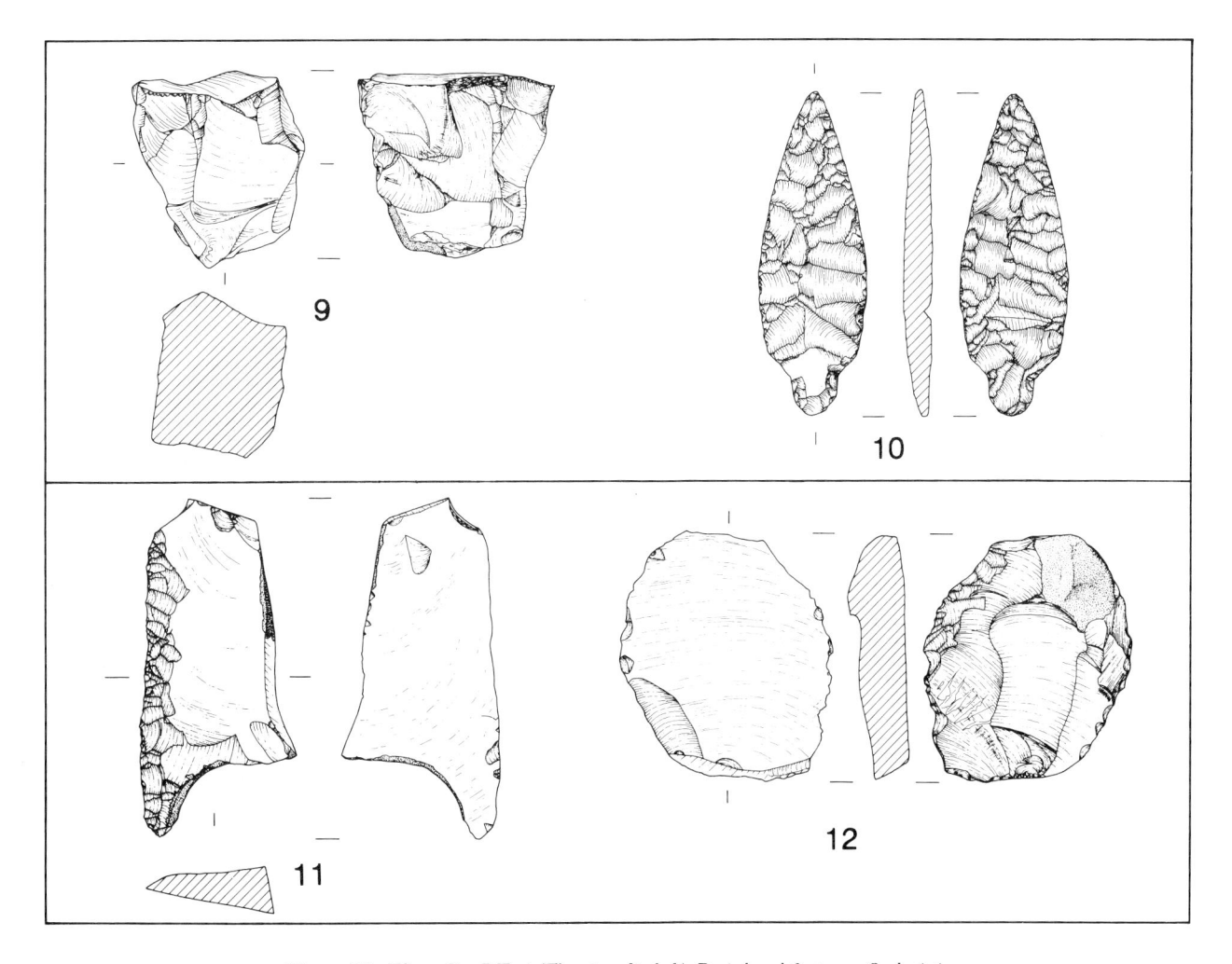

Figure 33: Flint: Site VI a) The ring ditch b) Peripheral features. Scale 1:1.

Peripheral features

Thirty three pieces were recorded from the various contexts in this group. Most would seem to be residual.

The fill of the palisade trench, Context 1006, produced a broken secondary flake and a seemingly water rolled flint chunk. Context 1007, the fill of the ?Roman linear ditch produced a retouched knife (SF 944) on a dark grey, secondary, blade – like flake. This exhibits fine retouch on the left edge, dorsal face (Fig. 33, 11). Two cores weighing 3 and 4gms respectively, a chunk and one complete and one broken inner flake were also recorded from Context 1007.

Other linear ditch fills produced a range of lithic finds. Context 1037 yielded a grey rolled flint chunk. Context 1048 produced two plough struck chunks of flint, two broken and two complete secondary flakes and one complete inner flake, while a light grey flint chunk (SF 847) was recorded from Context 1056. A broken secondary and a broken inner flake and a shattered fragment from a ?keeled core came from Context 1113.

The excavated backfill of the original evaluation trench (Context 1011) produced a scraper fragment and a complete secondary flake, while the topsoil from the trench's initial excavation produced a scraper (Fig. 33, 12; SF 28), one chunk, one chip a fragmentary utilised inner flake and a complete secondary flake with some possible thermal damage.

The two pits, F108 and F32, produced three broken

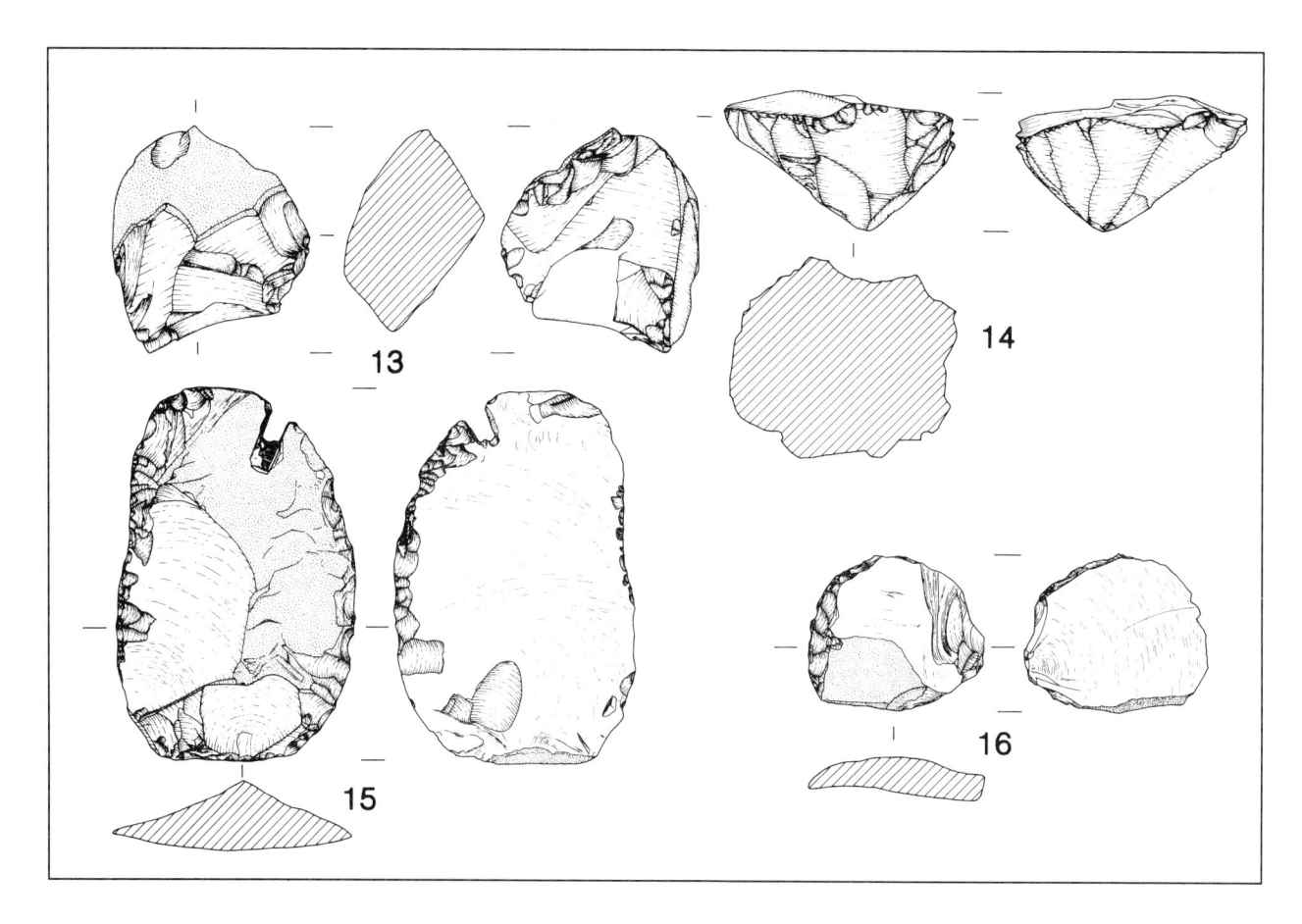

Figure 34: Flint: Site VI silt over ring ditch. Scale 1:1.

flakes (Contexts 1019 and 1061). Context 4005 (F40) produced a complete secondary flake. Two lithic finds also came from the pit which produced the gold hoard. These include a rolled inner flake (SF 957) and a fragment from a shattered, multi-directional core.

SILT OVER RING DITCH

Cores/Core Fragments

Sixteen fragments and 6 complete cores (SF 449, 328, 738, 391, 530, 245) were recorded. All 6 complete cores come from Context 1005. All are in varying shades of grey flint and all with the exception of SF 530 (opposed platform core) and SF 391 (single platform worked all way around circumference) show evidence for multi-platform working. The multi-platform example SF 449 has been re-used as a hammer stone. Cores range in weight from 52gms to 10gms with a mean weight of 28.8gms. Only two examples are illustrated (Fig. 34, 13 and 14; SF 245 and SF 391). All of the fragmentary cores come from Context 1005.

Scrapers

Three side and end scrapers (SF 531, SP 299, SP 305 (Fig. 34, 15) one fragmentary side scraper (SF 529) and one end scraper (SF 302, Fig. 34, 16) were recorded. Three are on secondary flakes and two are on inner flakes. All were from Context 1005. Complete scrapers range in length from 51mm to 20mm with a mean length of 30.5mm and in breadth from 35mm to 14mm with a mean breadth of 23mm. Weights range from 16gms to 2gms with a mean weight of 12.5gms.

Miscellaneous Retouched/Utilised Pieces

Eight pieces show possible evidence for utilisation/retouch – SF 186, 369, 310, 159, 519, 389, 307, and 279. All are from Context 1005. SF 310, 519, and 389 are fragmentary. Four pieces, SF 369, 279, 307, 389 are on secondary flakes while the remainder are on inner flakes. None are illustrated. Complete utilised flakes range in length from 34mm to 24mm with a mean length of 30mm and in breadth from 25mm to 10mm with a mean breadth of 19.6mm.

Chips and Chunks

Eighty six chunks were recovered from Context 1005, fifty of which show abrasion and plough damage to a greater or lesser degree. Three pieces, SF 326, 601 and 640 show evidence for burning/thermal damage – SF 640 exhibits pot-lid removals.

Unretouched/Waste Flakes

Two hundred and sixty three waste flakes were recorded and these can be classified as follows:

	Complete	Broken
Primary Flakes	12	5
Secondary Flakes	70	117
Tertiary/Inner Flakes	18	41
TOTAL	100	163

Complete flakes range in length from 49mm to 10mm with a mean length of 23.32mm and in breadth from 50mm to 7mm with a mean breadth of 18.7mm. Although more flakes from this context group attain blade like proportions than in any of the other groups from the barrow, the general trend is still towards short squat flakes. One primary flake and six secondaries show signs of burning.

PLOUGHSOIL AND TOPSOIL

Cores/Core Fragments

Six shattered cores (SF 1, 2, 13, 14, 15, 90) and three complete examples (SF 29, 81, and one unstratified with no finds number.) were recovered. SF 1, 2, and 14 were also unstratified finds. All of the stratifed examples with the exception of SF 13, (from Context 1000) are from Context 1003. SF 1 and 2 are fragments from single platform cores, SF 13 is part of a small blade core and SF 14, 15, 90 are fragments from multi platformed pieces. All of the complete pieces are multi platform cores and range in weight from 8gms to 15gms with a mean weight of 11.3gms. None are illustrated.

Scrapers

Four fragmentary examples (SF 31, 47, 3, 4) and four complete scrapers (SF 51, 43, 445, 69) were recovered. SF 3 and 4 are unstratified finds, SF 31, 47, 69 and 445 come from Context 1000, SF 43 is from Context 1001 and SF 51 is from Context 1003. Four examples are illustrated (SF 31, 43, 51, 445; Fig. 35, 17–20). SF 43 and 445 (Fig. 35, 18 and 20) are small thumbnail type scrapers, as are the broken pieces SF 3 and 4. SF 31 is a fragmentary disc scraper which is broken almost in half (Fig. 35, 17). SF 47 is a broken side scraper, SF 51 (Fig. 35, 19) is a scraper on the distal end of a secondary flake and SF 69 is a side and end scraper. The four complete examples range in length from 28mm to 18mm with a mean length of 22.5mm and in breadth from 24mm to 15mm with a mean breadth of 18.8mm. Weights range from 8gms to 1gm with a mean weight of 3.6gms.

Knives

One possible example was recorded from Context 1000 (SF 36; Fig. 35, 21). This is on a heavy, fresh, light grey secondary bladelike flake. The right edge, dorsal face shows evidence for heavy utilisation.

Arrowheads

One example from Context 1000 was recorded (SF 3; Fig. 35, 22). This is a small, possible, chisel shaped arrowhead with pressure flaking on both faces and a definite thickened base. The edges show traces of plough damage.

Miscellaneous Retouched/Utilised Pieces

Five complete flakes/blades (SF 16, 56, 70, 422 and one unstratified piece without a finds number) and three broken examples (SF 77, 94, 711) were recorded. SF 56 comes from Context 1003 and the remainder are all from Context 1000. All show varying degrees of utilisation/retouching on one or both edges. Only the blade, SF 16

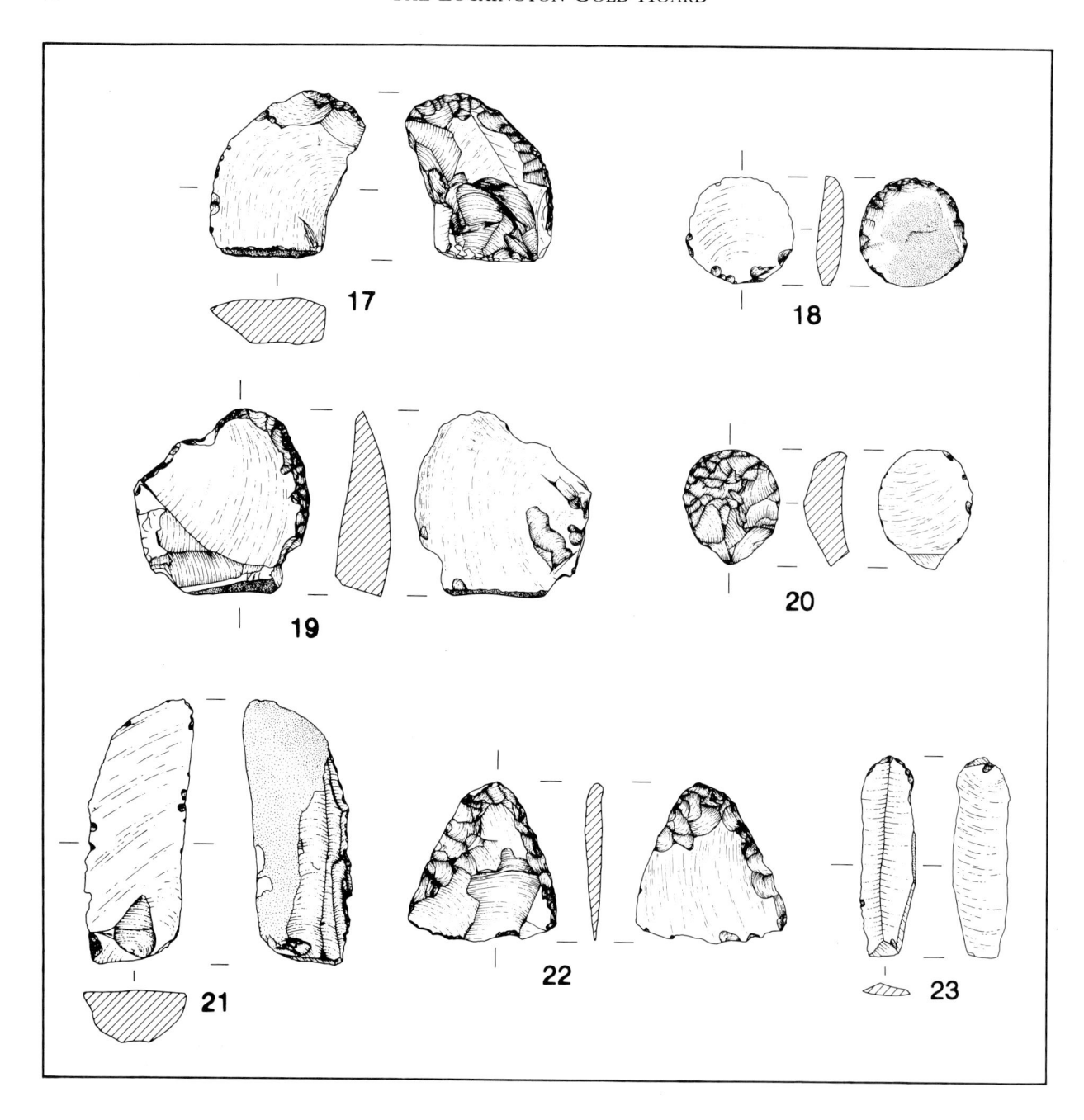

Figure 35: Flint: Site VI ploughsoil. Scale 1:1.

is illustrated (Fig. 35, 23). Complete examples range in length from 35mm to 24mm with a mean length of 31.2mm and in breadth from 29mm to 8mm with a mean breadth of 16.8mm.

Blades/Bladelets

Two broken blades (SF 14, and 99) and one broken bladelet (SF 147) came from Contexts 1000 and 1003 respectively. SF 14 is truncated at the distal end while

THE FLINT

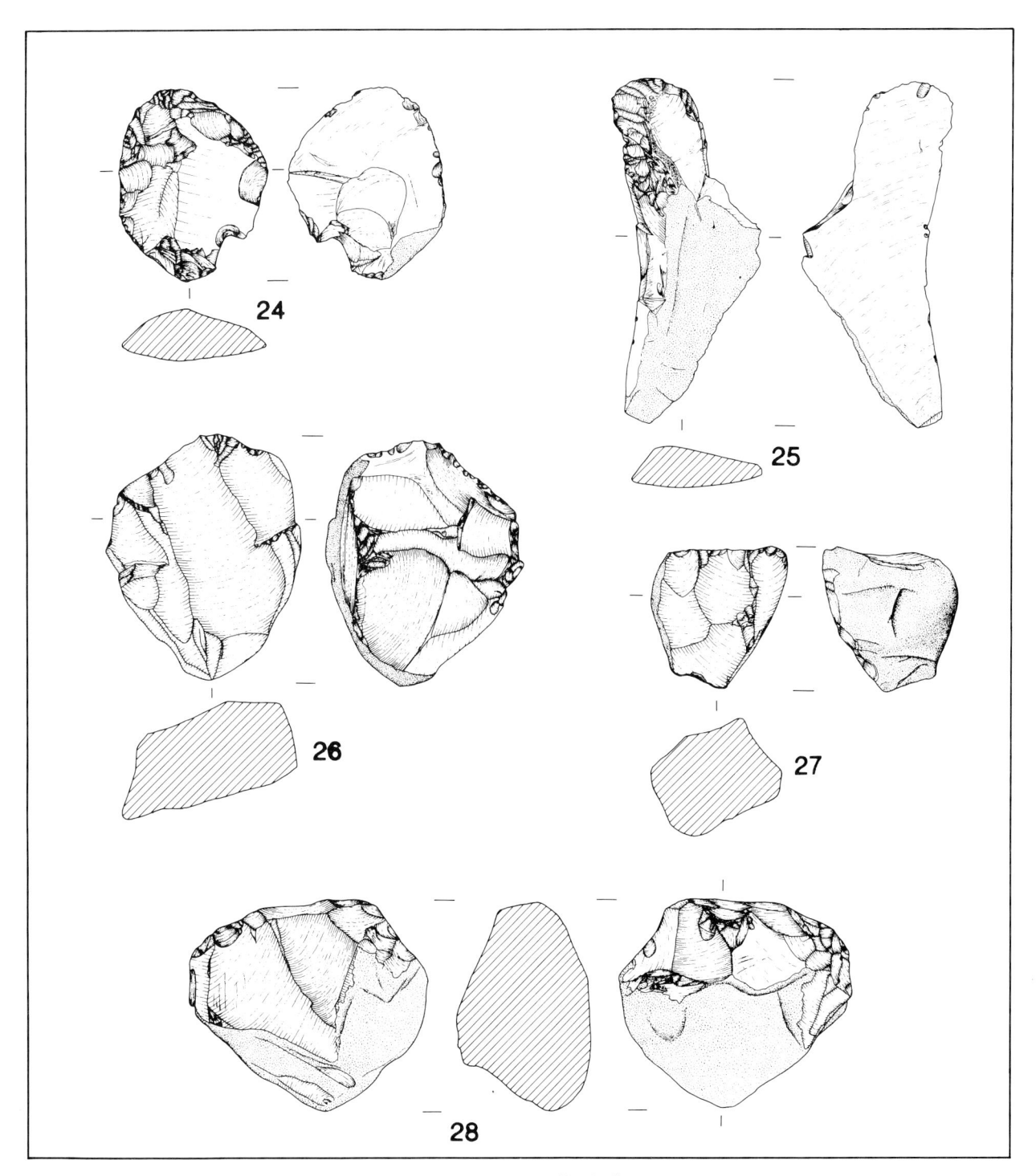

Figure 36: Flint: Site V. Scale 1:1.

the other examples are broken at both the distal and bulbar ends.

Chips/Chunks

One chip (SF 151) was recovered from Context 1003. Five chunks were unstratified (SF 16–20), fifteen came from Context 1000 and fifteen came from Context 1003. Thirteen examples show clear plough damage to a greater or lesser degree, while six (SF 59, 145, 16, 126,39,157) show possible evidence for previous flake removals and may be fragments from shattered cores.

Natural Flakes

One was recorded (SF 93) from Context 1003.

Unretouched/Waste Flakes

One hundred and twenty one examples can be categorised as follows:

	Complete	Broken
Primary Flakes	3	1
Secondary Flakes	52	36
Tertiary/Inner Flake	10	19
TOTAL	65	56

Fifty nine (43 compete and 16 broken) were recovered from Context 1003, forty seven (13 complete and 34 broken) came from Context 1000 and fourteen (8 complete and 6 broken) were unstratified. One inner flake (SF 135) from Context 1000 was burnt and two secondary flakes (SF 27 and 182) both from Context 1003 are from core rejuvenation. Complete flakes from all contexts range in length from 37mm to 6mm with a mean length of 18.10mm and in breadth from 31mm to 3mm with a mean breadth of 16.64mm. Few flakes attain blade like proportions.

THE SITE V PIT GROUP

A total of 58 pieces of flint were recovered from the excavation of the Pit Group (Site V). With the exception of one brown secondary flint flake, all are in varying shades of grey and 41 finds retain pebble cortex to a greater or lesser degree.

Artefact categories are as follows:

TYPE	
Primary flakes	3
Secondary flakes	17
Tertiary flakes	8
Scrapers	6
Utilised/retouched	11
Cores/core frags	7
Chips/chunks	6
TOTAL	58

Technology

As on the barrow site the low representation of primary flakes and cores and core fragments would imply that primary knapping was not heavily represented in this small assemblage. An examination of extant bulbs of percussion and platform types on flakes can be used to gain an insight into technological processes, and these can be classified as follows:

Pronounced Bulb	Diffuse Bulb	Plain Bulb	Faceted Bulb	Cortical Bulb
17	17	16	5	15

From the above it can be suggested that both soft hammer techniques are present in equal measure. A brief discussion of the artefact categories is given.

Scrapers

Of the six recorded examples, three are discoidal in shape, one is on the side and end of a secondary flake, one is a side scraper and the sixth example is on the end of a secondary flake. One of the discoidal scrapers is illustrated (SF 55; Fig. 36, 24) as is the side and end scraper (SF 59; Fig. 36, 25). Scrapers range in length from 22mm–54mm with a mean length of 34mm and in breadth from 14mm–29mm with a mean breadth of 23mm.

Utilised/retouched flakes/blades

Eleven were recorded, and of these, five are blades and six are secondary flakes. The four complete retouched/utilised flakes range in length from 25mm–54mm in length with a mean length of 29mm and in breadth from 18mm–26mm with a mean breadth of 22mm. The four complete blades range in length from 24mm–32mm with a mean length of 28mm and in breadth from 9mm–12mm with a mean breadth of 11mm.

Cores/Core fragments

Of the seven cores recorded six retain pebble cortex to a greater or lesser degree and two display incipient re-cortication. Three are illustrated (SF 68, SF 74 and SF 28; Fig. 36, 26–28). Cores range in weight from 10grms–34grms with a mean weight of 21 grms, just slightly heavier than the mean weights recorded from the barrow excavation.

Waste flakes

Twenty eight were recorded and they can be classified as follows:

	Complete	Broken
Primary	2	1
Secondary	13	4
Inner	2	6
TOTAL	17	11

Complete flakes range in length from 14mm–40mm with a mean length of 26mm and in breadth from 12mm–34mm with a mean breadth of 21 mm.

Chips/chunks

Six irregular chunks were recorded.

DISCUSSION

The lithic material from the Lockington barrow throws up many points of interest in terms of assemblage formation and potential patterns of deposition. It is a tribute to the skill of the excavators that all of the material was plotted three dimensionally within context and this, it was hoped, would allow a detailed discussion of possible structured deposition across the site. Indeed an initial examination of the spatial plots of all flint finds suggests several discrete groupings of material across the mound and the deposits relating to the ditch. However, a comparison of the distribution plots of material from the topsoil, the silt over the ring ditch and the upper fills of the ring ditch shows a close correlation between flint patterning and the occurrence of medieval and post-medieval residual furrows plotted from the resistivity survey (Fig. 17). A similar phenomenon was noted by Healey at the Pipe Hole Farm, Eaton barrow in Leicestershire (Healey n.d., 37). It is suggested that only the material from the lower levels of the ring ditch, the mound and from pre-barrow contexts are in undisturbed locations.

This raises the important point about the relationship between the flint assemblage and the barrow and its related features. How did the material from the topsoil and the re-deposited silt and the mound material actually get into these contexts? Saville (1980, 21–22) has speculated on the problem of the formation processes that lie behind lithic groupings recorded from barrows. It may be that material was incorporated into the original mound in the course of its construction, from sources such as earlier or contemporary settlement in the immediate vicinity (cf. Bradley 1972, 196; Alexander and Ozanne 1960).

In the course of his work on the Deeping St. Nicholas barrow complex in South Lincolnshire, French has recently shown that this is highly likely. Here he suggested that to build a mound of 2m in height with a diameter of 15m would require some half a hectare of turf (1994, 103), and his micromorphological analysis of the mound soil, which incorporated the majority of the flintwork examined by Julian Richards, showed it to have derived from deposits that were similar to the preserved areas of buried soil at the site (1994, 103).

It may be significant in relation to the Lockington material that in terms of the mound and the ring ditch fill, lithic finds were concentrated in the extant turf 'core' (Contexts 1033/34 and 1035) and the upper levels of the ditch, in particular Context 1010. This might imply that the material had been incorporated into the mound in the way that French has suggested and that it had subsequently been spread by ploughing.

Further support for this may be seen in the occurrence of the three greenstone fragments (SF 898, 900, 934) from a polished axe in the mound make-up along with the presence of blades and blade segments in both the mound, and topsoil, and the fact that waste flakes with blade like proportions occur more in the mound material, redeposited silts and topsoil than elsewhere. All of these finds might suggest that the mound was made up of earth not just from the ditch but also from soils gathered from the surrounding area, incorporating earlier and contemporary cultural material possibly of Meso-lithic as well as Neolithic and Bronze Age date.

Turning to the contexts beneath the mound, both Neolithic and Bronze Age pottery was present (see page 52 above). The contents of F65, the pit with associated

Neolithic pottery and a radiocarbon date of 4375±80 BP (Uncal., see Table 1), were sieved, producing an overall total of 47 pieces of lithic material of which 24 were burnt. None of these pieces is chronologically diagnostic and only 17 flakes were complete, the remainder of the pieces being chips, chunks and broken flakes. Taken together this may represent debitage from an early episode of flint working that was later placed in the pit. However, unlike the material from the early Neolithic pits at Tattershall Thorpe in Lincolnshire (Healy 1983, 28–33) the complete flakes are mainly short and squat with only three examples attaining blade-like proportions.

The central scoop, F23 (Contexts 1041, 1043) produced only 17 pieces, again none of which are diagnostic. This total does however include a small core with multi-directional flaking and two utilised/retouched flakes.

The pottery sherd plots for the pre-barrow contexts highlights a concentration of ceramic finds south of the mound's centre (Fig. 8). This is not mirrored by the overall distribution of lithic finds from these contexts as this shows a high concentration in the NW quadrant around F65, and associated with Contexts 1044, 1046 and 1088. Recognisable tool forms come from Context 1046 which produced two scrapers and a fragment of a leaf shaped arrowhead, and Context 1088 which produced a scraper and a knife fragment.

As has already been noted there is a high percentage (over 50%) of broken pieces from the contexts beneath the mound and, unlike the ceramic finds, some 25% of the total material from this location was burnt. It has suggested that the ceramic material may have been deposited, as at Amesbury barrow 71, after the cremation of the human remains had taken place (see page 52 above). The lithic material may therefore be either contemporary with, or earlier than, the suggested cremation activities.

In terms of a general discussion of artefact typology and parallels, all of the scraper forms could be paralleled on any Neolithic and Bronze Age site in the Midlands. The chisel arrowhead from the topsoil would fit well into a general Grooved Ware/Late Neolithic context. Green has shown that chisel arrowheads may have a close association with the Woodland sub-style of Grooved Ware (1980, 108) and that they are the commonest type in late Neolithic flint mine contexts (1980, 103–110). Chronologically these arrowheads seem to have their origins in the forth millennium BC and they probably disappear from the record by c.2000 BC at the latest. Green has also hinted at an early Beaker association for these arrowhead forms (1980, 114).

The only anomalous find is the arrowhead SF 668 from Context 1010 in the ditch fill (Fig. 33, 10). Initially it was thought by the excavator and both authors that this was a leaf shaped arrowhead, possibly of Green's Type 3C (Green 1980, fig. 28, 71), which had subsequently been modified by the working of a tang at the haft end. No regional parallels for this could be found and on a detailed examination of the piece it really is impossible to say without doubt whether or not the tang is a secondary feature. It does not conform to the criteria for inclusion into Green's Sutton Type a category of unbarbed or vestigially barbed but tanged pieces. On balance it is suggested here that the arrowhead started life as a leaf shaped projectile point and was modified by subsequent re-working. As such it may again reinforce the multi-period aspect of the lithic assemblage from the site.

The cores from Lockington deserve further comment. Out of a total of 21 complete or identifiable core types from the cores and fragments recorded, 13 show multi-directional flaking, one is a keeled core, 5 are single platform cores, one is discoidal and one exhibits opposed striking platforms. The predominance of cores showing multi-directional flaking and keeled cores in the Midlands is something that other workers have noted. Indeed, Saville (1980) has suggested that the dominance of multi-platform cores is a distinct feature of prehistoric lithic assemblages away from the chalk. Healy records a similar situation at the prehistoric and Anglo-Saxon site at Nettleton Top in Lincs. (1993), while Chowne and Healy (1983, 43) recorded a high proportion of multi-platform cores at Anwick Fen also in Lincs. In the course of their discussion of this material they drew attention to Saville's work at Bourne Pool in Staffs where he noted a similar high occurrence multi-directional flaking. Moore and Williams, as early as 1975, in their discussion of lithic material from the Late Neolithic site at Ecton in Northants, also noted a high representation of multi-directional and keeled cores (1975, 20) and Julian Richards highlighted a similar situation at the Deeping St. Nicholas Barrow complex (1994, 58). The Lockington cores, then, are typologically not out of place in terms of a range of Late Neolithic/Bronze Age sites in the Midlands.

Lockington cores range in weight from c.5gms–52gms with a mean weight of 16.14 gms. Compared with other Midlands assemblages this is on the small size and probably reflects the dimensions of available flint pebbles in the vicinity. However, the Lockington material does compare very favourably with the cores from Newton Cliffs on Trent (Garton 1989) which shows a range of 12gms, 16gms and 18gms from various parts of the knapping area, with a mean weight of some 17.6 gms. At Nettleton Top mean core weight was c.40 gms, (Healy 1993, 15), at Anwick Fen the figure was 25gms (Chowne and Healy, 1983, 39), at West Ashby, Saville recorded a mean core weight of 37gms (1985) and at the Neolithic and later site of Tatershall Thorpe, Healy (1983) records mean core weights of 24, 26, 27, and 39 gms from various parts of the site. Maximum core dimensions at Lockington range from 20 -50mm with a mean maximum dimension of c.30mm. it is thus slightly smaller than the core range recorded from the Eaton, Leics. barrow (Healey, n.d., 37).

Only a small sample of the flakes from the silt over the ring ditch and the mound attain blade-like proportions and the possible reasons for this have been set out above. Healey, in her report on the lithic material from Eaton, Leics. records that the flakes from this site were 'small in size and squat in shape' (n.d., 37). This is a feature of most of the waste flakes from well reported Neolithic/Bronze Age assemblages off the chalk in the Midlands, and again probably reflects the size range of available raw material. The Lockington assemblage of waste material compares almost exactly with the metrical range of waste flakes from the late Neolithic/Bronze Age sites of Anwick Fen, Lincs. (Chowne and Healey 1983, 45), Ecton, Northants. (Moore 1975, fig. 10, 22), Weasenham Lyngs, Hockwold 93, and Reffley Wood (all Norfolk) (Petersen and Healy, 1986, 88), Fengate (Newark Rd.), Maxey, Barnack/Bainton (all in the Welland Valley) (Pryor and French 1985, 162) and Newton Cliffs in the Trent Valley (Garton *et al.* 1989). Detailed study of the typological and distributional aspects of the Lockington flint allows the following conclusions to be drawn:

a) The majority of the finds in the topsoil, mound, re-deposited silt and the upper levels of the ditch fill are probably the product of the material for mound con struction being obtained from a variety of locations as well as from the ditch.

b) The material has subsequently been disturbed by ploughing and aspects of the distribution pattern across the site shows a correlation with the pattern of ridge and furrow remains plotted from the resistivity survey.

c) Material from the deposits under the mound may relate to activities either earlier than or contemporary with the pre-barrow cremation activities.

d) In terms of overall chronology the material compares well with Neolithic and Bronze Age assemblages from other areas of the broad Midlands region.

THE CUP MARKED STONE

By Gwilym Hughes

A single object of worked stone was recovered from the fill of the ring ditch (F1) on its northern side approximately two metres to the southeast of the pit containing the hoard (Fig. 37 and Plate 20). The block is approximately triangular in shape, 250×210×120mm, with evidence for a series of eight shallow pits or 'cup-marks', between 20mm and 40mm in diameter and up to 5mm deep. The cup marks are pecked into one surface and appear to form two, slightly sinuous rows of four.

The block is composed of waterlain siltstone of Carboniferous or Permo-Triassic age (Rob Ixer pers comm). Its provinance is difficult to acertain but it is likely to be from one of the outcrops of millstone grit to the north of the site in southern Derbyshire. It forms a natural joint block with slickenedsides along the prominent joint plain. There are also traces of disseminated iron sulphide oxidised to limonite (red rust) on this side. The cup-marks are pecked onto the bedding plain. There is no obvious differential weathering of the joint surfaces which suggests that the carving has been undertaken on a block already detached from the bedrock.

Stones with carved decoration are widely associated with barrows (Ashbee 1960, 66–68; Bradley 1997, 42–3). They have been recorded in a number of different contexts within the structure of barrows and cairns, and frequently on stones built into, or over, graves or cists. Simple cup marks are the most widespread form, although numerous other motifs have been recorded. It has been suggested that the cup marked stone from Lockington is an outlier of a distinct western group with a distribution in the south-west of England and Wales (Bradley 1997, 146–8). The only other cup-marked stone known from Leicestershire is a fragment of mica-schist with eight cup marks from Tugby near Oakham (Vine 1982, 249 and 409). Other examples are known from the Derbyshire Peak District (Vine 1982, 409), including examples from the embanked stone circle at Barbrook (Barnatt 1990, 55–57). One of these was located near to a blocked entrance through the bank on the northeast; others were associated with a cairn and cist within the enclosure. Another recently excavated example of a cup marked stone in the east Midlands region is from Biddenham Loop (near Bedford). This was recovered from the fill of a pit thought to date to the Iron Age, but which was located 50m from a ring ditch (Holly Duncan pers comm).

It seems possible that the Lockington cup-marked stone may have fallen into the partially filled ring ditch and may have originated from the vicinity of the metalwork and pottery hoard. It is concievable that it may have been used as some form of marker stone indicating the location of the hoard. Bradley suggests that in some instances that there might be a relationship between the deposition of metalwork and rock carvings (Bradley 1997, 138).

The Cup Marked Stone

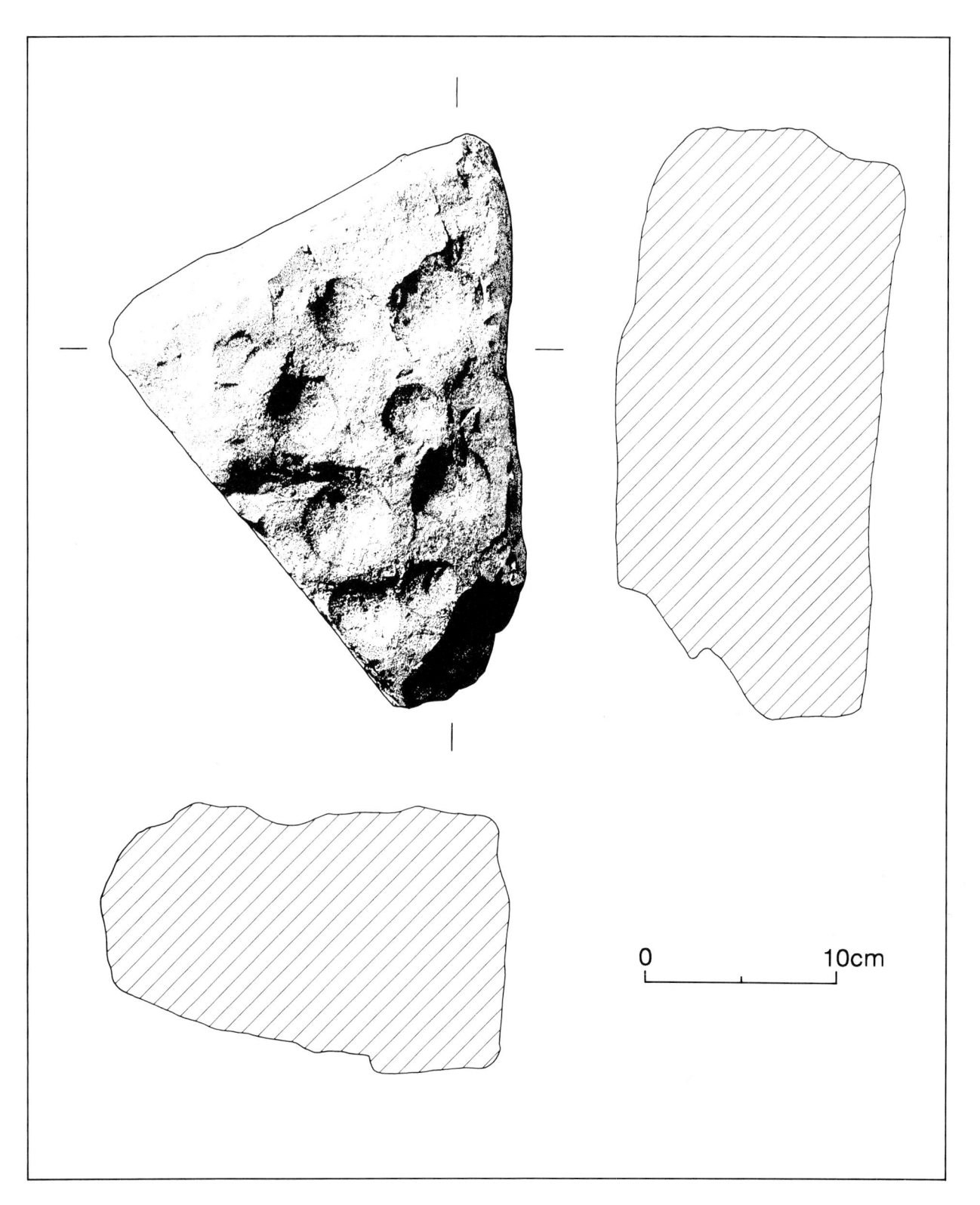

Figure 37: Cup marked stone.

THE CHARRED PLANT REMAINS

By Lisa Moffett and Angela Monckton

The barrow (Site VI)
By Lisa Moffett

Method

A total of forty samples were taken from selected dateable contexts. They were processed using 'bucket flotation' and the floating fraction (flot) decanted onto a 0.5mm mesh sieve. The flots were assessed by scanning the material under a binocular microscope at x10 and x20 magnification.

Results

Very little charred material other than wood charcoal was seen. A very small number of cereal grains were present in two samples from the mound make-up (1034 and 1035). These consisted of a fragment of unidentified wheat grain from 1035 (*Triticum* sp.), and from 1034 some unidentified wheat and four grains of emmer (*T. dicoccum* Schübl.), and a single hulled barley grain (*Hordeum vulgare* L.) which appeared to have germinated. A single grain of glume wheat (*T. dicoccum/spelta*) was found in the central pit in the mound (1043). The charcoal spread under the mound (1041) was sampled by grid squares of which only three were scanned for this assessment. These produced a grass culm base (the underground basal part of the stem), fragments of rhizomes and a single seed of blinks (*Montia fontana* ssp. *chondrosperma* (Fenzl) Walters), a small plant of damp ground. The mound cremation pit (1105) produced a fragment of hazel nutshell (*Corylus avellana* L.).

One of the ring-ditch samples (1010 section C) produced a thorn of sloe or hawthorn (*Prunus spinosa*/*Crataegus* sp.) and an unidentified grass seed (Poaceae indet.). A single grain of wheat was found in another ring-ditch sample (1013 section C). No charred remains other than wood charcoal were seen in any of the peripheral features. A few fragments of possible parenchymatous material were found in a few of the mound and ring-ditch samples.

The amount of material is too small to place an interpretation on. The most productive sample was from the mound make up and this was presumably derived from the surrounding land surface. The cereals from this sample are likely to be residual, indicating human activity but no more than that. The grass material in the charcoal spread (1041) could have been accidentally incorporated in the fire when the wood was burned or even used to start it.

Prehistoric ritual contexts occasionally have been known to yield unusual plant remains (e.g. Moffett 1991) but this is rare. Plants associated with normal domestic activities would not necessarily be expected in a ritual area with no other evidence of occupation, and their low occurrence at Lockington seems to be in keeping with this expectation.

The pit group (Site V)
By Angela Monckton

Method

Samples of 17 contexts varying in size from 5 to 157 litres were selected from those taken as having some potential to produce charred remains. They were wet sieved in a York tank with a 1mm mesh and flotation into a 0.5mm sieve. The sandy sediments gave reasonable recovery of charred material where present and a total of 646 litres was processed. The flotation fractions were air dried and all sorted with a stereo microscope at ×10 magnification.

Results

Charred cereal remains were found in small numbers in nine contexts being most numerous in cut numbers F84 and F182. Contexts (4) and (132) were from a pit (F84) with abundant charcoal observed during excavation (Table 4). The remains included a few chaff fragments (glumes and spikelet forks) some of which could be identified as emmer (*Triticum dicoccum*). A few grains of barley (*Hordeum vulgare*) were also found in this pit together with hazel nut shell (*Corylus avellana*) and a few charred seeds. Charcoal from this pit was identified by Graham Morgan of Leicester University as oak, poplar, hawthorn, hazel, blackthorn, field maple, ash and gorse and was dated to 1875 to 1805 cal BC and 1795 to 1645 cal BC (at 68% probability Beta-83721).

Context (175) from cut F182 was the most productive from the site with 108 items from a 5 litre sample. Both emmer and spelt (*Triticum spelta*) were found confirmed from diagnostic chaff (glumes) with chaff forming 62% of the remains, seeds mainly of grasses including brome grass (*Bromus hordeaceus* or *secalinus*) as 23% of the remains and a few cereal grains as 14% of the sample. The large grass seeds may have been gathered and used as part of the crop. Charcoal of hazel and blackthorn (det Graham Morgan) was dated to 1425 to 1260 cal BC (at 68% probability Beta-83722).

Cereal remains were found in six other contexts grouped together in Table 4; from context (137) there were a total of 15 cereal and wheat (*Triticum* sp) grains, three seeds of vetch or vetchling (*Vicia/Lathyrus*) and two seeds of wild radish (*Raphanus raphanistrum*) with evidence of bean or pea (*Vicia/Pisum*). Context (198) had a glume base of emmer or spelt (*Triticum dicoccum/spelta*) and one cereal grain, (265) had a glume base of emmer or spelt with two cereal grains and a possible fragment of bean or pea. Context (267) had a cereal grain and (288) had a cereal grain and a hazel nut shell fragment. Context (260) produced a single grain of a free threshing wheat identified as bread wheat type (*Triticum* cf *aestivum*) which with emmer is the main cereal of the Neolithic period and is found in small amounts with the glume wheats (spelt and emmer) in the Iron Age (Greig 1991). As a single find here it cannot be shown to be associated with the Bronze Age material. Contexts which were examined but produced no plant remains other than small charcoal fragments were (53), (57), (70), (201), (207), (238), (277) and (287).

Discussion

With the exception of cut F182 charred plant remains were at a low concentration and probably represent redeposited material. Wheat chaff and grains were identified as emmer from cuts F84 and F182 and glumes confirmed as spelt were found only in cut F182. A single grain of a free threshing wheat was also found but was unassociated with the other cereals. Barley was also present in cut F84, grains of a hulled, cultivated form were found. Other food plants were represented by hazel nut shell and a bean or pea fragment. A few charred seeds were also found probably as weeds of the crops. Charcoal from pit cut F84 and cut F182 dated to the bronze age give evidence that the cereal remains are also of this date. Emmer, spelt and hulled barley, as found here, are typical crops of the Bronze Age in England (Greig 1991). Remains from F182 have a high proportion of chaff which may suggest that this is waste from the preparation of glume wheat for consumption, the chaff being removed by fine sieving and disposed of by burning (Hillman 1981). The remains from F84 consist of more grains than chaff but numbers are small so the proportions may be affected by residual material, however the presence of these remains with burnt animal bone and large amounts of charcoal suggests this may also be waste from food preparation. The charcoal itself shows the exploitation of wood and scrub species.

Other finds from Leicestershire of the cereals found here include the neolithic pit circle at Oakham, Rutland, Leicestershire (Monckton 1999) which produced small numbers of charred cereal grains including bread type wheat (*Triticum* cf *aestivum*) although no chaff fragments were recovered from that site. The only find of charred cereal remains from the county from a site of Bronze Age date are those from Eaton round barrow (Paradine 1978) which include rye and spelt with wild radish but the possibility that these may originate from later activity in the area could not be excluded and was noted by the specialist at the time. Spelt of Bronze Age date on this site shows that it was in use in the area at this time, however the find of wild radish from F136, a plant which

Table 4: Charred plant remains from Site V.

Cut	F84	F84	F182	Rest	
Context	4	132	175	–	
Cereal chaff					
Triticum dicoccum Schubl s.f.	1	–	–	–	Emmer
Triticum cf *dicoccum* s.f.	2	–	–	–	cf Emmer
Triticum dicoccum Schubl gl.	2	1	15	–	Emmer
Triticum spelta L. gl	–	–	5	–	Spelt
Triticum cf *spelta* gl	–	–	5	–	cf Spelt
Triticum dicoccum/spelta s.f.	–	–	5	–	Emmer/Spelt
Triticum dicoccum/spelta gl.	1	–	34	2	Emmer/Spelt
Triticum sp rachis	–	–	3	–	Wheat
Cereal grains					
Triticum dicoccum Schubl	2	–	1	–	Emmer
Triticum cf *dicoccum*	4	1	–	–	cf Emmer
Triticum cf *aestivum*	–	–	–	1	Bread wheat type
Triticum sp	7	–	2	7	Wheat
Hordeum vulgare L. hulled	1	1	–	–	Barley
cf *Hordeum vulgare*	2	–	–	–	cf Barley
Cereal indet	28	12	7	12	Cereal
Cereal/Gramineae	2	–	5	4	Cereal/Grass
Other plants					
Corylus avellana L.	3	2	–	2	Hazel nutshell
Polygonum sp	–	1	–	–	Knotgrass
Rumex sp	2	–	–	1	Docks
Raphanus raphanistrum L	–	–	–	2	Wild radish pod
Vicia/Pisum	–	–	–	1	Pea/Bean
cf *Vicia/Pisum*	–	–	–	2	cf Bean/Pea
Vicia/Lathyrus	1	2	2	4	Vetch/Vetchling
Plantago lanceolata type	1	1	–	–	Ribwort plantain
Galium aparine L.	–	1	–	–	Cleavers
Carex 3-sided	3	–	–	–	Sedges
Gramineae large	–	–	15	–	Grasses, large
Gramineae small	–	1	–	–	Grass, small
Bromus sp	–	–	8	–	Brome grass
Danthonia decumbens (L) DC	–	2	–	–	Heath-grass
cf *Danthonia decumbens*	1	–	–	–	cf Heath-grass
Arrhenatherum elatius (L) tuber	1	–	–	–	Onion couch
Seed indet.	7	1	–	3	

Table 4: continued.

Other remains					
Cereal culm node	–	1	–	–	
Cereal culm	1	1	1	1	
Cereal/Gramineae culm	1	1	–	–	
Seed head/Flower bud	1	–	–	–	
Bark fragment	1	2	–	–	
Twig/Bud	1	2	–	–	
Thorn	1	–	–	–	
Stem fragment	2	4	–	–	
Charred fragment	+	+	+	+	
Uncharred seeds	+	+	+	+	
TOTAL	79	37	108	42	Total
Flot Vol (mls)	182	81	22	89	(mls)
Sample Vol (litres)	157	77	5	159	(litres)
Sample Wt (kg)	229	108	7	241	(kg)

Remains are seeds in the broad sense unless specified.

Key: s.f = spikelet fork; gl = glume base; + = present.

was first noted as a weed of cultivation in the Iron Age (Greig 1991), adds to the evidence for this plant in the county at this date although material from F136 was not itself dated so this cannot be confirmed. Emmer has previously been found in small quantities from the Iron Age site at Normanton le Heath (Monckton 1994) and from Roman levels at the Shires, Leicester (Moffett 1993), on both these sites it was found together with spelt which is the most common wheat of these later periods. The finds of emmer and spelt at Lockington may therefore be the earliest records of these glume wheats from the county to date and provide evidence of Bronze Age cereals from the county.

Conclusions

Charred plant remains including cereal grains and chaff fragments were found from samples from pits, mainly from cuts F84 and F182. The cereals were identified as wheat, including both emmer and spelt, and barley which were associated with charcoal dated by radiocarbon analysis to the Bronze Age. The use of these cereals and possibly the preparation of food is suggested on the site. Hazel nut shell fragments and fragments of pea or bean were also found. Although the total number of plant remains was small it can be concluded that wheat including emmer and spelt, barley, hazel nuts and legumes formed part of the diet during the period of use of the site.

THE POLLEN REMAINS

By J. Greig

A number of samples were collected from various contexts and processed for pollen analysis. The aim was to provide information on the prehistoric environment of the barrow, its contents or the means of construction. Two of the samples examined were collected from the immediate vicinity of the dagger (1012, sample nos 2 and 4) where it was thought that copper corrosion products might have preserved pollen. Samples were also collected from the mound deposits (1034 and 1035), the pre-mound deposits (1043 and 1044) and the fill of the ring ditch (1015).

Methodology

The soil samples were collected in the field by the writer. Some were also collected by the archaeological excavation team. A subsample of approximately 1 cm^3 was collected from each sample and processed for pollen analysis. Pollen preparation involved breaking down each sample in dilute alkali, sieving through a 75μm mesh, separating organic material by swirling on a 15cm watchglass, fine sieving on a 10μm mesh, acetolysis to remove cellulose and similar materials, staining and mounting. Pollen counts were done with a Leitz Dialux microscope, and pollen was identified using the writer's own reference collection.

Results

The buried soil samples did not contain enough pollen for a significant count. The scabbard samples did, however, and these pollen counts are listed below in Table 5. The two spectra show rather similar results, and can be considered as essentially the same thing.

Trees and woodland and heathland

There is rather little tree and shrub pollen, mostly *Alnus* (alder) and *Corylus* (hazel) with single grains from a range of other taxa. The signs of trees and woodland are therefore slight. There is, however, a substantial record from Ericales (heathers) which could either represent heathland in the vicinity or heathery material deposited. In the present-day agricultural landscape there is little heathland to be seen in the area today. However, the *Flora of Derbyshire* does record heather as present in the adjoining area (Clapham 1969), and its past presence is also shown by pollen results from two nearby sites at Hemington with Ericales records (although these are not necessarily contemporary with the Lockington barrow) (Greig 1997a and b).

Grassland and other open land

Much of the rest of the pollen, from herbaceous taxa, represents open, unwooded, land. There are grassland plants such as *Plantago lanceolata* (ribwort plantain), *Centaurea nigra* (knapweed) and Poaceae (grasses).

Cereal crops

Cultivated crops are indicated by a substantial pollen record from Cerealia type, which includes cereal crops. It raises the question whether these pollen spectra come mainly from pollen which was dispersed naturally in the atmosphere from a surrounding, farmed, landscape round the barrows, or whether plant material such as straw which contained this pollen was included in the hoard. In either case the results are likely to show aspects of the surroundings.

Other vegetations

There is practically no sign of other kinds of vegetation such as wetlands, which is only to be expected since these sediments are not waterlain.

Discussion

A somewhat similar picture to that from Lockington, with evidence of an open farmed landscape with little woodland remaining by the Bronze Age has been shown by pollen results from the Avon valley sites at Bidford on Avon and Beckford (Greig 1987, Greig and Colledge 1988). Such results may be representative of the parts of the landscape that were heavily occupied by this time, probably where better soil was more attractive to settlers. Some pollen diagrams, particularly those from the lowlands and the south, show signs of extensive woodland clearance around 3800 uncal BP (Berglund *et al.* 1996, p. 70). However, although there was extensive early prehistoric clearance of woodland in some places, woodland seems to have persisted for much longer in other parts of the landscape, as shown by pollen results from wetland sites near Lockington, as at Kirby Muxlow, Narborough and at Croft, near Leicester, where there is some Neolithic and Bronze Age woodland clearance, followed by much more in the Iron Age (Brown, 1999). These marshy areas where such peaty sediments developed would have been less suitable for farming and settlement than those on lighter soils, and the pollen results from such sites may not be fully representative of the more occupied parts of the landscape on better land.

Taphonomy

The pollen could have come from plant materials deposited with the hoard (such as cereals or straw, or possibly heather), or as part of the pollen rain from the general surroundings (such as tree pollen and the range of grassland herbs), or quite probably a mixture of both. This makes interpretation difficult, although even plant products would represent the surroundings to some extent.

Pollen from whole plant materials is suspected when the amounts of certain types are very large, for example the 23% cereal pollen in an Anglian cauldron at Garton (Stead 1991, 153). The 10% in sample 2 is more than would be expected in a natural pollen spectrum, for cereals disperse pollen sparingly, and does suggest plant material containing cereals as a source. This would have decayed together with the rest of the material, a process arrested by the copper salts released by corrosion of the dagger.

Pollen from the surroundings are suspected when higher proportions of wind pollinated plants with good pollen dispersal such as many trees, wild grasses and plantains are present. The range of pollen types does have the features of a natural spectrum, as with Iron Age bronzework at Kirkburn (Stead 1991, 153). The mechanism of preservation would be that pollen blowing around in dust would have been incorporated into the contents and would have been preserved where they were in contact with the bronze goods.

It is unlikely that the pollen associated with the dagger has been contaminated with modern pollen filtering through the overlying soil. Firstly, the soils at Lockington have been shown not to preserve pollen, so modern pollen would decay away in these conditions. Secondly, pollen tends to remain in the upper layers of a soil in which it is preserved with negligible amounts below 45–60cm (Dimbleby 1967, 127).

Conclusions

The results seems to indicate a partly natural pollen spectrum originating from the surroundings. The low tree pollen and signs of a large range of grassland plants and weeds suggest an open agricultural landscape. Some of the relatively large amount of cereal and heather pollen might also have come from whole plant materials such as bread, straw or heather incorporated into the hoard. These results add to the very small amount of evidence for the prehistoric landscape here.

Table 5: Pollen and spore counts from Lockington. Actual numbers of pollen grains and spores.

Taxon	sample <2>	<4>	common name
Ranunculus	–	1	buttercups
Thalictrum	1	–	meadow rue
Quercus	1	2	oak
Betula	1	–	birch
Alnus	4	7	alder
Corylus	11	5	hazel
Caryophyllaceae	5	4	pink family
Salix	–	1	willow
Ericales	15	8	heathers
Plantago lanceolata	13	6	ribwort plantain
Galium tp.	2	–	bedstraws
Sambucus nigra	–	1	elder
Dipsacaceae	6	3	scabious
Cirsium tp.	1	1	thistles
Centaurea nigra	1	2	knapweed
Cichorioidae	22	8	
Artemisia	1	2	mugwort
Aster tp.	2	2	
Cyperaceae	–	1	sedges
Poaceae <40 µm	43	15	grasses
Cerealia tp >40 µm	15	6	cereal type
Secale tp.	–	1	rye
Sparganium tp.	1	–	bur-reed
spores			
Polypodium	5	4	polypody
Pteridium	1	1	bracken
total	151	81	

THE BURIED SOIL AND MOUND MATERIALS

By Susan Limbrey

Study of the soils of the Lockington barrow was directed in the first instance at answering the excavator's questions about the characteristics of the central area of the barrow and of the mound materials and structure. It was initially intended that soil studies would be done in their entirety by Rebecca Roseff, who was responsible for environmental studies at the site, took most of the samples and recorded soil characteristics. Some additional sampling and was done by the excavator. I visited the site and made some supplementary observations on the soils, and when Rebecca Roseff moved to another job took over the post-excavation stage of the work. David Smith did the laboratory analyses and the resin impregnation of the micromorphology sample blocks, from which slides were prepared in the Soil Micromorphology Laboratory, University of Newcastle upon Tyne.

The following questions were to be addressed: what was the source of materials for the different components of the barrow mound? Was the buried soil complete, truncated, or covered by deposits associated with the barrow ritual? What could be learned from the characteristics of fill of the central feature? Was the intense 'reddening' of the soil in the central area due to burning? Was the charcoal deposit in situ? To these, the soil scientist adds: what was the soil type at the time of the barrow's construction and does this have any implications in terms of soil history and the soil resource of the time?

Methods

1. Detailed bench description of bag samples, of soil blocks before impregnation with resin, and of soil blocks initially taken for micromorphology but not processed, amplified soil descriptions done in the field. This was particularly useful because of the change of personnel between field and post-excavation stages. Terminology is after Hodgson 1974.

2. Particle size analysis, by sieve for sand fractions and SediGraph X-ray particle size analyzer for silt and clay down to 0.2 microns, to enable comparisons to be made between the different materials of the mound and between them and the buried soil and the filling of the central feature.

3. pH determination for information on the pedological environment in which post-depositional processes took place.

4. Oxidisable organic matter, as a further comparative measure. Potassium dichromate method (Avery and Bascombe 1974)

5. Micromorphological study was directed both at the soil history and at the comparison of materials and interpretation of phenomena affecting the sub-barrow surface and features. Undisturbed soil blocks taken in Kubiena tins were dried through acetone replacement, impregnated with Crystic resin by replacement of acetone, cured by stepwise temperature increase to 100°C. Study of thin sections was supplemented by 'microexcavation' and powder preparation from retained soil blocks. Micromorphological examination was by Olympus BX50 polarising microscope with epifluorescence facility, after using low power binocular microscope with incident and transmitted light with polarising insert for preliminary scans. High magnification ordinary

incident light was available using a metallurgical microscope. Micromorphological terminology is after Bullock *et al.* 1985.

Description of the Mound Materials and Buried Soil

The descriptions which follow are a combination of field description and bench study.

The soil developed over the barrow mound, context 1000

The soil was described in the field as having an A and a B horizon. Since it is clear that the long history of arable land use had truncated the mound, cutting across the three mound contexts and producing an homogenised soil of which the upper part only was the current plough soil, the lower part being the product of earlier deeper ploughing, it is better designated Ap1 and Ap2, differing in humus content and therefore colour.

Ap1: dark brown, 7.5YR 3/2 moist, 4/2 dry, sandy loam with many stones, moderately developed fine granular structure; consistency weak, slightly sticky, non swelling.
Ap2: dark reddish brown, 5YR 3/4 moist, reddish brown, 5YR 5/3 dry, most other characteristics as above, but structure less developed.

Mound materials

The three mound contexts, 1033, 1034, 1035, in apparent order of deposition, differed mainly in degree of iron staining and mottling, and in uniformity of their materials, with 1033 and 1034 being markedly more varied and having more intense staining, particularly so in 1034, and 1035 being more uniform, less mottled, and somewhat paler in colour. Textural characteristics in all three were produced by mixtures on a macroscopic scale of sand, loamy sand, and sandy loam, with some of the loamier soil being in the form of infillings to earthworm burrows penetrating from the recent topsoil, context 1000, and therefore affecting all three. Field descriptions comment on the more or less stone-free nature of these contexts, but these descriptions ignore the content of very small stones in the 2 to 6mm size grade, which are common, and frequent stones larger than this, in all of them (see table below). They are, nevertheless, very markedly less stony than the topsoil and, especially, the underlying gravels, the upper part of which, context 1046, is the B horizon of the buried soil. Field descriptions also use the term 'silty' in inappropriate ways. None of the soils have enough silt for this word to apply. Soil structure was poorly developed medium and fine granular, with the recent worm soil in better developed very fine angular blocky form, consistency was weak, and the soils slightly sticky, non-plastic and non swelling. The following descriptions of each of the mound contexts concentrate on what distinguishes between them, their colour characteristics.

1033: reddish brown to yellowish red, 5YR 4/4 to 4/6 moist, light brown, 7.5YR 5/4 dry, sand with a lesser component of dark reddish brown, 5YR 3/2 moist, brown, 7.5YR 5/4 dry, sandy loam, with in the sand component fine, sharp distinct red mottles and fine and medium sharp black dendritic mottles. Up to 25% more continuous staining, red, 2.5Y 3/6 moist, 5/8 dry and a range of less intense colours, and black, the black generally as streaks and mottles within the red.

1034: overall colour darker than 1033, colour formed by mixtures on various scales of dark reddish brown, 5YR 3/3, 3/4 moist, brown to dark brown, 7.5YR 5/4, 4/4 dry and reddish brown to yellowish red, 5YR 4/4, 4/6 moist, brown, 7.5YR 5/4 dry, together with prominent, fine and medium, diffuse and sharp red mottles, 2.5Y 3/6 moist, 5/8 dry, together with dark brown and black, up to 40% being stained and mottled soil; some mottling is in the form of multiple laminae, black within yellowish red, and laminar patterns sometimes include paler soil.

1035: more uniform than 1033 and 1034, brown to reddish brown, 7.5YR–5YR 4/4 moist, light brown, 7.5YR 6/4 dry, with common fine, sharp black mottles and common fine diffuse yellowish red, 2.5Y 3/6 moist, 5/8 dry, and fainter, mottles.

Buried surface contexts

The buried soil took different forms, manifest in three zones. In the first two, the upper horizon of the soil was distinct from the underlying gravels in its relatively low stoniness; these zones were present as the area of 'reddened material', context 1044, surrounding the central feature and charcoal deposit, and a zone further out, context 1088. The third zone lay further out again, where gravel, context 1046, immediately underlay the mound materials. This gravel also underlay contexts 1044 and 1088, forming the lower horizon of the soil in the other two zones, and so is described below as a lower horizon of the soil.

1044: the 'reddened material'. Description refers to the reddened material itself and the subjacent soil. The reddening is in fact iron panning in multiple thin layers, each from less than 1mm to 5mm, red and yellowish red, 5YR 5/8, and black, with light brown soil, 7.5YR 6/4, between and below them. The soil is a sandy clay loam, with weakly developed fine granular structure.

1088: an un-numbered sample was taken at a late stage in the excavation, and no micromorphological slide was prepared. A very thin iron pan had formed at or, probably, just below the buried soil surface. No clear boundary was detectable between the dark brown soil above the pan and the more mixed soil of the mound, context 1034, but about 5mm of grey soil, 7.5YR 7/2, was detectable above the pan in the dry sample. The iron pan was sharp at its upper surface, dark red, 2.5Y 3/6 moist and dry, less than 1mm, extending down 2 to 3mm as yellowish red, 5YR 5/6 moist, 6/8 dry, staining. Below this the soil was reddish brown and dark reddish brown, 7.5YR 4/4, 3/4 moist, light brown and brown, 7.5YR 6/4, 4/4 dry, with some grey and very dark brown inclusions and fine diffuse and very fine sharp reddish yellow mottling. Texture is sandy clay loam, structure weakly developed fine granular, consistency weak, slightly sticky, non swelling.

1046: gravel, overall colour yellowish red, 5YR 4/6 moist, with common very fine, sharp black mottles, very weak, very porous. Matrix consists of sand grains loosely enclosed and bridged by fine soil, pale reddish brown, stained brown and red.

Two further contexts were examined, 1043, the fill of the central feature, F23, and 1041, the charcoal layer which partly overlay it.

1041: the charcoal layer was a mixture of charcoal fragments and finely comminuted charcoal in a mixture of grey ashy material and yellowish red, 5YR 6/4, moist, light brown, 7.5YR 6/4 dry, soil, texture sandy clay loam, structure variable in relation to the materials with which it was mixed. Soil in contact with the charcoal and ash was not heat-reddened.

1043: The fill of the central feature (F23). This was a mixture on various scales, colours being reddish brown and dark reddish brown, 5YR 5/4, 4/4, 3/4 moist, very pale brown, light yellowish brown and yellowish brown, 7.5YR 7/4, 6/4, 5/4 dry, with fine sharp red and very fine sharp black mottles. Texture was very variable, sandy loam, sandy clay loam, with common stones, variably distributed, and structure determined by mixture of material.

Discussion of soils as described macroscopically

The colour variation and the mottling of all these materials is conspicuous. Matrix colour as observed in the field is amplified by bench description under low magnification, which shows the effects of faunal mixing on the millimetre scale, soil with more well formed microstructure and darker colour with a weaker, looser, paler and/or redder matrix, as well as recent vertical worm burrowing on a larger scale, which clearly introduces dark brown worm casts from the top soil. Throughout the mound structure there is much iron staining, from yellowish red and reddish brown through dark reddish brown to black, it being noticed that the black often lies within both linear and rounded stains of redder colours, and there are paler, iron depleted zones associated with the linear stain features. Comparing the three mound units, 1035 is notably paler and less red that the other two, and mottling is finer, more evenly distributed and less prominent; 1034 is overall darker and much more heavily stained. The similarity of the soil below the iron panning, 1044, and the soil in the zone outside the area of heavy iron panning, 1088, suggests that these are one and the same, the difference lying in the conditions and processes affecting their surface. These are identified as the A horizon of the buried soil in relatively undisturbed form, and 1046 as the B horizon. The fill of the central feature, 1043, has characteristics of the A horizon, but with an admixture of B horizon giving more colour and texture variability, including more stones, and the charcoal layer, 1041, shows incorporation of charcoal and ash into the top of this fill, partly by faunal action.

A further visual comparison is available following particle size analysis, that of the colour of the sand fractions. The sands are dominated by quartz and predominantly quartzose composite grains, and grains are to a large extent 'clean'. The colour of the gravel substrate reflects the dominant source of the materials in Triassic 'New Red' sandstones in which iron oxides coat the grains. Some of these coatings are retained in the soils, but much has gone. Only one of the top soil samples and the buried soil B horizon, have distinctly redder sand fractions. The other source of colouring is the presence of burnt grains, with colour reflecting the redder hue of haematite, which occur in all samples except the B horizon at a consistent low level.

Particle size analysis

(See Table 6). The analysis shows clustering of particle size distribution of mound and buried soil together. All these samples fall in the range 58–64% sand, 18–23% silt, 13–22% clay, sandy loams and sandy clay loams, but all close to the boundary between these two classes (18% clay). The similarity of the samples is further emphasised by their sharing a bimodal distribution in the sand-plus-silt fraction, with modes in medium sand and medium silt. The SediGraph analysis went down through the clay grade to 0.2 microns, and it is clear from the shape of the curves that there is a steady diminution of particle size from fine silt downwards, with little fine clay and no further mode in the clay grade. Texture of the fine soil had been recorded on the context record sheets in estimated percentages of sand, silt and clay. It is difficult to estimated percentages by hand, and the figures given consistently over estimate silt at 30 to 60 % and under estimate clay at 10%. Throughout the archaeological text, the word 'silty' features strongly, and this is again a subjective response to materials which are relatively fine textured when compared to the substrate, together with the application of terminology which has developed within archaeology and is more dependant on ideas about process of deposition than on the application of internationally established and clearly defined terms. Over-estimation of silt would be more understandable if the sand fraction had been dominated by fine sand, but this is not the case.

ORGANIC MATTER AND PH

The topsoil values for organic matter, 2.4–2.5%, are normal for cultivated soils of this kind under modern farming practice, provided there has not been a long period of continuous arable cropping with little or no manure input. The lower values from mound and buried soil are consistent with the evidence from redistribution of iron to produce the mottling and staining, which indicate vigorous activity by iron reducing and iron oxidising bacteria, metabolising organic matter in the original soils under conditions of restricted free oxygen availability. The differences in these values can probably be attributed to charcoal content, since the dichromate method does oxidise charcoal.

The slightly acid pH values are normal for a brown earth of this kind under modern agriculture with chemical input, but may not reflect the earlier condition of the soil (see below).

MICROMORPHOLOGY

Since many of the characteristics of the microstructure and pedofeatures of the buried soil and mound materials are common to all samples, these will be described first, followed by description and discussion of the phenomena distinctive of each context.

Microstructure and textural relationships

All samples share a sandy texture, are poorly sorted, and have an open to closed porphyritic and enaulic related distribution of the coarser fraction, dominated by medium sand, with a tendency to clustering of sand grains in linear and reticulate patterns. Sand and silt grains, rounded and sub-rounded, either have very thin, discontinuous coatings of fine material, or are clean. Included materials are burnt and unburnt angular flint fragments, in strong contrast to the rounding of the materials which are native to the soil, fragments of pottery, and fragments of charcoal. Microstructure is complex, with microaggregates dominating the fabric in intergrain, bridged grain and composite crumb forms, that is, microaggregates form loose fillings to voids and in all stages of amalgamation, with porosity vughy to spongy, and some large channels and chambers. Loose microaggregates are often darker brown than those amalgamated into crumbs. Groundmass is generally isotropic, with only very localised small areas of birefringence, which will be described below where it occurs in particular samples. Apart from the patterns formed by the coarser material, there are few and very localised textural pedofeatures, also described below. Mottling, impregnation, and nodule formation by iron and manganese oxides and humus is common to all samples, but varies strongly both locally within samples and between contexts: this is the dominant feature by which the contexts are differentiated in micromorphology, as it was in field interpretation and macroscopic description.

Table 6. Percentages are given in terms of 'fine soil': sand, silt and clay, with stones (above 2mm) being a percentage of this total.

context	sample	stones	c. sand	m.sand	f.sand	total sand	c. silt	m. silt	f.silt	total silt	clay	pH	OM
1000	27	11.1	9.1	36.8	16.8	62.7	7.1	8.9	4.1	20.1	17.2	6.1	2.4
	37	17.3	6.0	37.5	14.7	58.2	4.1	10.5	6.7	20.3	20.5	6.9	2.5
1035	26	18.8	11.2	36.4	13.5	61.1	3.9	10.5	5.7	20.1	19.5	6.7	0.8
1034	23	10.4	12.1	37.3	14.7	64.1	3.6	11.1	5.8	20.5	15.5	6.4	0.9
	24	7.8	9.6	38.1	13.7	61.4	3.9	10.0	5.0	18.9	19.7	6.6	1.2
	35	3.3	11.3	39.4	12.0	62.7	3.0	10.9	7.1	20.0	16.5	6.8	0.8
	34	11.0	10.4	38.9	14.5	63.8	3.6	12.7	6.5	22.8	13.4	6.9	0.8
1033	39	9.1	7.6	37.1'	14.7	59.4	2.0	8.9	7.3	18.2	22.3	6.8	0.9
	41	9.4	8.3	36.5	15.0	59.8	4.5	10.1	6.0	20.6	20.1	6.7	0.8
1043	47	20.2	9.4	35.6	14.3	59.3	3.3	12.2	6.9	22.4	18.4	6.5	1.0
1044	33	6.9	5.5	35.8	17.1	58.4	3.3	13.3	6.2	22.9	18.7	6.9	1.1
	48	0.8	10.5	38.4	14.1	63.0	3.8	11.3	5.6	20.7	16.9	6.6	1.2
1046	54	71.8	105	33.4	15.3	59.3	total silt plus clay: 40.7						

Topsoil: context 1000, samples 30 (upper part), 31 – Groundmass is brown, with darker brown microaggregates in voids, and with occasional channels having dark brown earthworm excrements. Evidence of recent biological activity include fine roots and partially humified roots and other organic fragments, and a solitary calcite granule of the type formed in the bodies of Arionid slugs. The lower part of the topsoil (sample 30) included an area of intense reddish brown to black impregnation. Locally, there was a dense scatter of micro-spherulites (see discussion below), not associated with humic/ferruginous impregnation or organic residues.

Mound: context 1035, samples 16 and 25 – Fabric light brown in incident light. Porosity lower than in topsoil. Frequent light reddish brown mottles, black impregnations and common nodules. Small patches of ash. Small and localised areas of reddish brown coatings, in part fragmented and incorporated into the fabric, both birefringent and isotropic, non-fluorescent in UV light.

Mound: context 1034, samples 15, 23, 27a, 28, 29, 30 (part) – Generally similar to context 1035, but with areas of intense black and reddish brown impregnations occupying 10 to 20% of the area generally but with localised concentrations 60% or more, and common concentric nodules, which in places form foci of further impregnation of the fabric. Short stretches of bands of black and reddish brown are partly fragmented.

Mound: context 1033, samples 14, 38, 40 – Similar to 1034, but with mottling and impregnation intense in localised areas but less general in distributed form. There are small areas of yellow material which fluoresce in UV light, some having fine organic and mineral inclusions, and occasional peds of birefringent soil. Towards the bottom of sample 40, which was taken from the lowest part of the context, there is a band of intense reddish brown impregnation in laminar form, fragmented but adding up to over 3 cm long and 0.5 cm deep. In part it is an impregnative pseudomorph of plant material, as the outer parts of a sandwich with impregnated soil in the middle. Spherulites are scattered in the adjacent soil and clustered densely among part of the plant material psuedomorph. They vary in diameter from about 25 microns down to about 5 microns, a wider range than those seen in other samples. The central area of the slide is occupied by an area of fragmented black impregnation surrounded by reddish brown, the outer edge of this being dense, with impregnative pseudomorphs of fragments of plant material accounting for part, but not all, of the area. The impregnated materials have been subjected to microfaunal comminution, there being microaggregates of both impregnated and non-impregnated soil scattered among the more coherent areas.

Buried soil: context 1044, samples 32, 48 – The samples did not include the heavily iron-panned zone forming the 'reddened material' at the surface of the horizon, which has been described macroscopically. Most of the micromorphological characteristics are the same as those of the mound materials, but macro-porosity is lower. Nodules of various sizes and intensity of impregnation, uniform and concentric, occur, and mottles and areas of black impregnation. There is a dense cluster of spherulites, not associated with mottling or impregnation but having within its area some bright yellow coatings to pores, mostly isotropic but with some bits birefringent, non-fluorescent.

Fill of central feature: context 1043, sample 47 – General characteristics are similar to mound materials and buried soil, but with areas differing in lightness or darkness of colour juxtaposed. There are mottles and black impregnations as in other slides, and an area of densely clustered spherulites associated with reddish brown isotropic amorphous material, as well as scattered in localised areas of the soil fabric. A few very small areas of amorphous yellow, isotropic, non-fluorescent material occur as segregations within the fabric, and there are a few very small yellow fluorescent granules. There are rather more burnt mineral grains in this context than in others.

DISCUSSION OF MICROMORPHOLOGY

The characteristics of the soil fabric, be it buried soil, feature fill or mound, are those of a soil whose structure as it now appears has been formed predominantly by soil fauna other than earthworms. The loose infillings in voids, and their aggregation and coalescence to form the groundmass of the soil, indicates continuity of such biological activity over a sufficient period to have reworked any earthworm-dominated structure which existed earlier in the soil's history, and while there are earthworm channels penetrating from the surface today, their infillings are being actively reworked by the smaller animals, probably dominated by enchytraeid worms.

The partially or completely clean surfaces of mineral grains show that there has been aggressive stripping of the iron oxide coatings which cover and cement the grains in the Triassic sandstones from which the terrace gravels are predominantly derived. The B horizon of the buried soil was not studied micromorphologically, but its colour and the mottling in both horizons shows that the iron oxide mobilisation was a feature of the A horizon, and together with the characteristic microstructure suggests a marginally podzolising soil at some stage in its history.

The intensity of iron/manganese staining, impregnation and nodule formation is related to the amount of organic matter in and on the soil prior to the construction of the mound. In both mound and buried soil, some iron staining and impregnation has a laminar form, with paler soil between the black and reddish brown laminae. In the mound, these laminar zones are localised and discontinuous, but the buried soil shows a degree of continuity of iron panning which in the field was described as reddening of the surface of the soil and questioned as being evidence of burning. The colour was, however, not that of a burnt soil, lacking the haematite, 10R, hue even when modified or diluted by later precipitation of the yellower hydrous oxides. In micromorphology preparation, no haematite was apparent, in either reflected or transmitted light, except for that in the scatter of burnt mineral grains and pottery.

The fill of the central feature, context 1043, was a mixed and disturbed version of the buried soil, having no characteristics which indicated included materials or activities which left their trace on the fill. The charcoal deposit is, however, distinctive, and its study shows that while there is a great deal of charcoal and evidence that ash was also present, the soil with which these materials are mixed is not burnt. To a large extent, the mixing is that of soil faunal turbation, introducing into the charcoal and ash deposit soil from overlying and underlying material.

A phenomenon which appears in the buried soil, and also in the mound materials and the feature fill, is the presence of microspherulites which appear to be formed of an iron oxide compound. They are identical in size and morphology to the calcite spherulites which are formed in the gut of certain grazing animals and preserved in calcareous or dry environments (Canti 1997, 1998), but their colour is that of the iron panning of the soil, with which they are sometimes but not always associated in these samples. Calcite could not survive in a soil of the pH here, indeed, Canti (pers. comm.) has found that the calcite spherulites, probably because of their very finely crystalline nature, dissolve very rapidly indeed in distilled water. The association of the spherulites here with partially humified organic material, and the intensity of iron panning and impregnation, indicates that they were deposited in a highly biologically and chemically active environment, in which oxygen was rapidly depleted by microbial activity. The only explanation for what appears to be a pseudomorphing of calcite by an iron oxide compound is that it was an extremely rapid process, a mobile iron/humus complex being able to impregnate the crystal structure before simple dissolution by organic acids in the dung, or rainwater, could occur. The chance of this happening is greater in a closed environment, such as that of a buried soil, than in dung left on the surface of a field, and until further studies are made of this phenomenon, the explanation is offered that the mound was constructed of, and buried, a soil that had very recently had animals grazing, or dung dumped, on it. Direct evidence of dung, however, in the form of fluorescent phosphatic residues in the soil, is sparse, there being only occasional small particles of such material present. It is possible, though, that phosphate has been leached, since it is at pH close to neutral that phosphate is most likely to be mobile.

Interpretation of the Nature of the Mound Materials and Buried Soil

Textural similarity of mound materials and the A horizon of the buried soil provides the primary evidence that the mound was built by gathering up topsoil. Topsoil from an outer zone must have been scraped up and dumped on of that of the inner area, the outer zone then having its truncated soil covered by soil from further out still. There was no evidence of turf cutting and placing, but turfy bits of soil would have been included, providing foci for the vigorous organic activity which resulted in the colour patterns. Around the central feature, where the mound was highest, oxygen most effectively excluded, and perhaps the greatest concentration of organic material placed as the construction began, the processes of iron panning, which are common in buried soils, were most intense. The fact that there was no iron panning over the central feature and charcoal layer can be attributed to the vegetated soil surface there having been destroyed by the feature, and probably also to the presence of ash, modifying chemical conditions.

It is perhaps worth returning to Fox's suggestion (Fox 1959) that a zone of iron panning concentric to the central feature under a barrow mound was attributable to trampling during a ritual dance. Without trying to reconstruct ritual, one can agree that activity associated with the central feature would have involved trampling, and if the surface carried a substantial cover of green vegetation, especially if wet or in the lushness of early summer, and was buried straight after this had been thoroughly trampled, the development of anoxic conditions promoting iron pan formation would undoubtedly be enhanced. I was dismissive of this idea (Limbrey 1975), but the intensity of panning at this site is persuasive.

There was no evidence of weathering of earlier mound materials before later ones were deposited.

Discussion of Soil Type

The site lies on a gravel island in the floodplain of the River Trent. Given the alluvial history of lowland rivers in Britain, it is probable that in the early Bronze Age the island was more extensive, and was either surrounded by the multiple channels of the river or was part of the continuous stretch of low terrace flanking the valley. The soils of these gravel islands and terraces today are mapped as typical brown earths of the Wick series. The Ap horizon over the mound and the B horizon of the buried soil correspond closely in description and analytical data to a profile at Weston on Trent, SK 419285, given in Reeve (1975). The A horizon of the buried soil, with its much lower stone content than the B horizon, corresponds to an uncultivated version of the same profile. There is no micromorphological evidence that the soil had been cultivated.

The Ap horizon over the mound is the product of a long history of arable cultivation, including medieval ridge and furrow. Since the mound as it remained was so low, the stonier nature of the top soil in comparison to the mound materials can be attributed to the plough casting soil over the mound from the surroundings, rather than to there having been a gravel capping. One sample of the top soil shared the more coloured sand grains with the B horizon, suggesting deep ploughing, or ridge and furrow, cutting into this horizon nearby.

As an agricultural resource, soils of this type are limited by droughtiness in summer, and in arable use, their predominant use these days, need attention to organic content to help in maintenance of nutrient supply and water retention, and to resist erosion. Under pasture, they stand heavy stocking and are not susceptible to poaching when carrying stock in winter.

The question of the history of these soils needs to be addressed. The clean sand grains suggest attack on iron oxides under marginally podzolising conditions, and the rapid diminution of particle size through fine silt and clay grades, suggests acid attack on minerals. If the results of pollen analysis are taken into account (Greig, this volume), albeit pollen preserved though association with the dagger, and therefore possibly not representative of general vegetation, a heathy vegetation on acid brown earth or brown podzolic soils is indicated. The fine dark brown mottling in the B horizon is consistent with a weakly developed podzolic Bhfe horizon. The presence of a worm sorted A horizon is evidence of a well established brown earth, and there is no micromorphological evidence of cultivation prior to the development of the worm sorted horizon. While there are earthworm channels and infillings visible both macroscopically and in thin section, these mostly originate from the recent surface, the void component of the microstructure being in the process of infilling by microaggregates typical of enchytraeid worms, not earthworms, and the whole fabric is formed of coalescing microaggregates of this kind. This phenomenon is characteristic of soils too acid to sustain an earthworm population, but is characteristic of acid brown earths and brown podzolic soils. It is therefore probable that the worm sorting had ceased, and the soil was, at the time of its burial, marginally podzolising. The pH found today, like that of the surrounding soils of this type, is likely to be the result of application of fertilisers.

It is therefore postulated that the gravel terraces and islands in the early Bronze Age carried a heathy vegetation and were of lower agricultural value than the present soil type suggests. Weakly developed podzols can be turned back into brown earths by cultivation, though this is only worthwhile for more than short term cropping if productivity can be enhanced by manuring, liming or marling. Intensive agriculture, therefore, which in pre-mechanised agriculture would be close to a farmstead or byre, the medieval strip system, with fallowing and renewal of topsoil by ridge building, or a system involving folding on land which could stand high stock density in winter, will maintain, or re-form, brown earths in these areas. The abundance of *heath* placenames in areas of the English midlands where sandy and gravelly parent materials support soils now in arable use, but showing signs of earlier podzolisation, attests to soil reclamation at times of land hunger. Archaeological, historical and placename evidence is needed to establish the detailed land-use and soil history if we are to draw soil maps of the past to illuminate changing agricultural economy.

THE SOIL PHOSPHATE ANALYSIS

By A. G. Moss

Introduction

The purpose of the phosphate survey was to determine the variation in phosphate levels between the fill of the pit containing the hoard and adjacent deposits. It was hoped that this would assist in the interpretation of the original contents of the pit and, in particular, if there was any suggestion that decayed human remains may have been present. A series of soil samples were collected from a transect (sample points a–l) across the pit containing the hoard the adjacent natural gravel and the fills of the nearby ring ditch. 26 samples were analysed including 12 replicates and 2 'blanks' (Table 7).

Method

Accurately weighed oven-dry soil samples of less than 2mm grain size were ground in an agate mortar and ignited at 240°C for 1 hour. This procedure converts organic P to inorganic forms (Andersen 1976). The samples were then digested for 1 hour in warm conc. HCl acid, centrifuged, the supernatant added to 250ml volumetric flasks, and diluted to volume with distilled water (Black 1965). 3ml aliquots were taken for analysis using a phosphatomolybdate colorimetric method (Murphy and Riley 1962) after neutralization with dilute ammonia and HCl (Black 1965) All glassware was carefully washed in dilute acid and distilled water.

Replicate samples were taken through the entire procedure and the results are presented as the mean and standard deviation (Table 7). All figures are expressed as micrograms (μg) of elemental phosphorus (P) per gram of oven dry soil.

Results

The range of phosphorus concentrations for the natural gravels (3 samples) was 384.02±22.55 to 693.42±28; 62 μg/g (mean = 509.68±162. μg/g). For the hoard pit (3 samples) the range was 563.66±1.07 to 577.39±33.62 μg/g (mean = 569.94±6.94 μg/g). For the ring ditch fill (6 samples) the range is from 349.34±19.21 to 914.94±24.43 μg/g (mean = 672.65±204.11 μg/g).

Discussion

The presence of a body may add as much as 50 μg/g to the soil (Hamond 1983). Given the large range of phosphorus concentrations here, this figure seems somewhat insignificant! Two things can be demonstrated though – a) that there is greater internal consistency within the gold hoard soil samples than in the other samples; this may reflect some kind of soil homogeneity compared with the mixed gravels on the one hand and the soil infill on the other. b) that taken as a whole there is no evidence of phosphorus enhancement in the gold hoard – all three sample types clearly overlap at 1 standard deviation. Statistical treatment of the data in terms of tests of significance were applied to the data but there was such variability in the gravel and infill data sets that the results were meaningless. The wide range of results in the ditch fill samples may be expected if soils from different horizons were mixed together; the lower results are consistent with the natural gravels. The higher results (samples g–j) may represent soils showing some cultural impact or may come from naturally enriched horizons.

It is possible that leaching may have removed some P from the soil, particularly organic P (organic matter was not visible in the samples). The impact is impossible to assess. Since much of the phospate from a corpse would be in inorganic form, there is no reason to suppose this would all be leached out: the presence of abundant ferric oxides in the samples would actually attract mobile phosphates (Barker 1975 cited in Bethell and Carver 1987), especially in acidic conditions (Cook and Heizer 1965 cited in Bethell and Carver 1987).

Conclusions

The soil type at Lockington appears to be similar to that described at Sutton Hoo by Bethell and Carver (1987) with acid sandy and gravelly types prevailing. At Sutton Hoo increased phosphorus was detected where a burial was suspected (the actual values were not available to this study). At Lockington there is a wide variation in phosphorus levels but there is no evidence of increased phosphorus in the pit containing the hoard. The chemical conditions of the site suggest that mobile phosphorus would be retained so it may be concluded that no inhumation has taken place here.

Table 7: Phosphate analysis of Lockington Gold Hoard.

Sample	Mean conc.P (µg/g)	St.Dev.	Mean conc. P
a	693.42	28.62	
b	384.02	22.55	
c	451.61	3.43	
Mean concentration of P in natural gravels			509.68±162.66
d	563.66	1.07	
e	568.78	17.26	
f	577.39	33.62	
Mean concentration of P in the hoard pit			559.94±6.94
g	914.94	24.43	
h	628.30	29.69	
i	7bo.57	31.59	
j	830.40	18.19	
k	562.39	4.86	
i	349.34	19.21	
Mean concentration of P in fill of ring ditch			672.65±204.11

CHARCOAL IDENTIFICATIONS

By R. Gale

Eight samples of charcoal were identified to indicate the taxa used for or associated with the cremation or burial of the interred remains. Juvenile stems/twigs, suitable for C14 dating, were isolated from samples 1041 and 1105.

Materials and Methods

Samples 104le and 1041f included large quantities of charcoal with some fragments measuring up to 30mm in the longitudinal axis. Both samples were scanned for juvenile or twiggy fragments and the remainder sub-sampled before examination (25% subsample for sample 1041e; 50% subsample for sample 1041f). The remaining samples included smaller quantities of material. In general the charcoal was in good condition although a few fragments were partially vitrified due to charring at excessively high temperatures (in the latter instance insufficient diagnostic structure remained for identification). Sample <51> 1101 included a lump of tarry, cinder-like material which was isolated from the rest of the sample after examination.

Charcoal fragments measuring >2mm square in cross section were prepared for examination. These were fractured to expose a fresh transverse surface and separated into groups based on the anatomical features observed using a ×2 hand lens. Representative fragments from each group were selected for further examination at high magnification. Additional surfaces were prepared by fracturing in the tangential and radial longitudinal orientations. These were supported in sand and examined using an incident-light microscope at magnifications of up to ×400. The anatomical characters were matched to prepared reference material.

Where possible the maturity of the wood was noted, i.e. narrow roundwood, sapwood and heartwood. The identified fragments were isolated (in labelled polybags) from the main sample.

Results

The results are summarised in Table 8. The taxa identified included:

Corylus sp.,   hazel
Fraxinus sp.,   ash
Prunus sp.,   native species include *P. avium* (cherry), *P. spinosa* (blackthorn) and *P. padus* (bird cherry)
Quercus sp.,   oak

Table 8 charcoal.

Abbreviations: s=sapwood (diameter >20mm); h=heartwood; r=roundwood (diameter <2mm)
The number of fragments identified is indicated

Sample	Corylus	Fraxinus	Prunus	Quercus	Comments
1034	2	–	–	98sh	
1035	3	–	–	27sh	
1043	–	4	?1	26sh	Some vitrified
1088<45>	–	–	–	18sh	
1101<51>	–	–	–	18sh	Also tarry, cinder-like substance
1041<43e>	–	–	2r	103sh	25% subsample
1041<43f>	2r	–	9r	98sh	50% subsample
1105 F65	4r	–	–	39sh	1herbaceous stem, partially vitrified

DISCUSSION

The barrow at Lockington has provided a rare opportunity for examining in detail Early Bronze Age funerary practices and associated ritual activity in a lowland context in the English midlands. The preservation of the deposits and the importance of the artefacts recovered exceeded all expectations. All this information can be put in the context of an ever increasing body of information from funerary monuments of this period from the region, and has implications for the interpretation of mortuary practices and ritual deposits elsewhere in Britain. In particular, the context for the metalwork finds is not in accord with conventional expectations. A rich group of this nature would normally be expected to accompany a burial within the mound, often in a primary position. In such circumstances, the group would conventionally be interpreted as grave goods symbolic of the high status of the buried individual. The Lockington evidence contributes to the current debate in which such 'straightforward' social interpretations are increasingly being questioned. Much recent work has instead focused on attempts to understand the social context in which funerary and other ritual deposits are placed and what they reveal about attitudes to death and the ancestors amongst the living community. This discussion will consider the evidence for the various structures and deposits at Lockington and will attempt to compare this with other sites in the region. An attempt will then be made to consider the nature of the possible mortuary ritual that was undertaken at Lockington during the Early Bronze Age.

Neolithic activity

The evidence for Neolithic activity at Lockington is fragmentary. Only one feature can be dated to the Neolithic with any degree of certainty. This pit (F65) is unusual in a number of respects. The fill contains burnt material including burnt pebbles and flint and traces of cremated bone. Although this could not be definitely identified as human, it is tempting to suggest that the deposit has been taken from a funerary pyre and tipped into the pit. The presence of Neolithic pits containing 'special' deposits on sites which subsequently become the focus for Bronze Age barrow cemeteries has been noted elsewhere. Regional examples include Bromfield (Stanford 1982) where the barrow cemetery was preceded by two pits containing fragments of Neolithic pottery and charcoal and associated with a date of 3640–3140 cal BC. At Meole Brace near Shrewsbury (Hughes and Woodward 1995), two ring ditches were associated with a group of pits containing Mortlake Ware pottery and associated with a date of 3610–2950 cal BC and at Wasperton, Warwickshire (Hughes and Crawford 1995) a ring ditch was preceded by pits containing late Neolithic pottery. The Bromfield and Meole Brace dates compare closely with the date of 3350–2750 cal BC from the Lockington pit. At all these sites there appears to have been a tendency towards the formal deposition of pottery in these features rather than the casual deposition of rubbish from a domestic occupation. The early features at all these sites, including the pit at Lockington, are not easily explained in terms of domestic activity. An alternative is to see these Neolithic deposits as the first 'marking out' of a ritual location which is often to retain its significance for many centuries (Buteux and Hughes 1995, 160).

The remaining evidence for Neolithic activity derives from the character of the flint assemblage both underlying the barrow and incorporated into the barrow mound. Two leaf-shaped arrowheads (one apparently reworked at a later date), a chisel arrowhead and three flakes from a greenstone axe all hint at Neolithic activity pre-dating the barrow. The presence of several of these items within the make-up of the mound itself maybe significant. It is tempting to suggest that the barrow builders deliberately incorporated material from an earlier phase of activity into the make-up of the mound. It is possible that the material may have derived from earlier nearby settlements possibly of Mesolithic as well as Neolithic and Bronze Age date (see above page 73). These were then incorporated into the mound and subsequently spread by ploughing. Perhaps these were viewed as 'ancestral deposits'; an interpretation that echoes the possible re-use of the Beaker vessels already discussed (see page 58 above).

The palisade gully

On stratigraphic grounds, the ring gully (F2) appears to belong to an early phase of the Early Bronze Age activity at the site. It seems likely that this ring gully formed the foundation trench for some form of palisade perhaps defining a circular mortuary enclosure 38m in diameter. The form of this feature suggests that it might have had a polygonal plan, possibly constructed from a series of prefabricated hurdles. The narrow breaks on the western side may have been entrances. However, it seems likely that the principal entrance was on the north side where only faint traces could be discerned. Comparable ring gullies have been recorded at Tucklesholme Farm, Staffordshire (Hughes 1991), and at Foston, south Derbyshire (Hughes and Jones 1995) and, slightly further afield, at Holt Site F, Worcestershire (Hunt *et al.* 1986, 25 and Fig. 9) and at Tandderwen, Clwyd (Brassil *et al.* 1991, 51). At all these sites the ring gullies were within the circuit of the ring ditches. It has been suggested that, if they held palisades, these structures may have formed structural elements associated with the mound construction such as revetments or kerbs (e.g. Brassil *et al.* 1991, 80). However, it would seem equally plausible that some at least could have represented pre-barrow mortuary enclosures pre-dating the construction of the mound. Support for such pre-barrow enclosures is provided by numerous examples of stake circles or post rings which were clearly dismantled before the construction of the barrow mound (Ashbee 1960, 60–66). In Leicestershire, examples have been recorded at Eaton and at Sproxton, where concentric circles of stake holes pre-dated the construction of a mound over a primary cremation (Clay 1981).

The hoard

The gold armlets, the dagger and the pottery vessels were placed in a shallow pit on the north side of the palisade gully. The location is associated with a particularly distinct break in the line of the gully suggesting an entrance. The objects represent an exceptional group. The close proximity of the barrow but the absence of a directly associated burial would appear to suggest that the group is interestingly placed between what would be conventionally described as a grave deposit and a hoard. The combination of items in the assemblage is also of great interest, uniquely combining elements that are derived from geographically and symbolically varied networks of exchange and interaction. Even the three pieces of metalwork are an unusual combination (see above page 44).

Both the bracelets and dagger belong to a set of metalwork classes which have been viewed as symbols of personal status, rank and display (Barrett 1985, 103–4; Needham 1988, 245). They are objects intended to be worn and it has been suggested that their frequent association with graves represents a particular form of 'interpersonal exchange' used to describe the relationships between the living and the dead (Barrett 1994, 121–123). Such objects also represent relatively small amounts of metal and suggest a limit to the disposal of a valuable resource for such personal objectives (Needham 1988, 245). By contrast axes, which were frequently deposited in hoards or as single finds, involve much larger quantities of metal by weight (Needham 1988) suggesting that these represent 'community' deposits with less restriction on the volume of metal consumed. Needham suggests that the exploitation of metal implements for ritual and ceremony may at first have reinforced pre-existing traditions linked to communal monuments and burial grounds. Eventually, the deposition of metalwork may have become itself the object of veneration and communal display. It has been suggested that such objects may have been important in 'competitive gift exchange'; a system used to establish social position through the accruement of debt obligations (Barrett 1985, 95–103). There are, of course, exceptions to these general observations about the content of hoards and grave groups. For example the large number of ornaments which accompanied a single axe in the hoard from Migdale (Piggott and Stewart 1958, GB 26) and the occasional axe from a Wessex grave such as Ridgeway barrow 7 (Drew and Piggott 1936) and Bush Barrow (Annable and Simpson 1964, plate no. 178). Some of these examples are clearly exceptional occurrences and have been seen as particularly important 'gift exchanges' (Barrett 1985, 105; 1994, 123).

The pottery vessels may also have been concerned with personal identity rather than with communal activity. They were clearly incomplete prior to their deposition and their condition suggests that they might have taken an active part in other aspects of the ritual. Alternatively, they may have been deliberately selected, possibly because of a former sacred association. It is suggested above that the pots may have been heirlooms or ancestral property (see page 58). It is even possible that the missing portions may have been reused as grog in newly manufactured vessels. In this way the identity and power associated with the pots might have been carried forward to new vessels for use by succeeding generations.

If these interpretations are to be accepted, then the Lockington metalwork and pottery would appear to represent a 'personal' rather than a 'communal deposit'. Traditionally, they would be interpreted as prestige goods representing the high status of an individual entering the world of the ancestors. However, in these circumstances, the group would normally be expected to directly accompany a burial. The association between a dagger and armlets have only been recorded in Britain on two definite occasions (see page 44 above). One of these recorded associations was from a burial context; a cist burial at Masterton, Fife (Henshall and Wallace 1963). The bronze armlets from Masterton bear a striking resemblance to Armlet 1 from Lockington. This group also included a necklace of jet beads. The only traces of bone at Masterton were inside the armlets and above the dagger, where the bone had been in contact with the metal oxide, and the enamel crowns of a few teeth to the south of the beads. More locally, the only association of a bronze armlet, in this case a penannular sheet armlet, and a Beaker is from what is described as a 'pit-burial' from near Knipton in northeast Leicestershire (note in Antiquaries Journal 15 (1935), 60–61).

In the circumstances, the absence of any trace of a corpse in the pit at Lockington may appear surprising. It seems unlikely that the acidic conditions would have removed all trace of a corpse. Animal teeth fragments had survived elsewhere on the site and one might expect similar survival of human enamel. The shape and size of the pit is also inconsistent with the former presence of an inhumation. Certainly, the tight clustering of the objects and the juxtaposition of the armlets and dagger suggest that they were not actually being worn by a corpse. Similarly the traces of burnt bone elsewhere on the site, and in particular under the mound, would suggest that at least some trace of a cremation would have survived. The pH level within the two contexts was similar. Therefore, the evidence seems to indicate that the objects were not in direct association with a burial. The possible role of the deposit is discussed later.

The close proximity of the cup marked stone to the hoard is clearly highly significant and it seems likely that the object formerly marked the location of the feature. At the very least, its presence would have ensured that the deposit was not disturbed during the construction of the later barrow mound and excavation of the ring ditch. Stones with carved decoration are widely associated with barrows (Ashbee 1960, 66–68). They have been recorded in a number of different contexts within the structure of barrows and cairns, and frequently on stones built into, or over, graves or cists. Simple cup marks are the most widespread form although numerous other motifs have been recorded. It has been suggested that the cup marked stone from Lockington is an outlier of a distinct western group with a distribution in the southwest of England and Wales (Bradley 1997, 146–8). Many examples of decorated stones within barrows, particularly in the north of Britain, appear to be reused fragments from much older, open sites. It has been suggested that this forms part of a process establishing a link between a particular people and particular places in the landscape (Bradley 1993, 42–44). The Lockington stone is such an isolated example it would be impossible to demonstrate the nature of such an association. However, it demonstrates a clear link with funerary ritual practices being carried out in other parts of Britain. In the north, the decorated faces of these stones normally faced the burial (Bradley 1993, 43). The Lockington stone was recovered, decorated face down, in the fill of the ring ditch although, it seems likely that the stone was not in its original position. Of particular relevance to Lockington may be a cup-marked stone set into the inner face of a stone kerb forming part of the Tregulland barrow in Cornwall. Two concentric rings of stake holes, apparently predating this kerb (Ashbee 1958) suggest a feature reminiscent of the postulated enclosure at Lockington. The Tregulland stone and timber ring also surrounded an enclosure containing elements of a Food Vessel cremation burial. Closer to Lockington are the cup-marked stones from the embanked stone circle at Barbrook (Barbrook II) in the Peak District (Barnatt 1990, 55–57). One of these was located near to a blocked entrance through the bank on the northeast. Others were associated with a cairn and cist within the enclosure.

Pre-barrow activity

The character of the activity preserved under the barrow mound is difficult to define. The function of the shallow, irregular-shaped central scoop (F23) is unclear. The fill is described above as a mixed and disturbed version of the buried soil (page 90). There was no evidence for any unusual inclusions or other deposits in this fill and there were no other internal features indicating the nature of the associated activity. It was initially thought that the yellow/red staining in the central area of the barrow platform, under the barrow core and around the shallow central scoop was associated with a burning episode, perhaps an *in situ* funerary pyre. However, no evidence for burning could be identified during the detailed soil analysis and the intensity of iron staining is now seen as a consequence of the amount of organic matter in the soil prior to the construction of the mound. Similarly, there was no indication that the layer of charcoal overlying the central scoop resulted from *in situ* burning even though there was evidence that ash was also present. It seems far more likely that this material was the remains of redeposited pyre debris, rather than an *in situ* pyre site (McKinley 1997, 137). A similar conclusion was reached for the charcoal deposit recorded under the mound of Site I at Lockington (Posnansky 1955a, 19) and the cremated bone under Barrow I at Swarkeston (Posnansky 1955b, 126). The flecks of cremated bone associated with this material were too small to be positively identified. If they are of human origin, than it is clear that only a very small, 'token' element of the cremated deposit is represented. Perhaps there was a deliberate intention to destroy identifiable bone before the deposition of the cremated material. The bone from the various cremation deposits at Bromfield and the southern ring ditch at Meole Brace (Barfield and Hughes 1998) was in a similar fragmentary condition. Another possibility is that the identifiable cremated bone was removed from the pyre site and deposited in an un-identified grave elsewhere. Meanwhile, the remaining pyre debris was redeposited over the central scoop and sealed by the barrow. It seems probable that this deposit was accompanied by the fragments of an Enlarged Food Vessel Urn. Although these fragments were recovered from several different contexts, they formed a linear scatter sealed by the mound. Elsewhere in the region, there is rather more evidence for an *in situ* pyre, notably at Barrow 15, Bromfield, Shropshire (Stanford 1995, 40–41). However, at some of these sites the absence of a substantial pit associated with the scattered cremation burial may explain the absence of any primary burial at ring ditch sites which have been subjected to greater erosion, such as at Foston, Derbyshire (Hughes and Jones 1995).

An unusual and clearly significant phenomenon was the presence of microspherulites in the buried soil and in the fill of the central scoop. The soil analysis suggests that these indicate the presence of grazing animals or a dump of animal dung. Furthermore, it is suggested that the survival of this material could only have occurred if the deposition of the dung was immediately followed by the construction of the mound. In any other circumstances the spherulites would have dissolved due to the acidic soil or the action of rainwater. Consequently, the animals must have been present immediately prior to the deposition of the possible cremation deposit and the construction of the mound. One can only speculate what these animals may have been used for. Perhaps they were former possessions of the deceased to be paraded as a display of wealth and status. Perhaps they were subsequently divided up between the inheritors or slaughtered as part of a funeral feast.

The barrow and ring ditch

It seems likely that the core of the barrow is composed of topsoil scraped from the upper part of the A-horizon of the old ground surface and heaped in a mound over the central scoop, the redeposited pyre debris and the cremation pit. This would explain the absence of this distinctive, less stony, sandy loam from the peripheral areas of the barrow platform where only the gravely B-horizon of the pre-barrow soil had survived. The date from the redeposited pyre debris (1870–1520 cal BC) provides a *terminus post quem* for the construction of the mound. There was no evidence for turf stacking such as that recorded at the Swarkestone Barrows in south Derbyshire (Posnansky 1955b, 126 and Plate II; Greenfield 1960). However, the mottled and stained, and relatively stone free composition of the mound core suggests the former presence of decayed vegetation. The core of the barrows at Site I, Lockington (Posnansky 1955a, 19) and at Site 1, Aston-on-Trent, southern Derbyshire (Reaney 1968, 71–2) appear to be similar 'scrape barrows'. The deposition of additional material and the gravel capping may represent a subsequent enlargement of the barrow. There was no indication of the time that may have elapsed between these two episodes. However, the enlargement of the barrow may relate to the redefinition of the ring ditch represented by the recut. The original cut for the ring ditch had been allowed to almost fully silt up before this redefinition suggesting the passing of a considerable period of time. A similar redefinition of silted-up ring ditches in Leicestershire has been recorded at Cossington Site 1 (O'Brien 1976) and Tixover (Beamish 1992).

The sandy silt (1005) overlying the upper fill of the ditch recut (1010) almost certainly represents material removed from the top of the mound and redeposited over the top of the ditch by medieval and modern ploughing. The large number of flint flakes and cores from this deposit (just under 50% of the total assemblage from the site) presumably also originated from the upper part of the mound. This might suggest the deliberate deposition of flint material on the surface of or within the mound, or possibly flint working activity on the top of the barrow.

Later activity

The barrow appears to have become the focus for at least two linear boundaries with probable origins in the Iron Age. At least one of these boundary ditches crosses over the centre of the barrow, suggesting that the barrow may have been used as a marker in the landscape. However, the evidence that the sanctity of the site may have still been recognised derives from the apparent deliberate deposition of Late Bronze Age and Iron Age pottery in earlier contexts. This occurs not just in the upper fills of the ring ditch surrounding Site VI but perhaps more significantly in the pit containing the ceramic plug on Site V (F84). It seems highly unlikely that the deposition of fragments from a Late Bronze Age jar in a pit already containing an earlier special deposit was simply coincidence. Similar reuse of a Neolithic/Early Bronze Age feature in the Late Bronze Age is known from the site of Wasperton in Warwickshire. Perhaps this later deposition was a reference to the continued sanctity of the site and it may be that the surviving monuments of the Early Bronze Age provided material for the elaboration of new myths. Such an interpretation of apparent 'continuity' may explain the reuse of a large number of prehistoric sites in later periods (Bradley 1987; 1993, 113–129).

THE NATURE OF THE EARLY BRONZE AGE MORTUARY RITUAL AT LOCKINGTON

The chronological sequence of the Early Bronze Age activity at Lockington is very poorly defined. The earliest feature appears to be an enclosure, represented by the palisade gully, which pre-dates the construction of the ring ditch and mound. There appears to be a close spatial association between the gold hoard and this enclosure. It is even possible that the hoard was deposited at an entrance to the enclosure. What is unclear is the time interval between the deposition of the hoard and the mortuary ritual represented by the fragmentary remains preserved beneath the barrow mound. This problem is further complicated by the possibility of further phases of activity between the deposition of the hoard and the construction of the barrow which have not survived in the archaeological record.

A long chronology is suggested by both the radiocarbon dates and by the artefact typology. It has already been suggested that the dagger is best dated to *circa* 2200–1900 BC and the armlets to *circa* 2100–1700 BC. Needham makes a strong argument that the damage suffered by the dagger may suggest deposition by an individual from Amorica during the course of a single lifetime (see page 44 above). This would suggest a date of between 2100 and 1900 BC for the deposition of the hoard. By contrast the radiocarbon date (1870–1520 cal BC at the two sigma level) for the deposits under the mound and the fragments of Enlarged Food Vessel Urn suggest a much later date for the pre-barrow mortuary ritual.

Consequently, it is possible that at least two quite distinct events are represented by the sequence. The first would be represented by the construction and use of the enclosure and the deposition of the hoard. It is possible that this was not directly related to the events associated with a later funerary ritual and the construction of the barrow. It has already been suggested that, taken individually, the objects that comprise the hoard would not seem out of place in a grave context even though the combination of objects is extremely unusual and even though no human remains were actually present. The hoard may have been a specific deposit with ritual intent and one suggestion is that it was intended as a cenotaph or memorial. Perhaps the corpse was not recovered following the events surrounding the death or was required elsewhere. This would imply that the cremated fragments preserved under the barrow may have belonged to a completely different, and perhaps much later, funerary ritual. Another possibility suggested above (page 45) is that the peripheral location of the hoard allowed for its subsequent retrieval and that perhaps subsequent events prevented this original intention from being carried out. It has been suggested that this might explain the rare survival of such deposits in the archaeological record.

Alternatively, a significant period of time may have passed between the manufacture of the objects comprising the hoard and their final deposition in the pit. The objects may have been heirlooms and may have remained in circulation for several generations. Support for the use of at least some of the objects as heirlooms is suggested by the possible reuse of the pottery vessels (see above page 58). It remains possible that the deposition of the hoard, the construction and use of the pre-barrow enclosure, the central redeposited pyre debris and the construction of the barrow mound may all have been components of a single, protracted and highly specialised funeral.

It is possible that the palisade may have surrounded activities associated with the liminal stage of the funeral (Van Gennep 1960), perhaps the storage or display of the corpse in a mortuary enclosure prior to the lighting of the funeral pyre. The parading or stockading of animals within the enclosure then preceded the scattering of the ashes in the central area. The survival of microspherulites associated with the dung of these animals indicates that the construction of the barrow mound immediately followed this mortuary activity and represents the final act of incorporation.

The objects in the hoard could not have accompanied the corpse throughout the funeral rites because they clearly were not burnt by the pyre. Instead they may have been careful buried on the threshold of the mortuary enclosure. This highly significant location would have marked out the point of entry into the world of the dead. It is noticeable that this position is also directly north of the central area of the postulated mortuary enclosure. This orientation, calculated by taking the midpoint between the midsummer sunrise and sunset, is frequently considered to be of importance to contemporary populations (Aubrey Burl pers comm).

In this way the final resting place of the remains of the corpse and the accompanying burial items became spatially removed from each other. The final deposition of a token of the debris taken from the pyre site, the rite of incorporation, is followed by the construction of the mound and the excavation of the ring ditch. The superimposition of the ring ditch over the ring gully suggests that by this time the palisade, surrounding the earlier mortuary enclosure, had been removed.

At Lockington, the apparent spatial separation between the final deposition of the cremation burial and the 'grave goods' is difficult to reconcile with the argument that such objects directly reflect the status of the individual in life. However, the assumption that the social roles once held by the deceased determines the nature of the burial ritual has been questioned (Barrett 1991, 121–122). Instead, it has been argued that the presence of grave goods has more to do with the structure of the funeral and the nature of the accompanying social transactions than the status of the deceased (Barrett and Needham 1988, 130). Burial rituals are the means by which the living renegotiate relations of obligation, affinity and inheritance. In particular, cremation burials may be less likely to be accompanied by grave goods because of the temporal and spatial distance between the rites of liminality and the rites of incorporation. By the time of the final burial many of the social transactions may have already been played out. This has been used to suggest a possible relationship between the deposition of daggers or rapiers in rivers or bogs and contemporary 'poor' cremation burials during the Middle Bronze Age. That is the transfer of authority during the liminal phase, associated with the dagger deposition, was divorced from the incorporation phase, the consignment of the cremated remains to the place of burial (*op cit*, 133). It could be argued that, at Lockington, the two phases of the funerary rite were not so far removed, either spatially or temporally. Consequently, the final deposition of the 'rich' artefacts was relatively close to the final deposition of the 'poor' cremation burial. Clearly there is a need to view the Lockington group, not as a conventional hoard or grave group, but as a highly specialised form of ritual deposit which may have formed part of a complex and intricate funerary ritual.

The evidence for a comparable, complex ritual

sequence from elsewhere in the region is hampered by the poor level of survival. The majority of ring ditch/barrow sites in the river valleys of the midlands have been badly truncated by subsequent agricultural activity. However, the ring gullies recorded at other sites in the region, hint at the possibility of comparable pre-barrow mortuary enclosures (see above). Where traces of a barrow mound has survived, primary cremation burials (possibly redeposited pyre debris) scattered on the old ground surface have been recorded at Swarkeston (Barrow II), Lockington (Site I) and Bromfield (Barrow 10). At Lockington (Site I) the bronze objects (a knife dagger and an awl) and pottery fragment (possibly from a Food Vessel) appear to have been placed with the cremation burial after the pyre. By contrast the flintwork (including four flint knives and an arrowhead) appears to have been subjected to intense heat (Posnansky 1955a, 20). Although no trace of a ring gully was identified at any of these sites, the extent of the excavation outside the circuit of the ring ditch was extremely limited.

Comparable deposits of artefacts, unaccompanied by a burial, are extremely rare. Several unusual context types, including non-grave mound deposits, are discussed by Needham (1988, 241–242). However, as for hoards, these are dominated by axes (*op cit*, Table 4). A possible exception is the group of rich artefacts scattered around the surface of a flint cairn within the Clandon barrow, including a dagger and gold, lozenge-shaped plate (Drew and Piggott 1936). No mention is made of an associated burial and the assumption that this was a grave group has been questioned (Needham 1988, 241). The implication is that this might also be a non-grave mound group.

Another non-grave dagger group was recorded at the Caerloggas I ring cairn in Cornwall, where part of a decorated dagger, a piece of amber and other artefacts were scattered around a natural moorstone within a small embanked enclosure. The excavator suggests that the deposit within a pit beneath the moorstone was a ceremonial, dedicatory deposit (Miles 1975, 42–43) and that the dagger and amber fragments were votive offerings (*op cit*, 72). It has been suggested that the deposition of these artefacts and the earthwork at Caerloggas represented the translation of a natural feature (the moorstone) into the world of human culture (Bradley 1993, 28–9).

Although neither of these examples are directly comparable to Lockington, they demonstrate the potential complexity and variety of ritual that sometimes accompanies the deposition of such artefacts and demonstrates that such activity need not be directly accompanied by human remains. At Lockington, Site VI is only part of a complex at which a variety of different social transactions are likely to have been played out. Although there are superficial similarities with the barrow at Site I, there are also a number of differences. At Site I there was no trace of any pre-barrow structure but there was a direct association between the grave items, the bronze knife dagger and the flint daggers, and the central cremation burial. However, it is difficult to know how to begin to interpret the enigmatic pits belonging to Site V. The primary deposit within one of the pits (F84) contained a particularly interesting assemblage of artefacts including Beaker sherds, a ceramic pulley-shaped object and cremated bone, one fragment of which was identified as pig. The radiocarbon date suggests that this deposit may have been contemporary with the activity associated with Barrow VI. Without excavation, one can only guess at the nature of the ritual that was carried at the other sites in the complex. The internal pit circle at Site II, the double ditch at Site IV and the oval shape of the ring ditches at Sites III and VII all suggest a variety of different activities (Fig. 2). It may be misleading to see this complex simply as a burial ground. The cemetery at Lockington may have formed an important social role for a scattered community whose settlement sites are ephemeral and dispersed (or so our inability to locate them suggests). Furthermore, the pollen evidence from the vicinity of the dagger hints at the possibility that the cemetery was located in an open, cultivated landscape. This provides rare evidence for a close relationship between a ritual centre and possible early Bronze Age settlement suggesting that the contemporary population may have favoured the light, easily drained soils of the valley gravels. Ritual centres at such locations may have served as focal points in a social landscape where relationships of authority and dependence between individuals and lineages, and between the community and the wider social world, would have been negotiated (Buteux and Hughes 1995). It is at such sites that the identity of the community itself would have been forged and reworked.

Acknowledgements

The excavation of Site VI was directed by Gwilym Hughes on behalf of BUFAU and the excavation of Site V by James Meek on behalf of the Leicestershire Archaeological Unit. The principal members of the

BUFAU field team were, K. Allen, M. Allen, K. Baker, A. Bennet, R. Burrows, S. Barfield, E. Carter, R. Cuttler, H. Fawbert, M. Hewson, L. Jones, D. Moscrop, E. Newton, K. Nicholl, E. Ramsay, M. Ridgeway, B. Robinson, Dr R. Roseff, L. Salmon, and J. Sterenberg.

Thanks to K. Challis, J. Walker (Nottingham University Consultants Limited), G. Goodman (Scott Wilson Kirkpatrick), Anne Graf (Leicestershire County Council), T. Rogers (Highways Agency), Dr A. Brown, P. Wilson, M. Cooper (English Heritage), P. Leach, S. Buteux (Birmingham University Field Archaeology Unit), P Clay (Leicester Archaeological Unit), Dr S. Limbrey and Dr L. Barfield (Department of Ancient History and Archaeology, University of Birmingham) who all provided valuable assistance and advice during the course of the excavation. Further helpful comments were provided by Joan Taylor (University of Liverpool), M. Canti (Ancient Monuments Laboratory), Dr C. Salisbury and Graeme Guilbert (Trent and Peak Archaeological Trust).

The figures are by Nigel Dodds and Mark Breedon apart from the illustrations accompanying the metalwork report which are by Phil Dean (British Museum).

Particular thanks are due to Anthony Read (Conservation Department, Leicester Museum), who responded so rapidly to the request for assistance with the excavation of the pit group, and to Graeme Norrie (Department of Ancient History and Archaeology, University of Birmingham) for photographing the artefacts. Alan McPherson and a film crew from English Heritage kindly shot a video of the excavation in progress and Stuart Coulson took a series of aerial photographs of the site.

The co-operation of the farmer Mr J. Hardy and the landowner, Mr C.H.C. Coaker, was much appreciated.

Ann Woodward is extremely grateful to the following friends and colleagues who commented at length on the two partial pottery vessels from the hoard: Arthur ApSimon, Humphrey Case, Alex Gibson, Ian Kinnes, Ian Longworth, Stuart Needham and David Tomalin.

Angela Monkton is grateful to Lisa Moffett for help with the identification of the plant remains on Site V, to the Site V director, James Meek, for information and to Ian Baxter and Catherine Prasad for efficient processing of the samples.

Stuart Needham would like to thank the following individuals whose assistance was fundamental to the research on the metalwork. First and foremost was the draftsmanship of Phil Dean. At the beginning he benefited from the help of the Leicestershire Museums Service, notably Bob Rutland and Anthony Read, who allowed study of the dagger still in their care and provided information on the recovery process and early conservation work. Pursuit of the armlet parallels necessitated a visit to the National Museums of Scotland, Edinburgh, where every assistance was extended by Alison Sheridan, Trevor Cowie and Ian Scott. It was good fortune that between the initial research and final submission, the important find from Ingleby Barwick came to his attention; Blaise Vyner kindly showed a draft of his report on the armlets and associations and Richard Annis (Tees Archaeology) gave permission to mention them ahead of publication. He was also indebted to Professor Jacques Briard for his kindness in offering opinion and details on Breton daggers not yet fully published, while Dirk Brandherm came to the rescue with his recent analysis of the classification and chronology of relevant Iberian daggers. Fruitful discussions on the significance of the Lockington context were had with Gwilym Hughes. Further research queries on matters of composition and technology were aided through discussion with Ian MacIntyre, Duncan Hook and Paul Craddock. Finally, Kate Down and Judy Cash gave valued help with the inputting. Keith Matthews carried out the FTIR analysis and Caroline Cartwright the charcoal identification.

BIBLIOGRAPHY

Alexander, J., Ozanne, P.C. & Ozanne, A. 1960. Report on the investigation of a round barrow on Arreton Down, Isle of Wight. *Proceedings of the Prehistoric Society* 26, 263–302.

Allen, C.S.M., Harman, M. & Wheeler, H. 1987. Bronze Age cremation cemeteries in the East Midlands. *Proceedings of the Prehistoric Society* 53, 187–222.

Almargo Gorbea, M. 1976. La espada de Entrambasguas aportación a la seuencia de las espadas del bronce an el norte de la península Iberica. In *XL Aniversanio del Centro de Estudios Montañeses, Tomo III*, 455–77. Santander: Institución Cultural de Cantabria.

Anderson, J. 1886. *Scotland in Pagan Times: the Bronze and Stone Ages.*

Anderson, J. 1900–1. Notice of a hoard of bronze implements, and ornaments, and buttons of jet found at Migdale, on the estate of Skibo, Sutherland. *Proceedings of the Society of Antiquaries of Scotland* 35, 266–275.

Andersen, J.M. 1976. An ignition method for determination of phosphorous in lake sediments. *Water Research* 10, 329–331.

Annable, F.K. & Simpson, D.D.A. 1964. *Guide Catalogue of the Neolithic and Bronze-Age Collections in Devises Museum.* Wiltshire Archaeological and Natural History Society.

Armbruster, B.R. 1995. Rotary motion – lathe and drills: Some new technological aspects concerning Late Bronze Age gold work from south western Europe. In G. Morteani and J.P. Northover (eds), *Prehistoric Gold in Europe: Mines, metallurgy and manufacture*, 414. Kluwer Academic Publishers.

Ashbee, P. 1958. The excavation of Tregulland Barrow, Treneglos Parish, Cornwall. *Antiquaries Journal* 38, 174–196.

Ashbee, P. 1960. *The Bronze Age round barrow in Britain.*

Avery, B.W. & Bascombe, C.L. (eds) 1974. *Soil Survey Laboratory Methods.* Soil Survey Technical Monograph No. 6. Harpenden: Soil Survey of England and Wales.

Balquet, A. 1994. Les tumulus de l'Age du Bronze dans les Côtes-d'Armor. La fiabilité des données anciennes. *Antiquités Nationales* 26, 45–74.

Bamford, H.M. 1982. *Beaker domestic sites in the Fen Edge and East Anglia.* East Anglian Archaeology Report 16.

Barclay, A. and Glass, H. 1995. Excavations of Neolithic and Bronze Age ring-ditches, Shorncote Quarry, Somerford Keynes, Gloucestershire. *Trans. Bristol and Gloucestershire Arch. Soc.* 113, 21–60.

Barfield, L. & Hughes, G. 1998. *The excavation of a double ring ditch at Meole Brace, Shrewsbury, third interim report.* BUFAU, Unpublished Report No. 344.2.

Barker, H. 1975. Report on phosphate analysis carried out in connection with the cenotaph problem. In R. Bruce-Mitford, (ed) *The Sutton Hoo Ship Burial.* British Museum.

Barnatt, J. 1990. *The henges, stone circles and ringcairns of the Peak District.* Sheffield: Archaeological Monographs 1.

Barnatt, J. 1994. Excavations of a Bronze Age unenclosed cemetery, cairns, and field boundaries at Eagleston Flat, Curbar, Derbyshire 1984, 1989–90. *Proceedings of the Prehistoric Society* 60, 287–387.

Barrett, J.C. 1985. Hoards and related metalwork. In Clarke, D.V., Cowie, T.G. & Foxon, A. *Symbols of power at the time of Stonehenge*, Edinburgh.

Barrett, J.C. 1994. *Fragments from Antiquity.* Oxford.

Barrett, J.C. & Needham, S.P. 1988. Production, circulation and exchange: problems in the interpretation of Bronze Age bronzework. In Barret, J.C. & Kinnes, I.A. (eds) *The Archaeology of Context in the Neolithic and Early Bronze Age: Recent Trends.* Sheffield, 127–140.

Beamish, M. 1992. Archaeological excavations along the Anglian water pipeline at Tixover (SK 97 01). *Trans. of the Leicestershire Archaeological and Historical Society* 66, 183.

Benton, G.M. 1923. The Bronze Age burial at Benton. *Trans. Essex Archaeological Society* 16 (new ser.), 144.

Bethell, P.H. & Carver, M.O.H. 1987. Detection and enhancement of decayed inhumations at Sutton Hoo. In Boddington, A, Garland, A.N. & Janaway, R.C. (eds) *Death, Decay and Reconstruction: Approaches to Archaeology and Forensic Science.* Manchester: University Press.

Bewley, R.H., Longworth, I.H., Browne, S., Huntley, J.P. & Varndell, G. 1992. Excavation of a Bronze Age cemetery at Ewanrigg, Maryport, Cumbria. *Proceedings of the Prehistoric Society* 325–354.

Black, C.A. *et al.* 1965. *Methods of Soil Analysis* Vol.2, 1038–1039. American Society of Agronomy.

Boast, R. 1995. Fine pots, pure pots, Beaker pots. In Kinnes, I. & Varndell, G. (eds) *Unbaked Urns of Rudely Shape.* Oxford: Oxbow Monograph 55.

Bourhis, J.R. & Briard, J. 1985. Analyses de cuivres du Chalcolithique et du Bronze Ancien de la France. In J. Briard (ed), *Paléometallurgie de la France Atlantique, Age du Bronze (2)*, 165–180. Rennes, Travaux du Laboratoire Anthropologie-Préhistoire-Protohistorie-Quaternaire Armoricains.

Bradley, R. 1972. The Flint Industry. In E. W. Holden, A Bronze Age cemetery barrow on Itford Hill, Beddingham, Sussex. *Sussex Archaeological Collection* 110, 93–104.

Bradley, R. 1987. Time regained – the creation of continuity. *Journal of the British Archaeological Association* 140, 1–17.

Bradley, R. 1993. *Altering the Earth*. Edinburgh: Society of Antiquaries of Scotland Monograph Series No.8.
Bradley, R. 1997. *Rock art and the prehistory of Atlantic Europe*. London, Routledge.
Bradley, R. & Ellison, A. 1975. *Rams Hill*. Oxford: British Archaeological Reports, British Series.
Brandherm, D. 1995. Beiträge zur Bewaffnung der Steinkupfer- und älteren Bronzezeit auf der Iberischen Halbinsel. Freiburg, Doctoral thesis.
Brassil, B.S., Owen, W.G. & Britnell, W.J. 1991. Prehistoric and Early Medieval Cemeteries at Tandderwen, near Denbigh, Clwyd. *Archaeological Journal* 148, 46–97.
Briard, J. 1965. *Les Dépôts Bretons et L'Age du Bronze Atlantique*. Université de Rennes, thèse.
Briard, J. 1968. Un tumulus du Bronze ancien à Lescongar Plouhinec (Finistère). *Gallia Préhistorie* 11, 247–259.
Briard, J. 1970a. Un tumulus de Bronze ancien: Kernonen en Plouvorn (Finistère). *L'Anthropologie* 74, 5–55.
Briard, J. 1970b. Les tumulus de l'Age du Bronze de Plouvorn-Plouzévédé (Finistère). *Bull.Société Préhistorique Française* 67, 372–385.
Briard, J. 1984. *Les Tumulus d'Armorique*. L'Age du Bronze en France – 3. Paris, Picard.
Briard, J. 1991. Les premiers cuivres atlantiques en France. In C. Eluère & J.P. Mohen (eds), *Découverte du Métal*. Picard.
Briard, J. 1995. Les relations entre l'Armorique et la Méditerranée au Chalolithique et à l'Age du Bronze. In R. Chenorkian (ed), *L'Homme Méditerranéen: mélanges offerts à Gabriel Camps*, 403–409. Aix-en-Provence, Université de Provence.
Briard, J. & Bourhis, J. 1984. La paléométallurgie du Nord-ouest de la France; spectrographie des bronzes. In J. Briard (ed), *Paléométallurgie de la France Atlantique – Age du Bronze (1)*. Rennes, Travaux du Laboratoire Anthropologie-Préhistoire-Protohistoire-Quaternaire Armoricains.
Briard, J., Bourhis, J., le Goffic, M. & Onnée, Y. 1981. Préhistoire au pays de Guerlesquin: les tumulus du Bronze de la Croix-Saint-Ener à Botsorhel. *Bulletin de la Société archéologique du Finistère* 109, 15–34.
Briard, J. & Mohen, J.P. 1974. Le tumulus de la forêt de Carnoët à Quimperlé (Finistère). *Antiquités Nationales* 6, 46–60.
Briard, J. & Mohen, J-P.1983. *Typologie des Objects de l'Age du Bronze en France, Fascicule II: Poignards, Hallebardes, Pointes de Lance, Pointe de Flèche, Armement Défensif*. Paris, Société Préhistorique Française. Commission du Bronze.
Briard, J. & Verney, A. 1996. L'Age du Bronze Ancien de Bretagne et de Normandie: actualité. In C. Mordant & O. Gaiffe (eds), *Cultures et Sociétés du Bronze Ancien en Europe*, 565–578. Actes du 117e Congrès National des Sociétés Savantes (Clermont-Ferrand, 1992). Paris, Comité des Travaux historiques et scientifiques.
Britnell, W. 1982. The excavation of two round barrows at Trelystan, Powys. *Proceedings of the Prehistoric Society* 48, 133–202.
Britton, D. 1961. A study of the composition of Wessex culture bronzes. *Archaeometry* 4, 39–52.
Britton, D. 1963. Traditions of metalworking in the Later Neolithic and Early Bronze Age of Britain: part 1. *Proceedings of the Prehistoric Society* 29, 258–325.
Brown, A.G. 1999. Characterising prehistoric lowland environments using local pollen assemblages. *Quaternary Proceedings* 7, 585–594.
Burgess, C.B. 1979. The background of early metalworking in Ireland and Britain. In M. Ryan (ed), *The Origins of Metallurgy in Atlantic Europe; proceedings of the 5th Atlantic Colloquium*, 207–214. Dublin, Stationery Office.
Burgess, C.B. 1980. *The Age of Stonehenge*. London, Dent.
Berglund, B.E., Birks, H.J.B, Ralska-Jasiewiczowa, M and Wright, H.E. (eds) 1996. *Palaeoecological events during the last 15000 years; regional syntheses of plaeoecological studies of lakes and mires in Europe*. Wiley, Chichester.
Bullock, P., Federoff, N., Jongerius, A., Stoops, G. & Tursina, T. 1985. *Handbook for Soil Thin Section Description*. Albrighton: Waine Research Publications.
Buteux, S. & Hughes, G. 1995. Reclaiming a wilderness: the prehistry of lowland Shropshire. *Transactions of the Shropshire Archaeological and Historical Society* 70, 159–164.
Butler, J.J. & Waterbolk, H.T. 1974. La fouille de A.E. van Giffen à "La Motta"; un tumulus de l'Age du Bronze Ancien à Lannion (Bretagne). *Palaeohistoria* 16, 107–149.
Callander, J.G. 1918–19. Discovery of (1) a short cist containing human remains and a bronze armlet, and (2) a cup-marked stone at Williamston, St Martins, Perthshire. *Proceedings of the Society of Antiquaries of Scotland* 53, 15–24.
Canti, M.G. 1997. An investigation of microscopic calcareous spherulites from herbivore dung. *Journal of Archaeological Science* 24, 219–232.
Canti, M.G. 1998. The micromorphological identification of faecal spherulites from archaeological and modern materials. *Journal of Archaeological Science* 25, 435–444.
Case, H. 1956. Beaker pottery from the Oxford region: 1939–1955. *Oxoniensia* 21, 1–21.
Case, H. 1993. Beakers: deconstruction and after. *Proceedings of the Prehistoric Society* 59, 241–268.
Chowne, P. & Healy, F. 1983. Artefacts from a prehistoric cemetery and settlement at Anwick Fen, Lincs. *Lincolnshire History and Archaeology* 18, 37–46.
Christie, P.M. 1967. A barrow-cemetery of the second millennium BC in Wiltshire, England. *Proceedings of the Prehistoric Society* 33, 336–366.
Clapham, A.R. (ed) 1969. *Flora of Derbyshire*. Derby: County Museum and Art Gallery.
Clarke, D.L. 1970. *Beaker Pottery of Great Britain and Ireland*. Cambridge: University Press.
Clark, D.V., Cowie, T.G. & Foxon, A. 1985. *Symbols of Power at the time of Stonehenge*. Edinburgh: HMSO.
Clarke, D.V. & Kemp, M.M.B. 1984. A hoard of Late Bronze Age gold objects from Heights of Brae, Ross and Cromarty District, Highland Region. *Proceedings of the Society of Antiquaries of Scotland* 114, 189–198.
Clarke, R. 1995. *The Lockington barrow cemetery Leicestershire. An archaeological assessment*. Leicestershire Archaeological Unit, Unpublished Report 95/07.
Clay, P. 1981. *Two multi phase barrows at Sproxton and Eaton, Leicestershire*. Leicestershire Museums, Art Galleries and Record Services, Archaeological Report No.2.
Clay, P. 1986. Excavation of Neolithic – Early Bronze Age Pit circles at Burley Road, Oakham – interim report. *Transactions of the Leicestershire Archaeological and Historical Society* 61.
Clay, P. 1992. An Iron Age farmstead at Grove Farm, Enderby, Leicestershire. *Transactions of the Leicestershire Archaeological and Historical Society* 66, 1–82.

Cleal, R. 1995. Pottery fabrics in Wessex in the fourth to second millennia BC. In I. Kinnes and G. Varndell (eds), *Unbaked Urns of rudely shape*. Oxford: Oxbow Monograph 55.

Clifford, E. 1937. The Beaker Folk in the Cotswolds. *Proceedings of the Prehistoric Society* 3, 159–163.

Coffyn, A. 1985. *Le Bronze Final Atlantique dans la Péninsule Ibérique*. Paris, Publications du Centre Pierre.

Coles, J. 1968–9. Scottish Early Bronze Age metalwork. *Proceedings of the Society of Antiquaries of Scotland* 101, 1–110.

Cook, S.F. & Heizer, R.F. Studies on the Chemical Analysis of Archaeological Sites. *University of California Publications in Anthropology* 2.

Cowell, M.R. 1998. Coin analysis by energy dispersive x-ray fluorescence spectrometry. In W.A.Oddy & M.R. Cowell (eds), *Metallurgy in Numismatics* 4, Royal Numismatic Society, London, 448–60.

Craddock, P.T. 1985. Three thousand years of copper alloys. In P.A. England & L. van Zelst (eds), *Application of science in examination of works of art*, the Research Laboratory of the Museum of Fine Arts, Boston, 59–67, plus microfiche.

Davies, E. 1957. An interesting Bronze Age discovery made near Nefyn, Caernarvonshire, in A.D. 1691. *Archaeologia Cambrensis* 106, 117–118.

Dimbleby, G.W. 1967. *Plants and archaeology*. Baker, London.

Douglas, J. 1793. *Naenia Britannica*.

Drew, C.D. & Piggott, S. 1936. Two Bronze Age barrows excavated by Mr. Edward Cunnington. *Proceedings of the Dorset Natural History and Archaeology Society* 58, 18–25.

Edwards, K.J. 1983. Phosphate analysis of soils associated with the Old Kinord field and settlement sytem, Muir of Dinnet, Aberdeenshire. *Proceedings of the Society of Antiquaries of Scotland* 113, 6520–627.

Eogan, G. 1994. *The Accomplished Art: gold and gold-working in Britain and Ireland during the Bronze Age (c.2300–650 BC)*. Oxford: Oxbow Monograph 42.

Forde-Johnston, J. 1958. The excavation of two barrows at Frampton in Dorset. *Proceedings of the Dorset Natural History and Archaeological Society* 80, 111–131.

Forde-Johnson, J. 1965. The Dudsbury barrow and vessels with shoulder grooves in Dorset and Wiltshire. *Proceedings of the Dorset Natural History and Archaeological Society* 87, 126–141.

Fowler, M.J. 1953. Beaker sherds from Stenson, Derbyshire. *Derbyshire Archaeological Journal* 73, 121–6.

Fox, C., 1959. *Life and Death in the Bronze Age*. London: Routledge and Kegan Paul.

Fox-Strangways, C. 1905. *The Geology of the Country between Derby, Burton-on-Trent, Ashby-de-la-Zouch and Loughborough*, Mem. Geological Survey, London.

French, C.I.A. 1994. Excavation of the Deeping St. Nicholas barrow complex, South Lincs. *Lincolnshire Archaeology and Heritage Report Series* No.1.

Gallay, A. 1996. Le concept de culture du Rhône: repères pour un historique. In C. Mordant & O. Gaiffe (eds), *Cultures et Sociétés du Bronze Ancien en Europe*, 271–286. Actes du 117e Congrès National des Sociétés Savantes (Clermont-Ferrand, 1992). Paris, Comité des Travaux historiques et scientifiques.

Gallay, G. 1981. *Die kupfer- und altbronzezeitlichen Dolche und Stabdolche in Frankreich*. Prähistorische Bronzefunde VI, 5. Munich.

Galloway, T.L. 1919–20. Prehistoric Argyll – report on the exploration of a burial cairn at Balnabraid, Kintyre. *Proceedings of the Society of Antiquaries of Scotland* 54, 172–191.

Garton, G. *et al* 1989. Newton Cliffs: a flint working and settlement site in the Trent Valley. In Philips, P. (ed) *Archaeology and Landscape Studies in N. Lincs*. Oxford: British Archaeological Reports, British Series 208, 81–181.

Gerloff, S. 1975. *The Early Bronze Age daggers in Great Britain and a reconsideration of the Wessex Culture*. Prahistorische Bronzefunde Abteilung VI Band 2, Munich.

Gerloff, S. 1993. Zu Fragen mittelmeerländischer Kontakte und absoluter Chronologie der Frühbronzezeit in Mittel- und Westeuropa. *Praehistorische Zeitshrift* 68, 58–102.

Gerloff, S. 1995. Bronzezeitliche Goldblechkronen aus Westeuropa. In A. Jockenhövel (ed), *Festschrift für Hermann Müller-Karpe zum 70. Geburtstag*. Bonn.

Gerrish, E.J.S. 1983. The prehistoric pottery from Mam Tor: further considerations. *Derbyshire Archaeological Journal* 103, 43–6.

Gibson, A.M. 1982. *Beaker domestic sites: a study of the domestic pottery of the late third and early second millennia BC in the British Isles*. Oxford: British Archaeological Reports.

Gibson, A. & McCormick, A. 1985. Archaeology at Grendon Quarry, Pt. 1. *Northamptonshire Archaeology* 20, 23–67.

Gillan, J. 1860–2. Notes on some antiquities in the parish of Alford, Aberdeenshire. *Proceedings of the Society of Antiquaries of Scotland* 4, 382–386.

Giot, P-R. 1951. New light on the 'Armorican' Early Bronze Age 'dagger-graves'. *Proceedings of the Prehistoric Society* 17, 226–228.

Giot, P.R., Bourhis, J. and Briard, J. 1966. *Travaux du Laboratoire d'Anthropologie Préhistorique, 1964–5*. Rennes.

Gray, H.St.G. & Prideaux, C.S. 1905. Barrow-digging at Martinstown, near Dorchester, 1903. *Proceedings of the Dorset Natural History and Archaeological Society* 26, 7–39.

Green, C., Lynch, F. & White, H. 1982. The Excavation of Two Round Barrows on Launceston Down (Long Chrichel 5 and 7). *Proceedings of the Dorset Natural History and Archaeological Society* 104, 39–58..

Green, H.S. 1980. *The Flint Arrowheads of the British Isles*. Oxford: British Archaeological Reports, British Series.

Greenfield, E. 1960. Excavation of barrow IV at Swarkestone. *Derbyshire Archaeological Journal* 80, 1–48.

Greig, J. 1987. *Site VIII: The late prehistoric surroundings of Bidford upon Avon, Warwickshire*. Ancient Monuments Laboratory Report 170/87.

Greig, J. 1991. The British Isles. In W. van Zeist, K. Wasylinkowa and K-E. Behre, *Progress in Old World Palaeoethnobotany*, Rotterdam, Balkema.

Greig, J. 1997a. *Assessment of plant remains from Chapel Farm, Hemington, Leicestershire (CHF)*. Report 97.02.

Greig, J. 1997b. *Plant remains from Hemington Bridge, Leicestershire*. Report 97.03.

Greig, J. and Colledge, S. 1988. *The prehistoric and early medieval waterlogged plant remains from multiperiod Beckford sites 5006 and 5007 (Worcestershire) and what they show of the surroundings then*. Ancient Monuments Laboratory Report 54/88.

Guilaine, J. & Briois, F. 1984. L'épée de Lafage (Saint-Amadou, Ariège). *Bull. Société Préhistorique Française* 81, 122–125.

Harbison P. 1969. *The daggers and halberds of the Early Bronze Age in Ireland*, Prähistorische Bronzefunde VI, 1. Munich.

Harding, A.F. 1990. The Wessex connection: developments and

perspectives. In *Orientalish-Ägäische Einflüsse in der Europäischen Bronzezeit,* 139–54. Mainze: Römisch-Germanisches Zentralmuseum Monograph 15.

Hamond, Y.W. 1983. Phosphate analysis of archaeological sediments. In T. Reeves-Smyth, & F. Hamond, (eds), *Landscape Archaeology in Ireland.* Oxford: British Archaeological Reports, British Series.

Hartmann, A. 1970. *Prähistorische goldfunde aus Europa,* Studien zu den Anfängen der metallurgie, III, Berlin.

Hartmann, A. 1982. *Prähistorische goldfunde aus Europa II,* Studien zu den Anfängen der metallurgie, V, Berlin.

Healey, E. 1981. The flintwork. In Clay, P. *Two Multi-phase Barrow Sites at Sproxton and Eaton, Leicestershire.* Leicestershire Museum, Art Galleries and Records Service Archaeological Report No. 2, 16–17 and 37–41.

Healy, F. 1986. The flint. In F. Petersen, & F. Healy, The excavation of two round barrows and a ditched enclosure on Weasenham Lyngs, 1972. In A.J. Lawson, Barrow Excavations in Norfolk, 1950–1982. *East Anglian Archaeology* 29, 70–102.

Healy, F. 1983. Struck Flint. In N. Field, & K. Leahy, Prehistoric and Anglo-Saxon Remains at Nettleton Top, Nettleton. *East Anglian Archaeology* 27, vol. 1.

Henshall, A.S. 1964. Four Early Bronze Age armlets. *Proceedings of the Prehistoric Society* 30, 426–429.

Henshall, A.S. & Wallace, J.C. 1963. A Bronze Age cist burial at Masterton, Pitreavie, Fife. *Proceedings of the Society of Antiquaries of Scotland* 96, 145–54.

Herity, M. 1969. Early finds of Irish antiquities from the minutebooks of the Society of Antiquaries of London. *Antiquaries Journal* 49 Part 1, 1–21.

Hillman, G. 1981. Reconstructing crop husbandry practices from charred remains of crops. In R. Mercer, *Farming Practice in British Prehistory,* Edinburgh University Press.

Hoare, R.C. 1812. *The Ancient History of South Wiltshire.* vol.1. London.

Hodges, R., Thomas, J. & Wildgoose, M. 1989. The barrow cemetery at Roystone Grange. *Derbyshire Archaeological Journal* 109, 7–16.

Hodgson, J.M., 1974. *Soil Survey Field Handbook.* Soil Survey Technical Monograph No. 5. Harpenden: Soil Survey of England and Wales.

Hook, D.R. Freestone, I.C., Meeks, N.D., Craddock, P.T. & Moreno Onorato, A. 1991. The early production of copper alloys in south-east Spain. *Archaeometry , 90* eds. Pernicka, E. & Wagner, G.A., 65–76, Basel: Birkhauser Verlag.

Hughes, G. 1991. *The excavation of a ring ditch at Tucklesholme Farm, Staffordshire.* Unpublished BUFAU Report.

Hughes, G. 1996. Lockington. *Current Archaeology* No. 146 Vol. 13, No. 2, 44–49.

Hughes, G. & Crawford, G. 1995. Excavations at Wasperton, Warwickshire, 1980–1985 introduction and Part I: the Neolithic and Early Bronze Age. *Transactions of theBirmingham and Warwickshire Archaeological Society* 99, 9–45.

Hughes, G. & Jones, L. 1995. The excavation of a ring ditch at Foston in the Dove Valley. *Derbyshire Archaeological Journal* 64.

Hughes G. & Woodward, A. 1995. A ring ditch and Neolithic pit cluster at Meole Brace, Shrewsbury. *Transactions of the Shropshire Archaeological and Historical Society* 70, 1–22.

Hughes, R.G. 1961. Archaeological sites in the Trent Valley, South Derbyshire. *Derbyshire Archaeological Journal* 81.

Hundt, H-J. 1971. Der Dolchhort von Gau-Bickelheim in Rheinhessen. *Jahrbuch des Römisch-Germanischen Zentralmuseums Mainz* 18, 1–50.

Hunt, A.M., Shotliff, A. and Woodhouse, J. 1986. A Bronze Age barrow cemetery and Iron Age enclosure at Holt. *Transactions of the Worcestershire Archaeological Society* 3rd Series 3, 7–36.

Junghans, S., Sangmeister, E. & Schröder, M. 1974. *Kupfer und Bronze in der frühen Metallzeit Europas.* Berlin: Studien zu den Anfängen der Metallurige, 2, 4.

Keevill, G.D. 1992. Life on the edge: archaeology and alluvium at Redland's Farm, Stanwick, Northants. In S. Needham & M.G. Macklin (eds), *Alluvial Archaeology in Britain,* 177–184. Oxford, Oxbow Monograph 27.

Kinnes, I.A. 1994. *Beaker and Early Bronze Age Grave Groups.* British Bronze Age Metalwork, Associated Finds Series A17–30. London: British Museum Press.

Kinnes, I.A., Gibson, A., Ambers, J., Bowman, S., Leese, M. & Boast, R. 1991. Radiocarbon dating and British Beakers: the British Museum programme. *Scottish Archaeological Review* 8, 35–68.

Kinnes, I. & Varndell, G. (eds), 1995. *Unbaked urns of rudely shape.* Oxford: Oxbow Monograph 55.

Knight, D. 1992. Excavations of an Iron Age settlement at Gamston, Nottinghamshire. *Transactions of the Thoroton Society of Nottinghamshire* 96, 16–90.

Krause, R. 1988a. *Die endneolithischen und frühbronzezeitlichen Grabfunde auf der Nordstadtterrasse von Singen am Hohentweil.* Stuttgart, Landesdenkmalamt Baden-Württemberg.

Krause, R. 1988b. Ein alter Grabfund der jüngeren Frühbronzezeit von Reutlingen. *Fundberichte aus Baden-Württemberg* 13, 199–212.

Leaf, C.S. 1935. Two bronze age barrows at Chipenham, Cambridgeshire. *Antiquaries Journal* 15, 61.

Limbrey, S. 1975. *Soil Science and Archaeology.* London: Academic Press.

Longworth, I.H. 1984. *Collared Urns of the Bronze Age in Great Britain and Ireland.* Cambridge: University Press.

Losco-Bradley, S. 1984. Fatholme, Barton-under-Needwood, Staffordshire. *Proceedings of the Prehistoric Society* 50, 402.

Losco-Bradley, S. Forthcoming. Excavations on an Iron Age cropmark at Swarkestone Lowes, Derbyshire. *Derbyshire Archaeological Journal.*

Lynch, F. 1993. *Excavations in the Brenig Valley. A Mesolithic and Bronze Age landscape in North Wales.* Bangor: Cambrian Archaeological Monograph.

McKinley, J. 1997. Bronze Age 'barrows' and funerary rites and rituals of cremation. *Proceedings of the Prehistoric Society* 63, 129–145.

Macgregor, M. 1976. *Early Celtic Art in North Britain.* 2 vols. Leicester University Press.

Martin, A. 1900. Les sépultures armoricaines du bronze à belles pointes de flèche en silex. *L'Anthrologie* 11, 159–78.

May, J. 1970. An Iron Age square enclosure at Aston upon Trent, Derbyshire: a report on excavations in 1967. *Derbyshire Archaeological Journal* 90.

Maynard, G & Benton, G.M. 1921. A burial of the Early Bronze Age discovered at Berden. *Transactions Essex Archaeological Society* 15 (new ser.), 278–286.

Meek, J. 1995. *The excavation of a pit complex at Lockington-Hemington, Leicestershire.* Leicestershire Archaeological Unit, Unpublished Report 95/98.

Megaw, J.V.S. & Simpson D.D.A. (eds) 1979. *Introduction to British Prehistory.* Leicester University Press.

Menghin, W. & Schauer, P. 1977. *Der Goldkegel von Ezelsdorf: Kultgerät der Späten Bronzezeit.* Germanisches Nat. Museum.

Miles, H. 1975. Barrows on the St. Austell Granite, Cornwall. *Cornish Archaeology* 14, 5–81.

Moffett, L. 1991. Pignut tubers from a Bronze Age cremation at Barrow Hills, Oxfordshire, and the importance of vegetable tubers in the prehistoric period. *Journal of Archaeological Science* 18, 187–191.

Moffett, L.C. 1992. Charred Plant Remains. In D. Knight, Excavation of an Iron Age settlement at Gamston, Nottinghamshire. *Transactions of the Thoroton Society of Nottinghamshire* 96, 79–83.

Moffett, L.C. 1993. *Macrofossil Plant Remains from The Shires Excavation, Leicester*. Ancient Monuments Laboratory Report 31/93 (E.H.)

Moore, R.G. 1975. The flint. In Moore, R.G. & Williams, J.H. A Late Neolithic site at Ecton. *Northamptonshire Archaeology* 10, 3–31.

Monckton, A. 1994. The Plant Remains. In J. Sharman, R. Thorpe & P.N. Clay, An Iron Age Site at Normanton le Heath, Leicestershire. *Transactions of the Leicester Archaeological and Historical Society.*

Monckton, A. 1999. The Charred Plant Remains. In P. N. Clay, Neolithic-Early Bronze Age Pit Circles and their Environs at Burley Road, Oakham, Rutland. *Proceedings of the Prehistoric Society* 64, 293–330.

Mount, C. 1997. Adolf Mahr's excavations of an Early Bronze Age cemetery at Keenoge, County Meath. *Proceedings of the Royal Irish Academy* 97 (C), 1–68.

Munro, R. 1882–3. Notice of the discovery of five bronze celts and a bronze ring at the "Maidens", near Culzean Castle, Ayrshire. *Proceedings of the Society of Antiquaries of Scotland* 17, 433–438.

Murphy, J. & Riley, J.P. 1962. A modified single solution method for the determination of phosphate in natural waters. *Analyt Chim Acta* 12, 162–176.

Needham, S.P. 1979. The extent of foreign influence on Early Bronze Age axe development in southern Britain. In M. Ryan (ed) *The Origins of Metallurgy in Atlantic Europe; proceedings of the 5th Atlantic Colloquium*, 265–293. Dublin: Stationery Office.

Needham, S.P. 1988. Selective deposition in the British Early Bronze Age. *World Archaeology* 20, 229–248.

Needham, S.P. 1990. The Penard-Wilburton succession: new metalwork finds from Croxton (Norfolk) and Thirsk (Yorkshire). *Antiquaries Journal* 70, 253–270.

Needham, S.P. 1996. Chronology and periodisation in the British Bronze Age. In K. Randsborg (ed.), *Absolute chronology: archaeological Europe 2500–500 BC.* Acta Archaeologica 67, 121–140.

Needham, S.P. forthcoming a. Power pulses across a cultural divide: cosmologically driven acquisition between Armorica and Wessex. *Proceedings of the Prehistoric Society* 66.

Needham, S.P. forthcoming b. The development of embossed goldwork in Bronze Age Europe. *Antiquaries Journal* 80.

Needham, S.P. and Hook, D.R. 1988. Lead and lead alloys in the Bronze Age – recent finds from Runnymede Bridge. In E.A. Slater & J.O. Tate (eds), *Science and Archaeology Glasgow 1987*, 259–274. Oxford: British Archaeological Reports, British Series 196.

Needham, S.P., Lawson, A.J. & Green, H.S. 1985. *Early Bronze Age hoards*. British Bronze Age Metalwork, Associated Finds Series A1–6. London, British Museum Publications.

Needham, S.P., Leese, M.N., Hook, D.R. & Hughes, M.J. 1989. Developments in the Early Bronze Age metallurgy of southern Britain. *World Archaeology* 20, 383–402.

Neugebauer, J.W. 1995. Drei- frühbronzezeitliche Metalldepots der Aunjetitz-Kultur Niederösterreichs. In B.Schmid-Sikimić & P Della Casa (eds.), *Trans Europam: Beiträge zur Bronze- und Eisenzeit zwischen Atlantik und Altai, Feschrift für Margarita Primas*, 45–47. Bonn.

Norfolk Museums Service 1977. *Bronze Age Metalwork in Norwich Castle Museum*. Norfolk Museums Service (2nd ed.).

NUCL. 1994. *A564 (T) Derby Southern Bypass: archaeological brief.*

O'Brien, C. 1976. Excavation at Cossington – an interim report. *Transactions of the Leicestershire Archaeological and Historical Society* 51, 56–57.

O'Ríordáin, S.P. 1951–2. Lough Gur excavations: the Great Stone Circle (B) in Grange Townland. *Proc.Royal Irish Academy* 54, 37–74.

O'Ríordáin, B. & Waddell, J. 1993. *The Funerary Bowls and Vases of the Irish Bronze Age*. Galway University Press.

Ottaway, B. 1974. Cluster analysis of impurity patterns in Armorico-British daggers. *Archaeometry* 16, 221–231.

Paradine, P.J. 1978. The Plant Remains. In P. N. Clay. *Two multiphase barrow sites at Sproxton and Eaton Leicestershire*. Leicestershire Museums Archaeol. Rep. No. 2. p. 43.

Piggott, S. 1938. The Early Bronze Age in Wessex. *Proceedings of the Prehistoric Society* 4, 52–106.

Piggott, S. 1973. *A history of Wiltshire, Volume 1 Part 2*. London: Victoria History of the Counties of England.

Piggott, S. and Stewart, M. 1958. *Early and Middle Bronze Age grave-groups and hoards from Scotland*. London: Inventaria Archaeologica GB25–34.

Posnansky, M. 1955a. The excavation of a Bronze-Age round barrow at Lockington. *Transactions of the Leicestershire Archaeological and Historical Society* 31.

Posnansky, M. 1955b. The excavation of Barrow II at Swarkestone. *Derbyshire Archaeological Journal* 76, 10–26.

Powell, T.G.E. 1953. The gold ornament from Mold, Flintshire, North Wales. *Proceedings of the Prehistoric Society* 19, 161–179.

Pryor, F. & French, C.I.A. 1985. The Fenland Project 1. Archaeology and Environment in the Lower Welland Valley. *East Anglian Archaeology* 27, vol. 1.

Reaney, D. 1968. Beaker burials in South Derbyshire. *Derbyshire Archaeological Journal* 88, 68–81.

Reeve, M.J., 1975. *Soils in Derbyshire II*. Soil Survey Record No. 27. Harpenden: Soil Survey of England and Wales.

Richards, J. 1994. The worked flint. In C.I.A. French, Excavation of the Deeping St. Nicholas barrow complex, South Lincs. *Lincolnshire Archaeology and Heritage Reports Series* No. 1, 57–61.

Ritchie, J.N.G. 1967. Balnabriard Cairn, Kintyre, Argyll. *Trans. Dumfriesshire and Galloway Natural History and Antiquarian Society* 44, 81–98.

Royal Commission 1964. *An Inventory of the Ancient Monuments in Caernarvonshire, Volume III: West*. The Royal Commission on Ancient and Historical Monuments in Wales and Monmouthshire.

Russell-White, C.J., Lowe, C.E. & McCullagh, R.P.J. 1992. Excavations at three Early bronze Age burial monuments in Scotland. *Proceedings of the Prehistoric Society* 58, 285–324.

Saville, A. 1972–73. A reconsideration of the prehistoric flint assemblage from Bourne Pool, Aldridge, Staffs. *Trans. of the South Staffordshire Archaeological and Historical Society* 14, 6–28.

Saville, A. 1980. Five flint assemblages from excavated sites in Wiltshire. *Wiltshire Archaeological Magazine* 72/73, 1–27.

Saville, A. 1985. The Flint Assemblage. In N.A. Field, A multi-phase barrow and possible henge monument at West Ashby, Lincolnshire. *Proceedings of the Prehistoric Society* 51, 103–136.

Schauer, P. 1986. *Die Goldblechkegel der Bronzezeit: Ein Beitrag zur Kulturverbindung zwischen Orient und Mitteleuropa.* Bonn, Römisch-Germanisches Zentralmuseums Mainz, Monograph 8.

Seton, G. 1854–7. Note regarding two bronze rings, recently dug up near Stobo Castle, Peebleshire, the seat of Sir G. Graham Mongomery. *Proceedings of the Society of Antiquaries of Scotland* 2 (2), 276–278.

Sheridan, A. & Northover, P. 1993. A Beaker period copper dagger blade from the Sillees River near Ross Lough, Co Fermanagh. *Ulster Journal of Archaeology*, 56, 61–69.

Simpson, D.D.A. 1968. Food Vessels: associations and chronology. In J.M. Coles & D.D.A. Simpson (eds), *Studies in Ancient Europe: essays presented to Stuart Piggott*, 197–211.

Simpson, W.G. 1976. A barrow cemetery of the second millennium BC at Tallington, Lincolnshire. *Proceedings of the Prehistoric Society* 42, 215–240.

Smirke, E. 1865. Notice of two golden ornaments found near Padstow and communicated to the Institute by favour of H.R.H. The Prince of Wales, K.G. *Archaeological Journal* 22, 275–277.

Smith, M.A. 1957. *Bronze Age hoards and grave-groups from the N.E. Midlands.* Inventaria Archaeologica GB 19–24. London.

Stanford, S.C. 1982. Bromfield, Shropshire – Neolithic, Beaker and Bronze Age sites, 1966–79. *Proceedings of the Prehistoric Society* 48, 279–320.

Stanford, S.C. 1995. Barrow B15 and nearby features. In Hughes, G., Leach, P. & Stanford, S.C. 1995. Excavations at Bromfield, 1981–1991. *Transactions of the Shropshire Archaeological and Historical Society* 70, 35–49.

Stead, I.M. 1991. *Iron Age cemeteries in East Yorkshire. English Heritage Archaeological Report 22.* London: English Heritage/British Museum.

Stratascan. 1993. *A report for Trent and Peak Archaeological trust on a Geophysical Survey – Derby Southern Bypass.*

Sterner, J. 1989. Who is signalling whom? Ceramic style, ethnicity and taphonomy among the Sirak Bulahay. *Antiquity* 63, 451–9.

Stevenson, G.H. and Miller, S.N. 1911–2. Report on the excavations at the Roman Fort of Cappuck, Roxburghshire. *Proceedings of the Society of Antiquaries of Scotland* 10 (4th ser.), 446–483.

Stevenson, R.B.K. 1956. The Migdale hoard bronze necklace. *Proceedings of the Society of Antiquaries of Scotland* 89, 456–7.

Taylor, J.J. 1974. The gold box from "La Motta", Lannion. *Palaeohistoria* 16, 152–163.

Taylor, J.J. 1980. *Bronze Age goldwork of the British Isles.* Cambridge University Press.

Taylor, A.F. & Woodward, P.J. 1985. A Bronze Age barrow cemetery, and associated settlement at Roxton, Bedfordshire. *Archaeological Journal* 142, 73–149.

Tomalin, D. 1988. Armorican vases à anses and their occurrence in southern Britain. *Proceedings of the Prehistoric Society* 54, 203–222.

Trent & Peak Archaeological Trust. 1992. *Archaeology of the Derby Southern Bypass. Implications of the construction of the bypass between Hilton and the M1.* Trent and Peak Archaeological Trust unpublished report.

Trent & Peak Archaeological Trust. 1993. *Derby Southern Bypass archaeological evaluations. Report on site investigations.* Trent & Peak Archaeological Trust unpublished report.

Trollope, E. 1857. Antiquities and works of art exhibited. *Archaeological Journal* 14, 92–93.

Uenze, O. 1938. *Die Frühbronzezeitlichen Triangulären Vollgriffdolche.* Berlin.

Vandkilde, H. 1988. A Late Neolithic hoard with objects of bronze and gold from Skeldal, Central Jutland. *Journal of Danish Archaeology* 7, 115–135.

Vatcher, F.deM. and Vatcher, H.L. 1976. The excavation of a round barrow near Poor's Heath, Risby, Suffolk. *Proceedings of the Prehistoric Society* 42, 263–292.

Van Gennep, A. 1960. *The rites of passage.* London.

Vine, P.M. 1982. *The Neolithic and Bronze Age Cultures of the Middle and Upper Trent Basin.* Oxford: British Archaeological Reports, British Series 105.

von Brunn, W.A. 1959. *Die Hortfunde der frühen Bronzezeit aus Sachsen-Anhalt, Sachsen und Thüringen.* Berlin, Deutsche Akademie der Wissenschaften zu Berlin Schriften der Sektion für Vor- und Frühgeschichte, Band 7.

Voruz, J-L. 1996. Chronologie absolue de l'âge du Bronze Ancien et Moyen. In C. Mordant & O. Gaiffe (eds.), *Cultures et Sociétés du Bronze Ancien en Europe*, 97–164. Actes du 117e Congrès National des Sociétés Savantes (Clermont-Ferrand, 1992). Paris, Comité des Travaux historiques et scientifiques.

Walker, I.C. 1964–6. The counties of Nairnshire, Moray and Banffshire in the Bronze Age – part 1. *Proceedings of the Society of Antiquaries of Scotland* 98, 76–125.

Wardle, P. 1992. *Earlier Prehistoric Pottery Production and Ceramic Petrology in Britain.* Oxford: British Archaeological Report, British Series 225.

Waterman, D.M. 1948. An Early Bronze Age bracelet from Bridlington, Yorkshire. *Antiquaries Journal* 28, 179–180.

Watson, J. 1995. Mineral preserved organic material associated with metalwork from Gravelly Guy, Stanton Harcourt, Oxon. *Ancient Monuments Laboratory* Report No. 64/95.

Watson, J. forthcoming. Organic material associated with Bronze-Age metalwork from Barrow Hills, Radley, Oxon. *AML Report Series.*

Way, A. 1867. Notices of relics found in and near ancient circular dwellings explored by the Hon. W.O. Stanley, M.P. in Holyhead Island. *Archaeological Journal* 24, 243–264.

Way, A. 1868. Notices of relics found in and near ancient circular dwellings explored by the Hon. W.O. Stanley, M.P. in Holyhead Island. *Archaeologia Cambrensis* 14, 401–433.

Wheeler, H.M. 1979. Excavations at Willington, Derbyshire, 1970–1972. *Derbyshire Archaeological Journal* 99.

Whimster, R. 1989. *The emerging past: air photorfaphy and the buried landscape.* RCHME.

Whittaker, J.C. 1994. *Flintknapping: Making and Understanding Stone Tools.* University of Texas Press, Austin.

Wilson, D. 1863. *The Archaeology and Prehistoric Annals of Scotland* (2nd edition). Edinburgh, Sutherland & Knox.

Woodward, A. 1995. Vessel size and social identity in the Bronze Age of southern Britain. In I. Kinnes, and G. Varndell (eds), *Unbaked urns of rudely shape.* Oxford: Oxbow Monograph 55.

Woodward, P.J. 1980. A Beaker burial from Rimbury, Dorset. *Proceedings of the Dorset Natural History and Archaeological Society* 102, 99–100.

Woodward, P.J. 1991. *The South Dorset Ridgeway. Survey and Excavations 1977–84.* Dorchester: Dorset Natural History and Archaeological Society Monograph 8.

APPENDIX 1

Early Bronze Age Armlets in Britain and Ireland

(Nos. 1–44 in same order as Table 2)

A. ARMLETS OF KNOWN FORM					
	Provenance	NGR	Context/associations	Key references/Museum
1	Knipton, Leicestershire	SK 8130	Assumed grave; S3 Beaker. Found c. 1934 during ironstone quarrying.	Waterman 1948, fig. 2 Smith 1957, GB 20 Clarke 1970, fig. 955 no. 424 *Belvoir Castle (private)*
2	Bridlington Quay, East Yorkshire	TA 1766	Found 1891; no known associations.	Waterman 1948, fig 1 *Yorkshire Museum*
3	Normanton (Amesbury G41), Wiltshire	SU 1342	On arm of one of two adult inhumations in the barrow; also two child inhumations.	Hoare 1812, 160 Waterman 1948, fig. 3 Annable & Simpson 1964, no. 117 *Devizes Museum*
4	Carnoustie High Street, Angus	NO 5634	Found 1810 in one of "some stone coffins".	Henshall 1964, 426, fig. 1.1 *Carnoustie Town Council*
5	Castern, near Wetton, Staffordshire	SK 1055	Found with inhumation and "several instruments of flint" under large barrow excavated 1850.	Henshall 1964, 427, fig. 1.3 *Sheffield Museum J.93.573*
6	Mill of Laithers (1), west of Turriff, Aberdeenshire	NJ 7249	Recorded as coming from a grave with the butt of a flat axe.	Henshall 1964, 428 fig. 1.4 *NMS L.1962.139*
7–8	Fern, Auchnacree, Angus	NO 4663	Hoard found 1921: 2 armlets with 4 flat axes and 2 riveted daggers.	Piggott & Stewart 1958, GB27 *NMS DQ 261 and private*
9	The Maidens, Port Murray, Ayrshire	NS 2008	Hoard found 1883: armlet with 5 flat axes/chisels.	Munro 1882–3 Piggott & Stewart 1958, GB31 *NMS L.1950.4*
10–11	Kinneff, Kincardineshire	NO 8675	Grave disturbed in 1831: 2 armlets with Food Vessel and fragments of other rings "in association with an unburnt burial".	Munro 1882–3, 450 fig. 7 Anderson 1886, 59–60, fig. 67 Piggott & Stewart 1958, GB34 *NMS EQ 148–9*
12	Crawford, Lanarkshire	NS 9520	Grave - one of two cists found under a cairn 1850 contained armlet and N3 Beaker.	Munro 1882–3, 451–2, fig. 9 Anderson 1886, 58–9, fig. 65 Clarke 1970, fig. 674 no. 1702 *NMS EQ 139*

Appendix 1: continued

13	Ratho, Midlothian	NT 1370	Armlet fragments said to have been found with a Food Vessel.	Wilson 1863, 319, 454 Anderson 1886, 60–1 *NMS EQ 158–162*
14	Nether Glen, Glen Rothes, Morayshire	NJ 2552	Armlet possibly associated with a flat axe found the following year.	Walker 1964–6, 90 Coles archive, NMS *Elgin Museum 1953.23*
15–16	Near Stobo Castle, Peebleshire	NT 1837	Found 1855: possible cremation burial under a large boulder on top of which were the 2 armlets side by side and covered by a flat stone; a small piece of bronze found 10 yards distant in loose stones (?cairn).	Seton 1854–7 Anderson 1886, 57–8, fig. 63 Coles 1968–9, 89 *Lost*
17–22	Migdale, Sutherland	NH 6292	Hoard found prior to 1901: 8 armlets with flat axes, tubular beads, button covers, earrings, spacer-plate cover and jet buttons.	Anderson 1900–1 Callander 1918–19, 21 fig. 5 Piggott & Stewart 1958, GB 26 *NMS DQ 344–359*
23–24	Uppat, Sutherland	NC 8502		Britton 1963, 314 Coles 1968–9, 89 Coles archive, NMS *Dunrobin Castle*
25	Mill of Laithers (2), West of Turriff, Aberdeenshire	NJ 7249	Probably picked up on Mill of Laithers Farm prior to 1925, but only recently reported.	T Cowie, pers. comm. *NMS*
26–27	Windmill Fields, Ingleby Barwick, Cleveland	NZ 4413	Grave excavated by Tees Archaeology 1996: burial (no.6) of an adult female, crouched on right side; accompanied by two armlets, and at least 45 tubular bronze bead covers, 17 jet buttons, 80 jet disk beads, a jet fusiform bead and a stone bead.	Richard Annis and Blaise Vyner, pers.comm.
28–29	Migdale, Sutherland	NH 6292	Hoard (see 17–22 above).	(see above)
30	Mill of Laithers (3), West of Turriff, Aberdeenshire	NJ 7249	Probably picked up on Mill of Laithers Farm prior to 1925, but only recently reported.	T Cowie, pers. comm. *NMS*
31	Shorncote, Gloucestershire	SU 0296	Rectangular grave excavated 1990: armlet on one arm of vestigial crouched inhumation with S3 Beaker at head; also flint flake.	Barclay & Glass 1995 *BM P1994 4–2 7*

Appendix 1: continued

32	Williamstown, St Martins, Perthshire	NO 1530	Short cist discovered 1918 contained armlet fragments and human skeletal remains.	Callander 1918–9, fig. 3 Henshall & Walker 1962–3, 150 fig. 4 *Perth Museum*
33–34	Melfort, Argyllshire	NM 8314	Cist with extended inhumation found 1885; 2 armlets (1 lost) associated with jet spacer-plate necklace.	Anderson 1886, 57 fig. 62 Piggott & Stewart 1958, GB 25 *NMS DO 51*
35–36	Masterton, Pitreavie, Fife	NT 1284	Grave in cist excavated 1961: 2 fragmentary armlets with bronze dagger and small blade, and jet bead necklace.	Henshall & Wallace 1962–3 *NMS EQ 639*
37	Whitfield, Lisnakil, Co. Waterford	–	Possible grave disturbed in 1725; in a cist in a cairn an "earthenware vessel ... contained a golden bracelet ..."; another vessel found at the site.	Herity 1969, 11, pl. X *Lost*
38–39	Lockington, Leicestershire	SK 4627	Hoard - context described in this paper.	*BM P1996 9–1 1–2*
40	Cuxwold, near Caistor, Lincolnshire	TA 1701	Unknown.	Trollop 1857 *Lost*
41–42	Luggacurran, Co Laois	–	Possibly associated in a grave with a Bowl Food Vessel, one of 2 found 1881 in 2 short cists with unburnt bones and ? faience beads.	O'Ríordáin & Waddell 1993, 118 no. 301 *NMI 1881: 538, Wk 146*
43	Lough Gur stone circle B, Co Limerick	–	Excavated from position low in internal 'fill' of circle, just inside S. entrance.	O'Ríordáin 1951–2, 49, fig. 2.1
44	Redlands Farm, Stanwick, Northamptonshire	SP 9671	Excavated 1989, one of 3 Beaker inhumations inserted into axis of long barrow; with copper alloy basket ornament and fragmentary Beaker (? Southern).	G Keevill, pers. comm. Keevill 1992, 180 (*Oxford Arch Unit*)

Appendix 1: continued

B. POSSIBLE ARMLETS IN EBA CONTEXTS			
	Pen y Bonc, Anglesey	Grave group found 1828 in a "rock-grave" about 3 feet square; evidently included "bronze armlets" along with 2 urns, a jet spacer-plate necklace and V-bored button.	Way 1867, 257–8 Way 1868, 423–4 *Lost*
	Balnabraid, Argyllshire	Cist 5 contained a Cordoned Urn, bone toggle, flint flake and many fragments of sheet bronze, the larger of which bear repoussé decoration of closely set ribs in 2 motifs: transverse strokes between multiple bordering ribs, and chevrons.	Galloway 1919–20, 179 Ritchie 1967, 88, 90 fig. 5, 8 & 9 *Kelvingrove Museum, Glasgow*
	Pen-yr-Orsedd, Morfa Nefyn, Caernarvonshire	Found in 1691, "the handle of a tankard of brasse", at the same site as some inverted cinerary urns (one in a cist) and accessory vessels.	Davies 1957 Royal Commission (Wales) 1964, xxxix *Lost*
	Harlyn Bay, Cornwall	Original account of hoard/grave group, possibly in a cairn, noted an object "like a bit of a buckle" in addition to 2 gold lunulae and bronze flat axe.	Smirke 1865 *J Royal Institution of Cornwall* 2, 1866–7, xvi *Lost*
	"Col. Drax's barrow, Dorset Downs", Dorset	Burial found early 18th century AD in detached barrow: "entire skeleton" with Armorico-British dagger, knife and a piece "of very thin copper or brass gilt" – decorated with zigzag lines in two bands, all ? incised and outlined with pointillé. Depiction suggests extensive corrosion of edges – extant length c. 70 mm.	Douglas 1793, 150, 153 Gerloff 1975, nos. 122–123, pl. 46 B2 *Lost*
	Berden, Essex	Some years after discovery in 1907, a burial was described as extended inhumation with fragmentary S2 Beaker towards its feet; on left arm (verdigris stained) was "a narrow ring of flat section, thin ... as far as I can remember, two small 'ribs', or projections, which I thought were some kind of fastening". Said to be of small size. Clarke's 1970 depiction is conjecture.	Maynard & Benton 1921 Benton 1923 Clarke 1970, 388 fig. 894 *Lost*

APPENDIX 2

Armlets doubtfully of Early Bronze Age date (but sometimes considered to be)

Provenance	Context/description/comments	Key references
Moss of Tillychetly, Alfold, Aberdeenshire	" ... dug up, a good many years ago, a couple of brass armlets, of rather neat workmanship ... about 4 inches in diameter, and 1¾ inches in breadth ... fluted longitudinally, and enlarged and rounded off at the opening". 'Opening' seems here most likely to refer to break in a penannular form; more in keeping with massive Iron Age types than with known EBA ones.	Gillan 1860–2, 385 Coles 1968–9, 88 Macgregor 1976, nos. 248–9 *Lost*
Cairntable, near Muirkirk, Ayrshire	An armlet and ring "were found together under a boulder on the eastern margin of the east cairn on Cairntable" about 1933. Previously identified alternatively as EBA or Iron Age (although Macgregor was tentative). Given the treatment and likely (very worn) decoration of the terminals, the later date is preferred. The associated ring is rather crudely 'butt-jointed' by comparison with EBA group 2 armlets and need not imply similar date. [I am grateful for opinion from T Cowie].	Henshall 1964, 427 Coles 1968–9, 88 Macgregor 1976, no. 225 *NMS*
Cappuck, Roxburghshire	Penannular ribbed armlet found during 1886 excavations on site of Roman Fort. Although not dissimilar to some group 3 armlets, specific form and high zinc content (giving brass – Coles 1968–9, 97 Rx1) are not readily matched in EBA. Outer two ribs bulbous with flattish tops; central one slighter and more ridged; back totally flat. The terminals do not meet and are treated differently: one with steep 'cut' facet possibly reworked; other gently hammered, thinning profile and slightly splaying end. No decoration despite fine patina.	Stevenson & Miller 1911–2, 474, no. 5, fig. 11 Callander 1918–9, 22 fig. 6 Coles 1968–9, 89 *NMS*
'Ireland'	A sheet gold corrugated armlet with no recorded context. Three broad convex ribs meet at creases, giving cuspate profile more similar to occasional LBA ornaments than earlier ones (eg Heights of Brae – Clarke & Kemp 1984, 195 no. 9; Thirsk – Needham 1990). Beaded rims, perhaps rolled, evidently each decorated with fine zigzag line.	Herity 1969, 11–12, pl. Xb *Lost*

APPENDIX 3

Armorico-British daggers of unalloyed copper

Site	Type	References
BRITAIN		
Lockington, Leicestershire	Quimperlé	This paper
Bush Barrow, Wilsford G5, Wiltshire	Rumédon	Gerloff 1975, no. 113; Britton 1961, no. 5; Ottaway 1974, 229 no. 5
FRANCE		
Brun Bras, Saint Adrien, Côtes-du-Nord	? Quimperlé	Briard 1984, 225–6 no. 2; Briard & Bourhis 1984, 49 no. 2335
	Trévérec	Briard 1984, 225–6 no. 3; Briard & Bourhis 1984, 49 no. 2337
	Rumédon	Briard 1984, 225–6 no. 4; Briard & Bourhis 1984, 49 no. 2338
Bel Air (Plouguin), Landernau, Finistère	Rumédon	Gallay 1981, no. 330; Giot et al. 1966, MAL 11; Ottaway 1974, 229 no. 24
Kerguévarec, Plouyé, Finistère	Rumédon or Quimperlé	Giot et al. 1966, no. 45; Ottaway 1974, 229 no. 19; Gallay 1981, nos. 337–340, 360, 437
	Rumédon or Quimperlé	Giot et al. 1966, MAL 12; Ottaway 1974, 229 no. 25; Gallay 1981, nos. 337–340, 360, 437
Forêt de Carnoët, Quimperlé, Finistère	Quimperlé (x 3) (including 6 rivets analysed)	Briard & Mohen 1974; Junghans et al. 1974, nos. 21828–21836

List of Contributors

LYNNE BEVAN
Field Archaeology Unit
University of Birmingham
Edgbaston
Birmingham B15 2TT

DUNCAN HOOK
Department of Scientific Research
The British Museum
Great Russell Street
London WC1B 3DG

GWILYM HUGHES
Cambria Archaeology
Dyfed Archaeological Trust
Carmarthen Street
Llandeilo
Carmarthenshire SA19 6AF

ROWENA GALE
Folly Cottage
Chute Cadley
Andover
Hants SP11 9EB

JAMES GREIG
Department of Ancient History and Archaeology
University of Birmingham
Edgbaston
Birmingham B15 2TT

SUSAN LIMBREY
Department of Ancient History and Archaeology
University of Birmingham
Edgbaston
Birmingham B15 2TT

JAMES MEEK
University of Leicester Archaeological Services
University of Leicester
University Road
Leicester LE1 7RH

NIGEL MEEKS
Department of Scientific Research
The British Museum
Great Russell Street
London WC1B 3DG

ANDREW MOSS
School of Geography and Environmental Sciences
University of Birmingham
Edgbaston
Birmingham B15 2TT

LISA MOFFETT
Department of Ancient History and Archaeology
University of Birmingham
Edgbaston
Birmingham B15 2TT

ANGELA MONCKTON
University of Leicester Archaeological Services
University of Leicester
University Road
Leicester LE1 7RH

STUART NEEDHAM
Department of Prehistoric and Romano-British Antiquities
The British Museum
Great Russell Street
London WC1B 3DG

JACQUI WATSON
Centre for Archaeology
Fort Cumberland
Fort Cumberland Road
Eastney
Portsmouth PO4 9LD

DAVID WILLIAMS
Department of Archaeology
University of Southampton
Southampton SO17 1BJ

ANN WOODWARD
Field Archaeology Unit
University of Birmingham
Edgbaston
Birmingham B15 2TT

ROB YOUNG
School of Archaeological Studies
University of Leicester
University Road
Leicester LE1 7RH